Paper Toys
of the
World

by Blair Whitton

Published By  **HOBBY HOUSE PRESS, INC.**
Cumberland, Maryland 21502

DEDICATION

To Margaret Whitton, my wife, and Barbara Whitton Jendrick, my daughter, who both inspired me to collect over the years and encouraged me to write this book.

Additional copies of this book may be purchased at $24.95
plus $2.25 postage/handling from
HOBBY HOUSE PRESS, INC.
900 Frederick Street, Cumberland, Maryland 21502

ISBN: 0-87588-289-7

PREFACE AND ACKNOWLEDGMENTS

My wife Margaret and I, along with our daughter Barbara Whitton Jendrick, have always had an interest in collecting paper toys. We started some 35 years ago, and at that early period it was a secondary collection to Margaret's doll collection and my interest in toys. Barbara started collecting paper dolls as a child and continued with it into adulthood. She is an expert in this field. Over the years, we three have found scores of intriguing paper playthings. In the early years European boxed sets and American uncut paper toy sheets were more plentiful. There were a few other interested collectors at the time, but there was enough available material for everyone to share.

In America, girls have always had a deep interest in playing with paper dolls, and in their later years many of them continued to collect them. Strangely enough this interest did not apply to the other paper toys. In Europe there seemed to be an early and continuous interest in all types of paper collectibles.

In this country, a paper toy renaissance appears to have taken place in the past four or five years. A series of reproductions, particularly in the form of movable books, started the movement. Since then many original movables, along with many outstanding paper construction toys, have appeared on the market. Many of these new paper toys are on a par with those published in the 1800s.

While there seems to be a growing interest in paper toys in many parts of the world, there is very little published information available on them. With the exception of those on paper dolls, there are only a few books touching on the subject of these intriguing playthings. This is the reason for writing this study, the objective of which is to show the wide variety of paper toys that were published in years gone by, the creativity and talent of the artists who designed them, and the beauty and quality of color used by those who printed them.

While there is no way this vast field of paper toys could be covered in one book, this effort is a well-rounded start. It is hoped that others interested in any field of paper toy collecting will also publish and share their knowledge and collections. It is also hoped that those who casually leaf through the following pages, glance at the illustrations and read a caption here and there, will start again at page one and read this book word for word. If an interest is created and a desire to collect arises, the paper toy collecting field will offer them much satisfaction and pleasure.

I would like to take this opportunity to thank other collectors and institutions who shared either their paper toys or their knowledge, thus adding to the importance of this book: Jan Banneck; Herbert Hosmer; Helen Jo Payne; Seymour Merrall; Mrs. Stanley A. Weeks; and The Margaret Woodbury Strong Museum (Rochester, New York). Photographers Harry Bickelhaupt; Len Rosenberg; Tom Weber and Mike Radke of The Margaret Woodbury Strong Museum; and Barbara Whitton Jendrick, my daughter. For their research and translation assistance, my thanks to Elaine Challacomb, Kathryn Lazar, Anna Wang, Katie Nielson and Gerta Kyle, all of the Strong Museum's Library Staff.

An additional word of thanks should go to my long time friend and pioneer paper toy collector, Herbert Hosmer, for writing such an interesting introduction to this book.

My thanks, too for the interest and advice given me by Bettyanne Bethea Twigg in the development of this book.

I'm grateful to Gary R. Ruddell, Publisher, Hobby House Press, Inc., for accepting the challenge to publish *Paper Toys of the World*. My sincere thanks to A. Christian Revi who spent hours editing the text and captions and made them pleasant reading. Thanks should also go to Janet E. Smith, Director of Production at Hobby House Press, Inc., and the members of her talented staff for typesetting and laying out my book to make it readable and visually attractive. A sincere heartfelt thanks to you all.

Blair Whitton

RECOLLECTIONS OF PAPER TOYS

Cosy Cot Farm, published by Raphael Tuck & Sons. (See page 60).

The Pop-up Silly Symphonies, published by Blue Ribbon Books, Inc. (See page 75).

When Blair Whitton asked me to write an introduction to his new book on the history of paper and cardboard toys I found that a recollection of my own long life involved with these delightful and ephemeral treasures goes far back to my boyhood, during World War I, when I was about three or four. This first recollection must surely be of a Christmas morning at about that time, or just a bit later, when I went to our little local store with my father before breakfast to pick up the morning paper, only to find that we went especially to pick up a marvelous punch-out cardboard half-timbered house with a garage and other outbuildings. There was an array of separate trees and various shrubbery - everything snow covered and Christmasy. There was a sheet that

unfolded like a map defining where each of the pieces was to be placed. It showed an ice-covered pond fed by a brook. There was a bridge to put together to go over the brook to the pond, to skate on, snowy hills for sliding and a variety of people all dressed in bright winter costume to enjoy an outdoor Christmas morning. There were snow covered stone walls with large gates to surround this magical property. All this came in a large envelope with directions for assembling and a picture in full color on the outside of the envelope showing how it looked all put together. This first cardboard toy remembered from my boyhood came courtesy of one of the popular commercial bread companys –– Town Talk or Hatheway Bakers, I'm not sure which. However, if I were to

see it today I'd recognize it immediately, although some sixty five Christmases have slipped by since then.

I came by my love of cut-out paper and cardboard toys by "right of birth," so to speak, for I was the great grand nephew of John Greene Chandler, one of the first American engravers and lithographers to produce a variety of paper and cardboard toys and toy books. He lived from 1815 to 1879, and most of his adult life, even from boyhood, had been devoted to such work. Apparently apprenticed to the printing and engraving firm of Carter and Andrews here in Lancaster, Massachusetts, when he was about fourteen, he engraved and published a variety of toy books and also in his own company in Boston, Massachusetts, from 1836. His prolific years in cut-out toys were truly between 1850 and 1860 when he also became involved in the broad field of lithography and, for a while at least, with his brother, Samuel Ward Chandler. During that time he was responsible for some innovative American "firsts" –– *Fanny Gray* for Crosby Nichols, Boston, Massachusetts 1854; *Chandler's Paper Dolls of The Latest Paris Fashion* (a series of at least seven in 1857 and 1858); *The American National Circus*, c.1858 (an innovative boxed cut-out circus for Brown, Taggard and Chase of Boston, Massachusetts); and in 1858 and 1859 a remarkable movable print called *St. Nicholas* in one version and *Santa Claus* in another, in which when a string is pulled the beloved Saint suddenly descends and appears in the fireplace crossed legged with arms full of dolls, toys and games, and holding an American flag! Possibly adapted from a German print, it has on the back the familiar verses by Clement Moore. John Greene Chandler had an association with G. Du Bois for whom I have a wonderful trade card obviously designed by the firm. The Du Bois association may have been longstanding, for the last title of the Chandler's paper doll series, *The May Queen and Shepherdess*, bears the title "Du Bois' Paper Dolls." This may have been published after Chandler's eyesight began to fail, so that shortly after 1860 he was forced to give up serious work in cutting the wood blocks.

As a child, my grandmother (with whom we lived) still treasured her own childhood copies (shared originally with her brothers and sisters) of the works of her uncle John. These fragile toys were safely packed away in the bottom drawer of my grandmother's desk. On occasions of good behavior I was allowed to look at these wonderful toys, and under supervision to handle them –– but not to actually play with them.

So it is not hard to understand that my love for paper and cardboard cut-out toys was a natural one born of association from my first memories. John Greene Chandler's daughter, Miss Alice Greene Chandler, my grandmother and great aunts' older first cousin, still lived in Lancaster,

Massachusetts. A most remarkable and unique personage in her own right, she was strong-minded but witty and amusing, and completely individualistic in style of feature and dress. We, as small children, looked up to her as a kind of mystical godmother who could produce Christmas and birthday gifts requested of her at her suggestion, like no human family member that we were acquainted with. Her life had been devoted to library work, first in Lancaster where she served as librarian for ten years, then as a Library Trustee for forty five years. At her death, in 1935, she was Chairman of the Board of the Lancaster Library. She worked faithfully for the Massachusetts Library Commission, almost from its' beginning. She traveled all over Massachusetts to seek out the needs of little country and large city libraries, and reported back to the commission in Boston, Massachusetts. She was also a kind of trouble-shooter and frequently helped these libraries out of her own pocketbook since state funds were even then very limited.

When she died I had the good fortune to inherit, quite by accident, all the material relating to her father, John Greene Chandler! From this material I learned of Leopold Grozelier, a German lithographer who had been first in New York City but by 1854 was chief lithographer for the Chandler company. In that same year Grozelier married Sarah Peters of Andover, Massachusetts, who was a miniature painter on ivory. Sarah Peters became the first woman lithographer in Boston, Massachusetts with her own studio. I am quite sure that the exquisite paintings for *Fanny Gray*, so like miniatures on ivory in their original state, are her work, and though there is no evidence to support it they are dated 1853 –– a year earlier than the published boxed set.

So many engravers, lithographers, and publishers of cut-out and cardboard paper toys have had an association with publishing juvenile books, too, that it is intriguing to note that Chandler published various series of toy books with wood engraved illustrations from 1836 on, and by the 1850 period was involved in lithographic illustrations for juvenile books published

in Boston, Massachusetts. His most celebrated toy book was published in 1840 for the Fair sponsored by Sarah J. Hale, who was already the editor of *Godeys' Ladys Book* but still living in Boston, Massachusetts. This Fair was held in Quincy Hall, and at her suggestion women were trying to raise funds to complete Bunker Hill Monument. The Fair ran for one week in September 1840 and either at the Fair or sold at the Fair for the very first time, Chandler published *The Remarkable Story of Chicken Little*. Mrs. Hale reviewed it in the next to last of the seven issues of the Fair's official newspaper *The Monument*, and thus immortalized for the first time in America the never forgotten phrase "the sky is falling!" It is very possible that Chandler had known Sarah J. Hale from his early years at Carter and Andrews Company in Lancaster, Massachusetts, for in 1830 they advertised the publication of *The Ladies' Magazine* and Mrs. Hale as editor in Boston, Massachusetts. In January 1855, in Godey's book, Mrs. Hale reviewed the boxed paper doll *Fanny Gray* as a suitable gift for the holidays.

In my grandmother' desk drawer was the fragile and movable comical toy of the *Scissors Grinder* which had belonged to her father, G. F. Chandler, as a boy. He was J. G. Chandler's youngest brother, and being born in 1822 he probably had this delightful toy before 1830. It depicts the *Scissors Grinder* in many movable parts which, when a small appliance on the back is turned, animates everything –– his foot pushes the treadle which turns "the wheel" or "stone" on which he sharpens the knife. His hand and arm move the knife over the wheel, his eyes open and shut in amazement, and his mouth opens and closes in a jolly grin. It may be one of an imported series for "No. X" is engraved in the lower right-hand corner, but there is no other indication of the engraver, place, or date.

At about this time both of my great aunts (my grandmother's sisters) entertained me by making fabulous cut-outs for me. One was a magnificent Gothic castle (my choice) with round and square towers, crenellated walls and even a drawbridge. For some curious reason the inhabitants were all painted in watercolor and cut out and copied from illustrations from *The Arabian Nights* at my demand. There was a throne inside (the roof of the castle lifted off), with purple velvet cushions and a carpet of gold flecked silk, also a canopy bed, a copy of one in our old house, which had green satin curtains, spread and bolster! All these pieces were basically of cardboard cut out with knife blade and embroidery scissors, and I think there was a pond with celluloid ducks swimming on it's glass (over blue paper) surface, and all this because I was enchanted by Hans Christian Andersen's story *The Constant Tin Soldier*.

My grandfather's sister, who had inate ability as an artist, responded to my royal interests when I spent time after Sunday School in my great grandmother's house while the adults attended church. She drew and cut out for me a very splendid Queen in Coronation robes and crown — the first example was, alas, drowned when the local fish peddler, unmoved by my wish that he share my enthusiam for this marvelous creature, unfeelingly put the fish wrapped in wax paper down on top of her with disasterous results for the fish oil immediately soaked through. My grandmother put an end to her brief reign via the stove, but I must say she went up "in a blaze of glory." The next Sunday morning Aunt Emma made and cut out for me an even more grand and beautiful and majestic Queen, and her reign has been even longer than Queen Victoria's, for I have her still after more than sixty years! I must confess she was "lost" for some years between the pages of one of our four-volume set of Shakespeare, but that seemed like a safe place for her incarceration even though she turned up not long ago still safe between the pages of a photograph album I had been given when I left for preparatory school in New Hampshire, in the Autumn of 1926!

One exciting gift I recall from an early birthday, and I am very sure it was given me by cousin Alice Chandler, was a large book bound in hardcovers and filled with page after page of brilliantly colored soldiers in a variety of troops and regiments, with all kinds of military equipment to be cut out and assembled, and all associated with World War I. The book had a dust jacket of plain paper with a large round hole cut out of the center, so that a full color picture of the excitements contained in the book and illustrated on the outside cover was revealed to whet the appetite! This illustration may even have been somewhat like the one on the cover of the boxes and envelopes of Dennison Manufacturing Company paper dolls, which were jointed so arms and legs moved and were contained in three sizes with directions and vari-colored sheets of crepe paper with which to construct the costumes. On the cover of boxes and envelopes, children were illustrated sitting on the floor with open boxes of Dennison's paper dolls beside them, contents were spread about and the children were busy cutting out and pasting. The cover lay close by, and on that cover in diminishing size was the same illustration, and on that cover the same illustration growing smaller, and smaller, and smaller! Intriguing illusions!

Throughout my childhood there was fascinating cardboard and paper toys — farms, houses, zoos, in fact the whole real world seems to have been depicted in paper and cardboard to cut out and make or to assemble. One booklet I remember well was the *Movy-Dols* with sheet after sheet of familiar faces and the costumes for various roles — Mary Pickford, Douglas Fairbanks, Charlie Chaplin, Gloria Swanson, Marguerite Clarke and many others. There were magazines with sheets to cut out of all sorts, and also in the supplements in Sunday papers.

Ballerinas, and circuses and their performers were popular. Even Chandler had produced a ballerina with costumes to change for his *Chandler's Paper Doll* series of 1857. She was *Fairy Lightfoot*, obviously inspired by the American child dancers of the period — Mary Ann Lee and Augusta Maywood. Chandler produced board games too — *The Mansion of Happiness*, and the *Game of Coquette or The Suitors*, with dye cut figures to move about. Board games are a remote cousin to the more formal cut-out paper or cardboard toys.

When we had the fascinating task of clearing out Cousin Alice's house after her death, I found all kinds of cut-out and paper playthings that had appealed to her father as examples, or had belonged to her as a child. There were proof sheets and trial runs of the paper dolls and the circus, and a variety of books on the subject of engraving and lithography, as well as examples of the work of other publishers and engravers, infinite treasures, even his engraving tools! One last treasure may sum up the others. It was a portfolio of discs with figures encircling it in a kaliedescope of changes of movement. The portfolio was one of three which contained advertisements for their use, and informed the observer that these were Ackerman and Company's "FANTASCOPES= No. I, II, and III Series' - 96, Strand, London, July 1833." It further stated that "A looking glass and box may be had separate, price 8 s. extra." Alas, the looking glass and box were missing, but by spinning these discs on a pencil in front of a mirror one could animate dancers, acrobats, cyclists, strange beasts and familiar performing animals, and all the movement which made this early opitic toy a literal moving picture were later copied in various forms with original manner of movements in Sunday supplements, and on separate sheets to fascinate the eye and bewitch he or she who watched.

And so it all began, until today it is a brilliant videotape of magic memories that led me into the trials and successes, the thrills and highs and lows of the collector in the field of cardboard and paper toys. Blair Whitton's book, so long needed, will bring back joyful memories, or introduce a magic world of pleasures that will become a kind of combination toy theatre and magic lantern show of the story of these wonders of childhood, and of life — paper and cardboard toys!

Herbert H. Hosmer

The Toy Cupboard Theatre and Museum
October 30, 1985

Table of Contents

Chapter I.

PAPER MAKING AND PRINTING

The art of papermaking originated in China about 105 AD and remained a secret within that country for nearly five hundred years. At the beginning of the 7th century, this knowledge spread to Japan where the methods of making paper improved rapidly. Six hundred years later the art of papermaking moved westward from the Orient to the Mediterranean area, but did not reach Europe until the middle of the 12th century.

The first known form of printing, that of block printing, originated in Japan in the last quarter of the 7th century. Printing with blocks developed into a fine art, but further development of other forms of printing was non-existent. In all probability, this was due to the complexity of the Japanese language, which was made up of thousands of complicated ideographs. In comparison, mass production of movable type for the 15th century European alphabet of 23 letters was relatively simple. It was in Germany that printing as we know it today originated and progressed.

While scores of men in Europe were striving to speed book production through mechanization, Johann Gutenberg became the first person to assemble all the components of the printing process, such as type production, the making of paper and printing ink, and the building of a workable press. From this point on the demand by students for printed books increased tremendously. Following Germany's lead, the first Italian press appeared in 1464, and a year later one was established in Basel, Switzerland. Printing shops appeared in France and Holland in 1470, then in Spain, and later in England in 1476. William Caxton, the first of the English printers, published nearly all the important works of literature written in the English language before 1491. Nearly all the early printing shops became learning centers.

Scholars grouped together to express their views and interpretations, and by writing translating and helping with the printing, they were spreading grains of knowledge to people who were hungering for it.

Wooden hand presses were used from the 15th century until the last quarter of the 18th century. During the latter part of this long period many of the wooden parts of the press were replaced with those of iron. At the very end of this period they were completely constructed of cast iron. The two major faults of the wooden model were (1) the lack of stability caused by the loosening of joints, and (2) the slowness of operation. An early printer and one helper would average 250 sheets, printed on one side, per hour. News or notice sheets may have been printed faster, but careful work required a much slower rate.

Printing on the early hand presses utilized the use of wood blocks and copper plates. Each method had two or more different techniques, each technique having certain advantages and disadvantages. In wood block printing there were basically two methods, wood engraving and the wood-cut. Wood engraving is when the design is cut into the end grain. The block of wood is usually type high, which enabled it to fit easily into a press. Wood engraving usually produces a fine line result. A woodcut is when the design is cut into the face of the wood block and is often printed by hand; the end result is rather coarse. The coloring in these two procedures is done by hand or with stencils. Copper plate printing may consist of four techniques, some of which may be used in combinations. Engraving on copper is one of the oldest techniques used in printing. The lines of the design were cut directly into the plate with a

tool called a burin. This required a man with great manipulatory skill, high artistic ability, and patience. The second technique was that of hardground etching. This technique made use of an acid-resistant "hardground" made of asphaltum and beeswax. This preparation was coated on the surface of the copper plate and allowed to dry. The design was drawn in with an etching needle and, when finished, the plate was immersed in an acid bath. The depth of the design cut was controlled by the strength of the acid or by the length of time the plate was submerged. The advantage of this process over engraving on copper was a saving of time and money. It required an artist, not an artist trained as an engraver. The third technique was that of "stippling", it could be used in or with either of the previous procedures. It is obvious that stippling with acid compared to doing it with a burin wold be a time-saver, but the results might not be so fine. The last technique is called "aquatinting," which provided a method of shading. Aquatinting consisted of adhering powdered rosin onto a copper plate. The rosin dust was made to settle on the copper plate at the density required. It was then set on a hot surface where heat would melt the rosin causing it to adhere to the plate. After engraving the design, the plate was placed in an acid bath and the bite took place on the uncovered surface. Coloring in this process was always done by hand.

In 1797, a German by the name of Aloys Senefelder of Munich, Germany, discovered the printing process we call lithography. This process which depends upon the immescibility of grease and water, is the basis of all modern methods of offset printing. Early lithography was done with black ink, all color being applied by hand. Some successful color lithography was done in the late

1830s, but it did not come into wide commercial use until 1860. Color lithography was later called chromolithography, and for the remainder of the 19th century it became the popular method of color printing.

The early progress of the Industrial Revolution provided improved and new machinery that was activated by power from the steam engine. Printers were among the first to utilize this new power source. One of the biggest problems facing the printers at this point of time was the growing shortage of paper, due to the scarcity of rags. While the early paper of China, a thousand years before, had been made of wood fiber and reeds, the improvements in the quality of paper over the years required that it should have a rag content. When the then high speed steam driven press came into existance, the supply of existing rag pulp paper could not meet the demand of mechanization. While scores of men were attempting to rectify this problem, a German scientist, J.C. Schaffer, developed a vegetable pulp and fiber mixture that would satisfactorily replace the rag pulp in paper making.

Going back in time to discover when printing started in the United States, it is recorded that the first printing press in the Western Hemisphere was set up in Mexico City in the mid 1530s. In 1639, Stephen Day and his son Matthew built and operated the first printing press in the United States at Cambridge, Massachusetts. Ultimately, their press was taken over by Harvard College. Printing shops appeared in Virginia in 1682, in Maryland and Philadelphia, Pennsylvania, in 1685, in New York City in 1693, and in Connecticut in 1709. All paper used by these early printers was imported from Europe until William Rittenhouse, a German immigrant, built the first paper mill in 1690 at Roxboro, Pennsylvania. That area is now Germantown, a suburb of Philadelphia. It is recorded that in 1775 there were 50 printers in the 13 colonies. In 1871 the *American Encyclopedia of Printing* reported that there were 450 hand presses and 30 steam presses in operation that year. The lithographic printing process, which we will discuss later in regard to certain paper toys, was first used in the United States in 1818.

This very brief chapter on paper making and early printing is rather necessary as a background, as those two subjects are the basis of producing paper toys. Volumes of information on the subject of paper and printing, its origin, growth, and its resulting effects on the development and enlightment of the human mind are important. However, my primary purpose is to enlighten the reader to the many fascinating paper toys that were produced in the past.

CHAPTER II.

PAPER FOLDING & EDUCATIONAL CARDS

We go back to the Orient to find the origin of some of the earliest paper toys and games. Paper folding is the art of making objects out of paper without cutting, pasting or decorating. In Japan it is called *origami*, and the folded toys represent birds, fish, animals, flowers, and figures. Some outstanding examples are; a bird that flaps it's wings when it's tail is pulled, and a frog that hops when it's back is tapped. Interest in paper folding spread to Spain and South America, and eventu-ally the enthusiasm for this craft spread through-out the world.

Playing cards extended further back in time — their actual starting point is unrecorded. India and China both lay claim to the origin of the playing card, along with chess, dice and back-gammon. Conquering soldiers, seafaring men and gypsies spread the playing of cards from east to the west. The earliest cards were handmade, which made them too costly for any but the wealthy. The demand became so great that the publishers made them from either wood blocks or stencils, which brought them down in price. The first printing of playing cards appears to be around 1423, and from this point on the price per pack was within the reach of anyone desiring them. In the 15th century, playing cards were printed in Spain and Italy, and at a later date in Germany and France. A variant of the playing card, educational game cards, were originated by a German, Doctor Thomas Murner. In 1509, Murner invented a set of instructive cards for his young students to be used in the art of reasoning and learning. This idea was soon accepted in France, then in England, and later in America. Educational game cards received a popularity boost in 1644 when Cardinal Mazarin developed an instructional game of cards to quicken the learning process of Louis XIV of France. The king, a reluctant and rather slow pupil, was eight years old at the time. French printers published cards dealing with heraldry, the study of armor, and edged weapons. Later cards picturing outstand-ing personalities of ancient Greece and Rome, the art of warfare, military strategy, and the con-struction of fortifications, became popular. The subject of Napoleon's campaigns and later cards that ridiculed some of France's political leaders were favorites.

German publishers favored educational cards that dealt with geography, peoples of the world, costumes, astronomy, science and morality. **(Illustration 1.)** Educational cards dealing with

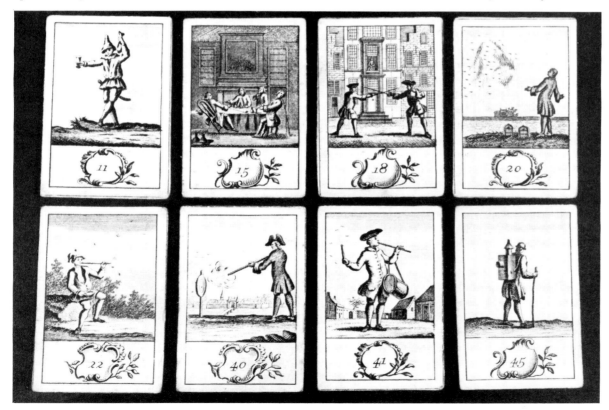

Illustration 1: Early deck of educational cards picturing trades, professions and recreational activities of the 1700s. The deck consists of 50 cards. Publisher unknown. Euro-pean c.1770. Card size 2¼ x 1½in (5.7 x 3.8cm). *Strong Museum Collection.*

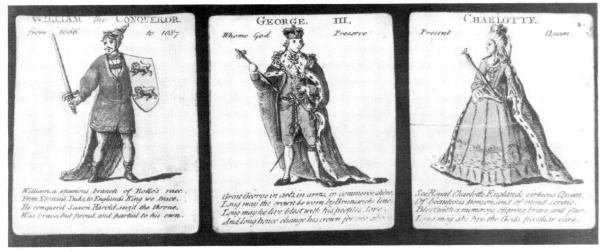

Illustration 2: Examples of cards from early deck illustrating British rulers from the time of William the Conqueror to Queen Charlotte, titled the *Royal Historical Game*. Publisher is unknown. Great Britain, c.1820. Card size 2 x 2½in (5.1 x 6.4cm). *Strong Museum Collection*.

mathematical and spelling subjects appeared in England. In the 17th and 18th centuries, political propaganda directed against the Catholic Church was printed in the form of playing cards in England. Towards the end of the 18th century a new form of playing card was issued consisting of what was called transformation cards. The game tested the artistic skill of each player, as each card had five points placed in predetermined spots that the player could draw a figure from. This type of transformation card was soon accepted all over Europe, and publishers in each country hired skilled artists to lay out dotted combinations that would intrigue artistically minded people to try and solve.

In 1795, a set of cards was issued called *The Elements of Astronomy & Geography*, by John Wallis of London, England. Wallis is known to have published "puzzle" cards around this date. Packs of 12 to 15 cards, engraved and hand colored, pictured a subject and a puzzle question. For example, the subject pictured might be a red plumed hat set on a low garden wall, with the question printed above it. "A well known place in London?" The answer, printed on the back, would be "Hatters Garden." We will learn more of Wallis as he was a prolific publisher of early games and

jigsaw puzzles during this period. Card games featuring past rulers with captions giving subject history and dates of reigns became popular. A fine example is the *Royal Historical Game* with illustrations of the British rulers from the time of William the Conqueror to Queen Charlotte. **(Illustration 2.)** Publishers like Wallis, C. Hodges, F. G. Moon and J. Evans & Son all produced card games of this type before 1850. Funny educational card games began to appear around this time, an example being *Trial by Jury*, with caricature courtroom characters and their families. Another type of game, *The Game of Counties of England*, contained illustrations of a town scene in each county, with information listing their important features and principal products or industries. Hundreds of card games appeared covering the above subjects, also birds, fish, animals, trees, flowers, music, A.B.C.s, and so on. **(Illustration 3.)**

While we know a wide variety of card games were published, we may wonder in what quantities they were printed. In C. L. Mateaux's book, *The Wonderland of Work*, he describes the workings of the tradesmen and manufacturers of Europe. One chapter deals with the making of various toys, and several paragraphs tell of the

Illustration 3: Early English A B C cards, publisher unknown, c.1850. Card size 2½ x 3in (6.4 x 7.6cm). *Strong Museum Collection*.

production of inexpensive game cards in England. In essence, he writes that most of the cards were manufactured in London, England, and that there were three types produced — halfpenny, penny and twopenny packs, all inexpensively made but well constructed. The average factory kept a large group of male and female workers busy, and used from five to six tons of paper annually. Each ton of paper consisted of 63,360 sheets, and on each sheet there were three "penny sets" printed. When the printed sheets were cut there would be a total of 190,000 packs of cards, or a total of 2,000,000 cards. The "halfpenny" cards were the smallest, since twice as many were printed on each sheet. The "twopenny" packs had fancy decorated backs, and because they were

more attractive than the other two packs, one would expect them to outsell the others. Not so, the two cheaper packs were by far the best sellers.

English card games were found in America until the time of the War of Independence. The first American to be documented as a manufacturer of cards was Jazamiah Ford of Milton, Massachusetts, who advertised his playing card manufactory in the early newspapers. One of the earliest card games published in America was *The Lottery of the Pious, or the Spiritual Treasure Casket*, dated 1744. The printer was Christopher Sower of Germantown, Pennsylvania. In Philadelphia, Pennsylvania, J. RIce's *Impenetrable Secret, or Young Ladys & Gentlemens Polite Puzzle* was a card game which established prin-

ciples of virtue and morality for both sexes. Many of the early American card games were similar to those published in England. W. & S. B. Ives of Salem, Massachusetts, manufactured *Dr. Busby* in the early 1830s. Bible card games, such as the *Scriptured History* and the *Battle For Palestine*, followed. These games included information as to the geographic locations of biblical places, facts about biblical characters, and quotes from the Bible. They were all well illustrated and very colorful. Noel's *Game of Music* and the *Allegrando Musical Game* were musical card games that required a knowledge of music reading to score in the game. Decks of cards with illustrations of characters from childrens' books followed. **(Illustration 4.)** Card games with themes of nature,

Illustration 4: Early American card game *Justice* based on the book *Uncle Tom's Cabin*. Published by V.S.W. Parkhurst of Rhode Island, in 1852. Cards measure 2½ x 1⅝in (6.4 x 4.1cm). *Strong Museum Collection.*

Illustration 5: Baseball card game published by the Lawson Card Company of Boston, Massachusetts, c.1900. Card size 2½ x 1¾in (6.4 x 4.4cm). *Strong Museum Collection.*

Illustration 6: Civil War cards depicting the various battles with detailed information, dates of battles, victor, leaders and casualties. Publisher unknown. American, c.1870. Cards measure 2¼ x 1½in (5.3 x 3.8cm). *Strong Museum Collection.*

politics, and sports appeared. **(Illustration 5.)** War games influenced by the Civil War followed. The *Game of Battle, North & South 1861-1863* consisted of 52 cards, each one illustrating a battle scene, its dates, who won the particular battle (the North or the South), and other pertinent facts about the war. **(Illustration 6.)** In the 1870s, games such as *Authors* became popular, and remained so, appearing in numerous variations up to World War II. In 1874, the F. A. Wright Company of Cincinnati, Ohio, issued *Logomachy, or War of Words.* This was a game that required thought and the ability to spell. It was a type of anagram game in which the players tried to outdo their opponents by spelling lengthy words

and phrases with the cards dealt to them. About 1900, comic strip characters appeared on cards. The first to appear was R. F. Outcault's *Yellow Kid*, followed a year later by *Buster Brown.* Some time later *And Her Name Was Maud* appeared which featured Fred Oppers stubborn mule along with other comic characters of the period. All were either being chased by the mule, or in turn they chased the mule. Included were *Buster Brown*, the *Katzenjammer Kids, Little Jimmy, Lulu & Leander, Foxy Grandpa, Happy Hooligan* and *Alphonse & Gaston.*

Possibly the reader would realize a broader view of the number of card games and their variations published by the big three of American

game publishers, by a comparison of the card games listed in their respective catalogs. McLoughlin Brothers of New York City, Milton Bradley of Springfield, Massachusetts, and Parker Brothers of Salem, Massachusetts, were the prominent publishers of paper toys and games in the United States. A comparison of their early catalogs dating from 1880 to 1900, and later versions from 1900 to 1920, will show that all three published similar card games on like subjects, differing only in the design art. However, each in their time published some totally original games.

The McLoughlin catalog of 1882 illustrated a number of card games. Among them was one of particular interest called *Conversation Cards.* The copy below the illustration reads: "Intended for people of small conversational powers. Six sets of cards, each set is devoted to special subjects of conversation, on marriage, on ladies & gentlemen, on loves & likes, on love, quizzical and comical. To bashful people, they are a great blessing, not only furnishing hours of amusement, but sometimes leading them to the gates of matrimony." **(Illustration 7.)** Games such as *Old Maid, The Golden Egg, Yankee Pedlar, Game of Authors, Game of Nations, Old Time Comic Conversation Cards, Centennial Presidential Game, Japanese Orcale, Game of Hens & Chickens, Pinafore Game, Old Maid & Bachelor, Game of Musical Authors, Grandma's Game of Useful Knowledge* and *Grandma's New Testament*, are pictured. The low priced decks, costing 12¢ to 20¢, are packaged in attractive pasteboard cases, while the more expensive decks, up to 60¢, were packed in wooden boxes. The 1882 catalog pictures 61 different card games. **(Illustration 8.)**

The later 1914 McLoughlin Brothers catalog pictured 84 card games, and many of these packs were issued in from three to six variations, offering a total of nearly 200 card games. Most of the games in the earlier 1882 catalog appear in this catalog, but in a different design. Some of the new games appearing were *Logomachy, the War of Words, Game of American Battles, Peter Coddle's Trip to N.Y.*, and the *Telegraph Messenger Boy.* These games were offered at 5¢ to 50¢. **(Illustration 9.)**

CONVERSATION CARDS................... Retail 20c. each.

These Cards are among the oldest and most popular of amusements. Originally intended for people of small conversational powers, they are now used by pleasure-seekers of all classes. The variety of conversations resulting from a single pack is immense. Each set is devoted to special subjects of conversation, making the entire series very perfect and desirable to each purchaser. To bashful people, they are a great blessing, not only furnishing an hour's amusement, but sometimes leading them to the gates of matrimony.

Illustration 7: A variety of Conversation Cards published by McLoughlin Brothers of New York City. Pictured as they appeared in McLoughlin's 1882 catalog.

CINDERELLA SERIES .... Retail 30c. each.

LITTLE RED RIDING-HOOD.

The game consists in fitting out Little Red Riding-Hood for her visit to her grandmother, and filling her basket with presents. The successful player is the one who contributes the most to this end. Recently revised and improved by the addition of a tee-to-tum.

COCK ROBIN.

Who killed Cock Robin? Who saw him die, etc., have been asked the world over. These questions, with their appropriate answers, are contained in the cards. The object is to play the proper answer to the question asked, each correct answer making a point in the game.

THE HOUSE THAT JACK BUILT.

Jack's house is the central card. As the game runs, Jack lived in this house, and offered to pay a large sum, for all the things named in the story of this wonderful place, as told by Mother Goose. The names of these things appear on the cards, and the lucky players get prices for them, varying with the different phases of the game.

MOTHER HUBBARD.

This game contains, besides the story of Mother Hubbard's Famous Dog, as told by Mother Goose, a new one written expressly for it, both of which are used in play. In the course of the game, the cards are made to supply omitted parts of the new story, and the context is often very ridiculous.

Illustration 8: A page from McLoughlin Brothers' 1882 catalog picturing four of some 61 card games offered that year.

Milton Bradley's 1896-97 catalog lists educational card games such as *The Little Object Teacher, Game of Dickens Revised, The Spelling School, Eclectic Authors,* and variations of *Authors.* **(Illustration 10.)** Other card games illustrated were *Watermelon, Peter Coddle's Trip to N.Y., Palmistry, I Don't Know, Aesop, Great Inventions,* and five variations of *Old Maid.* Bradley's 1909 catalog lists 94 card games ranging in price from 5¢ to 25¢. Included were the games mentioned above. All were published in five grades, the quality of each determined by the price level. **(Illustration 11.)** Bradley's 1918-19 catalog pictures 81 card games. The same games appeared, the following year in a new art format along with a general run of other games. The majority of the games were published in six grades or issues, the quality of each depending on the price level which started at 5¢ and reached a new high of 40¢.

George Parker started his game publishing

5 CENT CARD GAMES

No. 375¼.—PETER CODDLE SERIES—3 Kinds
By Mail 8c
OUT OF PRINT

Size, 5¼ x 4¼ inches

This is a strong combination of games, all well adapted to interest and amuse children. The titles are, Letters, Peter Coddle, and Authors.
Put up assorted in dozens

No. 4150.—UNCLE JOSH
By Mail 7c
OUT OF PRINT

Size, 3 x 4 inches

This is a simple game, but one that can be made to afford an immense amount of fun to a round party of young people.
Put up in dozens

No. 376A.—OLD MAID
By Mail 8c

Size, 3¼ x 4¼ inches

This edition of the popular game contains 36 round-cornered cards, printed in red and black. The designs are grotesque and amusing.
Put up in dozens

10 CENT CARD GAMES
No. 4210.—OLD MAID SERIES—3 Kinds

No. 372.—ILLUSTRATED AUTHORS
By Mail 17c

Size, 4¼ x 5¼ inches

These cards are round-cornered. The titles are, Illustrated Authors, Old Maid No. 2, and Peter Coddle's Trip to New York.
Put up assorted in dozens

No. 376.—OLD MAID GAME
By Mail 15c

Size, 4¼ x 5¼ inches

This is a first class edition of the oldest and most popular of all card games. There are 36 round-cornered cards in the pack.
Put up in dozens

No. 372B.—PETER CODDLE
By Mail 17c

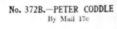

Size, 4¼ x 5¼ inches

The cards are 88 in number and, are used in connection with a funny story in which there are blanks to be supplied from the cards.
Put up in dozens

Illustration 9: McLoughlin Brothers offered these cards in their 1914 catalog. Many of these same card games were offered before 1900.

ECLECTIC AUTHORS.

This is a new game of Authors, comprising seventy-two cards. The portraits are not process work, but are finely printed from hand-engraved plates, made by the best engravers of the present day from pictures which have been selected as standard representations of leading writers in the English language.   Price, each, 25 cents.

AUTHORS IMPROVED.

As is well known by the trade, Authors Improved embraces peculiar patented features.

Each set comprises seventy-two cards, with portraits and ornamental borders on faces and beautifully engraved fancy backs.
Price, each, 50 cents.

AUTHORS, CLUB EDITION.

A set of Authors having fine portraits, with lithographed backs.
Price, each, 50 cents.

AUTHORS, HOUSEHOLD EDITION.

An elegant set of lithographed cards with beautiful designs, in a large box with lithographed label.   Price, each, 25 cents.

AUTHORS, PLAIN EDITION.

A very durable and pleasing game of Authors. A good set of thirty-three cards on buff ticket-stock, neatly lithographed, with a border.
Price, each, 10 cents.

FIVE CENT AUTHORS.

A new game of Authors, in a neat box, with illuminated label and lithographed cards.   Price, each, 5 cents.

Illustration 10: Milton Bradley's catalog of 1896-97 offered this selection of the game of *Authors*. Notice the price range and variety of designs in the packs offered.

business in 1883 with a card game he called *Banking*. In 1885 he issued his first catalog, a four-page folder, listing his game offerings which included such card games as *Banking, Famous Men, Speculation* and *Dr. Busby*. Two years later Parker issued a second catalog listing 125 items. Around the end of the 19th century he produced three new card games, *Pit, Flinch* and *Rook*,

which all proved to be good sellers up into the 1950s. *Rook* was published in several different forms. The Parker Brothers catalog of 1916-17 listed 44 card games which included the games mentioned above plus six variations of *Authors*, four of *Old Maid*, two of *Snap*, and others. **(Illustration 12.)**

Parker Brothers did not seem to publish

games in a series of grades to the extent that their two competitors did. However, their prices were competitive. Unlike the others, at least one quarter of their games originated within the company itself. They are still in business today, thriving and a leader in the game world.

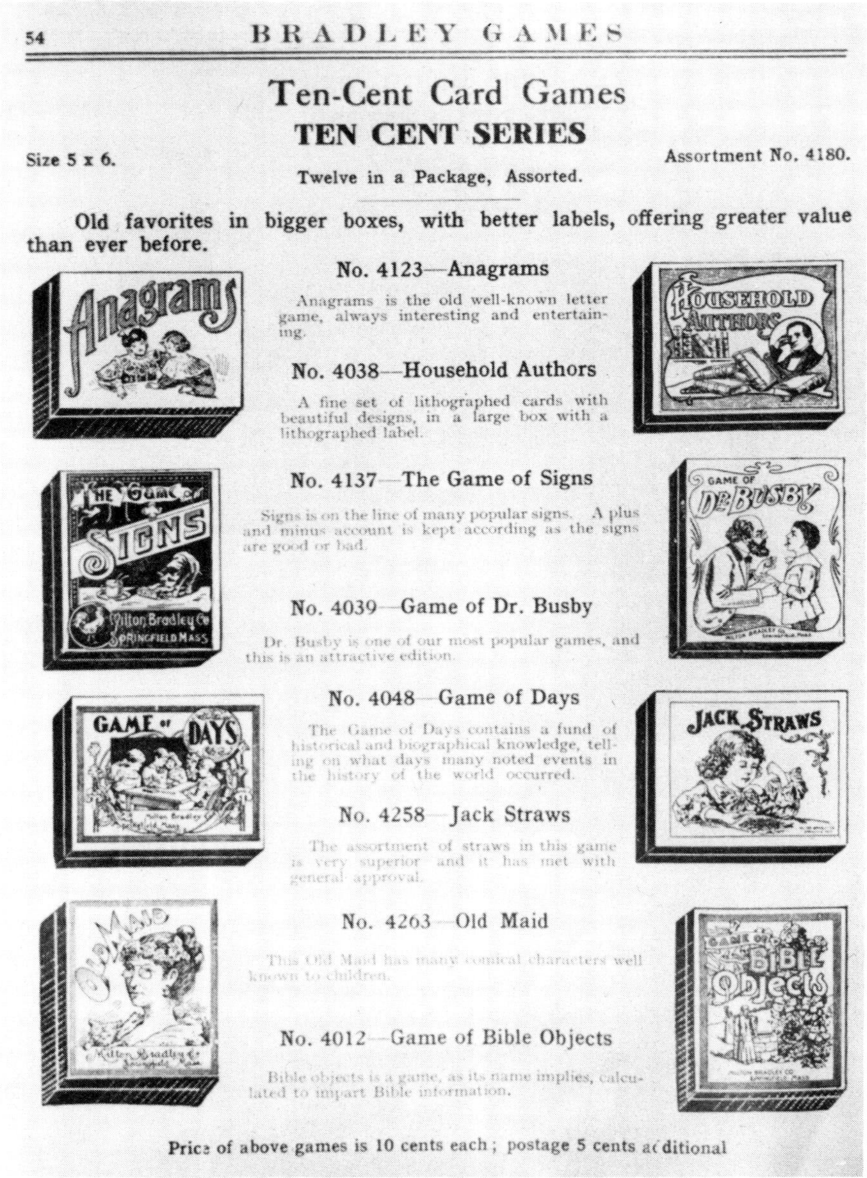

Ten-Cent Card Games
TEN CENT SERIES

Size 5 x 6.

Twelve in a Package, Assorted.

Assortment No. 4180.

Old favorites in bigger boxes, with better labels, offering greater value than ever before.

No. 4123—Anagrams

Anagrams is the old well-known letter game, always interesting and entertaining.

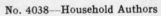

No. 4038—Household Authors

A fine set of lithographed cards with beautiful designs, in a large box with a lithographed label.

No. 4137—The Game of Signs

Signs is on the line of many popular signs. A plus and minus account is kept according as the signs are good or bad.

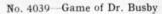

No. 4039—Game of Dr. Busby

Dr. Busby is one of our most popular games, and this is an attractive edition.

No. 4048—Game of Days

The Game of Days contains a fund of historical and biographical knowledge, telling on what days many noted events in the history of the world occurred.

No. 4258—Jack Straws

The assortment of straws in this game is very superior and it has met with general approval.

No. 4263—Old Maid

This Old Maid has many comical characters well known to children.

No. 4012—Game of Bible Objects

Bible objects is a game, as its name implies, calculated to impart Bible information.

Price of above games is 10 cents each; postage 5 cents additional

---

AUTHORS   Invented and first published in Salem

GREAT AUTHORS

No. 135 NEW. The best authors published. Entirely new plates. This is a game giving the most famous authors and poets, Shakespeare, Scott, Dickens, Longfellow, Tennyson, etc. It differs from our famous game of "Authors-up-to-Date" in that it deals with the standard authors rather than those contemporaneous with our time.

Beautifully made on the highest quality enamelled cardboard and completely illustrated.

Size 6½ x 5.   Price, 30 cents

Red Line Authors

No. 145 This is a very popular 25 cent Authors. Made with handsome plates in the best manner, and containing the masters of literature including leading modern writers such as Longfellow, Kipling, etc. Highly enamelled, round cornered cards, beautifully illustrated.

Price, 25 cents

Authors up to Date

No. 58 The largest selling Authors on the market. Entirely new plates, with the latest popular Authors of the day, such as Winston Churchill, William Dean Howells, Booth Tarkington, etc. Highly enamelled, round cornered cards, with fine half tone engraving and handsome bright colored backs.

Price, 30 cents

AUTHORS

No. 372 This is the best edition of Authors that is offered at a low price. It contains beautifully printed portraits of all the leading standard authors.   Price, 10 cents

50c. AUTHORS

Beautifully made cards from new plates on very highly finished cards of best quality. **Gold edges.**

Price, 50 cents

Gold-Medal Authors

Same cards in leatherette partition box ("Pit style.") Price, 50 cents

AUTHORS

No. 120 Containing such popular favorites as Dickens, Scott, Longfellow, etc., etc. Cards in this edition are not equal to the cards in Red Line or Authors up to Date.

Price, 20 cents

AUTHORS New 1911

No. 170 Showy new edition illustrated with half tone plates. Large box with handsome label. Size of box 8½ x 6½. Price, 25 cents

Shakespeare Game

No. 415 Played with cards bearing quotations from the plays of Shakespeare.   Price, 25 cents

Literary Salad

No. 166 A famous old game revived in new form. The cards bear popular quotations from the poets.

Price, 25 cents

Illustration 11: A page from Milton Bradleys' 1909 catalog offering a selection of 10¢ card games. This catalog listed 94 card games ranging in price from 5¢ to 25¢.

Illustration 12: Parker Brothers catalog of 1916-17 offerred this selection of the popular game of *Authors*. This same catalog pictured 44 card games.

Color Illustration 2: *Peep Show A.B.C. Blocks*, manufactured by McLoughlin Brothers of New York City, were patented in 1885. Twelve hollow blocks, each measuring 2¼in (5.8cm) square, one side has circular glass window exposing interior decoration. The remaining five sides are marked with alphabet letters. Box measures 8 x 10 x 2½in (20.3 x 25.4 x 6.4cm). *Photo by Harry Bickelhaupt.*

Color Illustration 1: The *Santa Claus Cube Puzzle* was manufactured by McLoughlin Brothers of New York City, and copyrighted in 1897. Twenty blocks, each measuring 2½in (6.4cm) square, made up six Christmas scenes. The box measures 13¼ x 10¾ x 2¾in (33.6 x 27.3 x 7.0cm). *Photo by Len Rosenberg.*

Color Illustration 3 A & B: *Telescopic View of The Great Exhibition*, printed by C. Moody, Holborn, London, England, dated 1851. Ten cut-out sections make up the main exhibition hall. Front face measures 6¼ x 6¾in and extends back 26in (15.9 x 17.1 x 66.0cm). **B**. Unusual camera shot through the peep hole. *Photo by Len Rosenberg.*

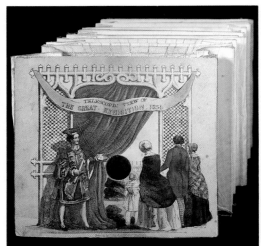

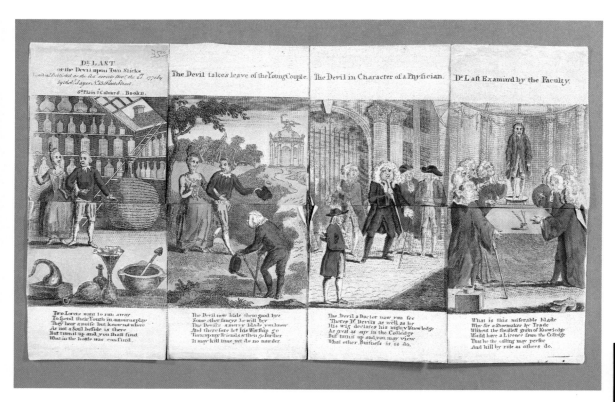

Two Lovers want to run away
To spend their Youth in amorous play
They hear a noise but know not where
Ar not a Soul beside is there
But turn it up and you shall find
What in the bottle was confin'd.

The Devil now bids them good bye
Some other fancye he will try
The Devil's a merry blade you know
And therefore let his Worship go
Turn up my friends & then go further
It may kill time yet do no murder

The Devil a Doctor now you fee
There's Dr. Devils as well as he
His wig declares his mighty Knowledge
As great as any in the Colledge
But turn it up and you may view
What other Business is to do.

What is his miserable blade
Who Sir a Shoemaker by Trade
Without the smallest grain of Knowledge
Would have a Licence from the Colledge
That he the calling may perfue
And kill by rule as others do.

Color Illustration 4: A Harlequinade titled *Dr. Last or the Devil Upon Two Sticks*, published by Robert Sayer, 53 Fleet Street, London, England, and dated 1776. Opens to a large sheet, 14½ x 12½in (36.8 x 31.7cm). It is folded three times vertically and twice horizontally. The brief story tells of two lovers who let the devil out of a bottle, he befriends them, then bids them farewell. The devil becomes a physician and creates turmoil among others in his profession. As Dr. Last he is examined by the faculty and found unsuitable to continue in the medical profession and is returned to the bottle of confinement. *Collection Herbert Hosmer. Photo by Len Rosenberg.*

Color Illustration 5: *The Hearty Old Boy, Who Always Looked The Same* was published by Dean & Son, Ludgate Hill, London, England, c.1865. Each page pictures Mr. Hodge in various stages of his life: as a soldier, a sailor, a storekeeper, a wealthy merchant, an Alderman, as Sir John Hodge and finally with the molded head. The preceding pages all have an oval cut-out at head level, exposing the molded head on the last page. Book size 10 x 6¾in (25.4 x 17.2cm). *Photo by Len Rosenberg.*

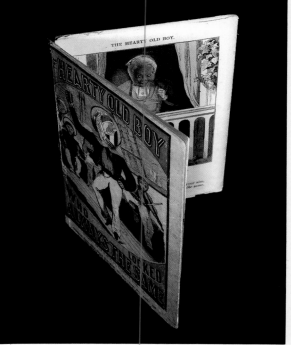

L'ange des fleurs. Die Blumenengel. The Flower Angels.

Le printemps à son retour
Chaque année est salué par nous,
Comme un ange qui apporte les fleurs,
Le bonheur, la joie pour tous.

Bringt ihr Füllhorn mit dem Lenze
Göttin Flora der Natur,
Flechten Englein Blumenkränze
Schmücken damit Wald und Flur.

When Flora, her horn of plenty, does bring
A tribute to Nature, in sweet time of spring;
Then Angels, they weave a ne'er-ending wreath
While blithely they spread it, o'er grove, mead and heath.

L'ange des fleurs. Die Blumenengel. The Flower Angels.

Le printemps à son retour
Chaque année est salué par nous,
Comme un ange qui apporte les fleurs,
Le bonheur, la joie pour tous.

Bringt ihr Füllhorn mit dem Lenze
Göttin Flora der Natur,
Flechten Englein Blumenkränze
Schmücken damit Wald und Flur.

When Flora, her horn of plenty, does bring
A tribute to Nature, in sweet time of spring;
Then Angels, they weave a ne'er-ending wreath
While blithely they spread it, o'er grove, mead and heath.

Color Illustration 6 A & B: One of eight moveable pages from a book published by Wilhelm Nitzschke of Stuttgart, Germany, 1870. Titled *The Flower Angels*, it contains a disc that when turned, transforms Flora's horn of plenty filled with Spring flowers and fruits to a circular array of small winged cherubs clinging to a garland of flowers. Page size 12¼ x 10in (31.1 x 25.4cm). *Photo by Len Rosenberg.*

Color Illustration 7: The *Columbus Panorama* was printed in Germany for The International News Company of New York City, c.1893. A three section fold-out featuring Columbus setting foot on the New World, Washington accepting the Declaration of Independence, and Lincoln announcing the Emancipation of the Slaves. This fold-out is 14in high and 32in wide (35.6 x 81.3cm). *Photo by Len Rosenberg.*

Color Illustration 8: *The Castle Tournament* was published by Bancroft & Company Ltd., of London, England, and printed in Czechoslovakia in 1961. A large pop-up, created and illustrated by V. Kubasta, it is beautifully done in strong colors. The double page pop-up is 12in high and 17½in wide (30.5 x 44.5cm). *Photo by Len Rosenberg.*

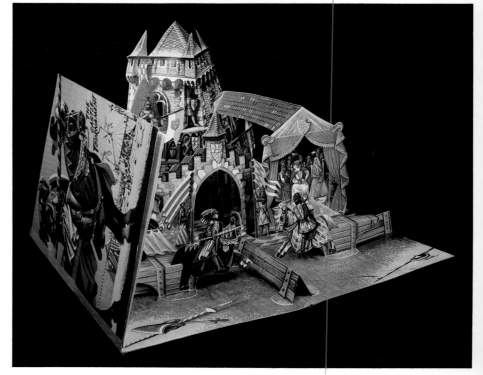

Color Illustration 9: "Attacked By the Giant Reptile" is one of three pop-ups from the book *Buck Rogers, Strange Adventures in the Spider-Ship*. It was published by Pleasure Books, Inc., of Chicago, Illinois, in 1935. An early space adventure illustrated with line drawings and excitingly portrayed in three colorful pop-ups. Opened it measures 6½in high and 16in wide (16.5 x 40.7cm). *Photo by Len Rosenberg.*

Color Illustration 10: "Tarzan Attacks the Crocodile" is the center spread pop-up in *The New Adventures of Tarzan*. A Blue Ribbon Press Book published by Pleasure Books, Inc., of Chicago, Illinois, in 1935. Three pop-ups picture "Tarzan Swinging Through the Trees," "Attacking the Crocodile" and "Tarzan & Ula in a Boat." This pop-up stands 6¾in high and 15½in wide (17.1 x 39.3cm). *Photo by Len Rosenberg.*

Color Illustration 11: "Ming the Merciless enters, riding between the jaws of death," is the center spread pop-up in the action book *Flash Gordon, Tournament of Death*. Art work by Alex Raymond, published by Pleasure Books, Inc. of Chicago, Illinois, and copyrighted in 1935 by King Features Syndicate, Inc. This fascinating pop-up is 6in high and 15½in wide (15.2 x 39.4cm). *Photo by Len Rosenberg.*

TOP LEFT: Color Illustration 12: Early French boxed set of soldiers titled *Le Garde National*, publisher unknown, c.1850. Unusual straight-sided soldier. Possibly four others are missing, as are parts of the military costumes. Figures may be dressed front and back. Single figure is 7in (17.8cm) tall. *Photo by Len Rosenberg.*

TOP RIGHT: Color Illustration 13: A boxed set titled *Tournament of The Nations, Series of Rockers*, copyrighted by Sam'l Gabrial Sons & Company of New York City and marked "Printed in Germany," c.1925. The highly embossed figures represent an Arabian Horseman, a French Chasseur, an Indian Cavalryman, a Russian Cossack, a German Uhlan, and a British Cavalryman. Figures average 8½in (21.6cm) tall. *Photo by Len Rosenberg.*

RIGHT: Color Illustration 14: *The Game of Battles*, produced by McLoughlin Brothers, New York City, c.1910. Game made up of 60 soldiers, two cannons, 30 wooden shells, two tents and two flags. A game for two or four boys, objects are divided equally, set up according to rules printed inside the cover, and firing starts. Object: to knock down opposing army. Each soldier stands 6in (15.2cm) tall. *Photo by Len Rosenberg.*

Color Illustration 15: *The Masquerade* is a magnificent boxed set published by F. Fechner of Guben, Germany, c.1850. Made up of four figures, each with three costumes and three separate heads or masks. Interchange of figures, heads, and costumes provides scores of masquerade possibilities. Figures stand 8in (20.3cm) tall. *Photo by Harry Bickelhaupt.*

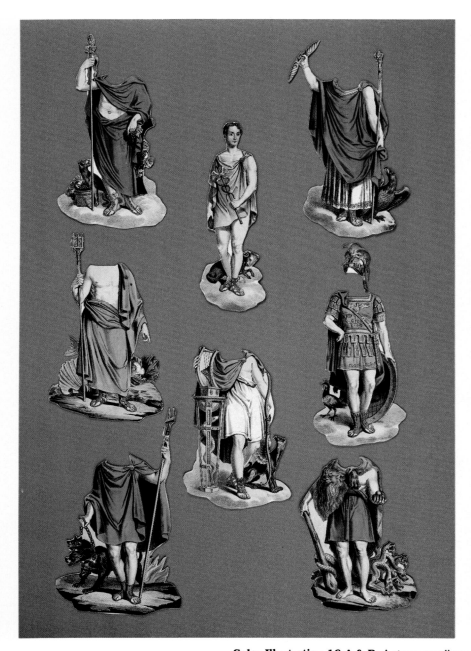

Color Illustration 16 A & B: A green cardboard slipcase titled *Mythologie* contains two matching folders containing these 16 figures. Published by H.F. Muller of Wien (Vienna), dated 1841. Included is a 72-page book, *A Conversation on Mythology for Young People*, printed in German and French. Figures average 8in (20.3cm) tall. *Photo by Len Rosenberg.*

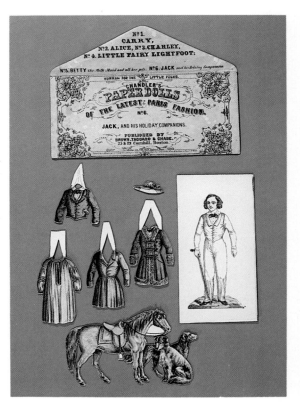

Color Illustration 17 A & B: *Little Fairy Lightfoot* and *Jack & His Holiday Companions* are examples of the work of John Greene Chandler of Massachusetts. These two sets were published by Brown, Taggart & Chase of Boston, Massachusetts, in 1857. *Little Fairy Lightfoot* stands 3½in (8.9cm) tall. The uncut figure of *Jack* is 4⅝in (11.7cm) tall. *Collection Herbert Hosmer, Photo by Len Rosenberg.*

Color Illustration 18: *Bessy & Kate* a rare uncut set of paper dolls published by R.A Hobbs of Lowell, Massachusetts, c.1885. Directions state: "Fold paper at top of the dresses and cut out front and back together, leaving a small space at the shoulder to rest on doll. The hat and cap must be folded at the top, cut out in the same way. Dresses and hats may be gummed at the sides." Backs of dresses are uncolored. Dolls are 4¼in (10.3cm) tall. *Photo by Len Rosenberg.*

Color Illustration 19: *Susie's Pets*, an uncut set of a little girl holding a puppy, a rabbit, a bird, a doll, and a basket of flowers. Published by McLoughlin Brothers of New York City, in 1858. These uncut sheets are extremely rare. *Susie* stands 6½in (16.5cm) tall. *Photo by Harry Bickelhaupt.*

Color Illustration 20: The characters of *Little Red Riding Hood* are enclosed in the above envelope which, when opened, has detailed directions on method of cutting out figures and the story of *Red Riding Hood.* The suggestion is made that a child, while reading the story, may act it out with the cut-out characters. Published by McLoughlin Brothers between 1864 and 1870. *Red Riding Hood* stands 7½in (19.0cm) tall. *Photo by Len Rosenberg.*

Color Illustration 21: Early hand colored paper doll set found in original grey and tan folder marked *Englische Puppe.* Published by J.L. Stahl of Nurenberg, Germany, c.1790. Pink booklet pictured (see text) has eight pages, each equipped with an identification label on a crossband which holds the various costumes in place. The doll stands 7¾in (19.7cm) high. *Photo by Len Rosenberg.*

LEFT: Color Illustration 22: *The Folding Doll House* produced by McLoughlin Brothers is a fine example of American color lithography in the late 1800s. Unfortunately, the red roof in the photograph has bleached out and does not do justice to this beautiful paper toy. The house is 18in high, 15¼in wide and 9½in deep (45.7 x 38.7 x 24.2cm). *Strong Museum collection. Photo by Tom Weber and Mike Radke.*

BOTTOM LEFT: Color Illustration 23: A hand colored uncut proscenium sheet published by W.G. Webb of St. Lukes, London, England, 1870. Webb did most of his own artwork and designing, coloring was done by the local cottage industry. This sheet measures 13½ x 17in (34.2 x 43.2cm). *Collection Herbert Hosmer. Photo by Len Rosenberg.*

BOTTOM RIGHT: Color Illustration 24: A lovely paper theater titled *Great Theater for Children.* Marked "A.K." on the box cover, it was made in Germany. There are four flats of scenery with matching side scenes, 44 characters and 24 accessories. Unfortunately the play book is missing. The stage front is 16in high and 28in wide (40.6 x 71.1cm). *Photo by Len Rosenberg.*

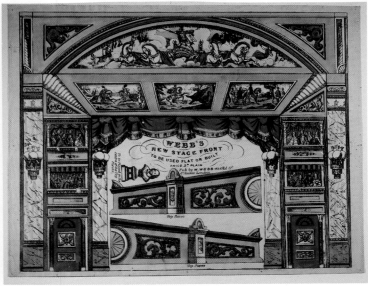

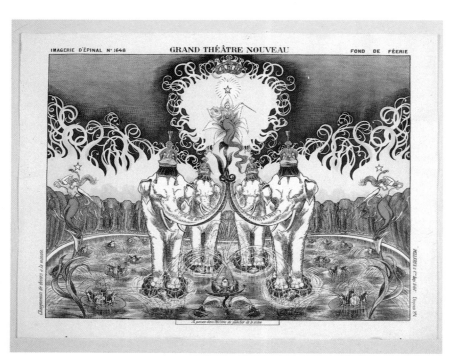

Color Illustration 25: A spectacular sheet of a back drop "Fond De Féerie" featuring four white elephants standing on the backs of turtles within a pool covered with frogs sitting on lily pads and gushing out water in fountain-like sprays. The elephants bring their trunks together and support a fairy sitting on a lily throne. An imaginative piece of artwork in a world of fantasy. Published by Pellerin of Epinal, France, c.1885. Size 16½ x 22in (41.9 x 55.9cm). *Photo by Harry Bickelhaupt.*

BOTTOM LEFT: Color Illustration 26: The four companion side pieces to the preceding bit of scenery, titled "Couliases De La Féerie," and equally as fantastic. Published by Pellerin & Cie. of France. Sheet size 16½ x 22in (41.9 x 55.9cm). *Photo by Harry Bickelhaupt.*

BOTTOM RIGHT: Color Illustration 27: A paper theater modeled after the famous Tivoli Theater in Copenhagen, Denmark. Alfred Jacobsen produced this toy theater in 1874. Pictured is a reproduction made in 1960. Its outstanding feature is the peacock curtain which slowly folds it's tail and sinks below stage level to reveal the open stage. This theater measures 13¼ x 17½ x 5¾in (33.6 x 44.5 x 14.6cm). *Collection Herbert Hosmer. Photo by Len Rosenberg.*

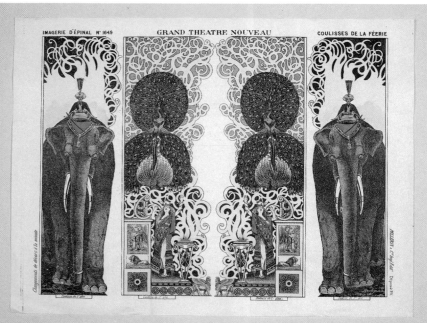

Color Illustration 28: *Schattentheater mit beweglichen Figuren*, roughly translated is shadow theater with jointed figures. Small trademark on box cover consists of an "A. & S." within a circle topped with a crown. Made in Germany, c.1910. Original box contains many jointed silhouette figures, with movement provided by stiff wires. Catalog contains numerous short sketches in German. Toy is 18in high, 24in wide (45.7 x 61.0cm). *Photo by Len Rosenberg.*

BOTTOM LEFT: Color Illustration 29: The *American Theater* was manufactured by McLoughlin Brothers and has a copyright date of 1901. It was still offered in the 1919 catalog. The highly colored proscenium measures 12 x 15 x 12½in (30.5 x 38.1 x 31.8cm). The photograph pictures the final scene of *Little Red Riding Hood*. *Photo by Len Rosenburg.*

BOTTOM RIGHT: Color Illustration 30: A fold-out panorama titled the *Great Menagerie*, published by J.S. Schrieber of Esslingen, Germany. Two of six panels are pictured, "Tigers & Monkeys" on the left and "Jumbo." The elephant has removed the hat of an enraged visitor who is swinging at him with an umbrella. Each panel is 13in high and 9in wide (33.0 x 22.8cm). *Photo by Len Rosenberg.*

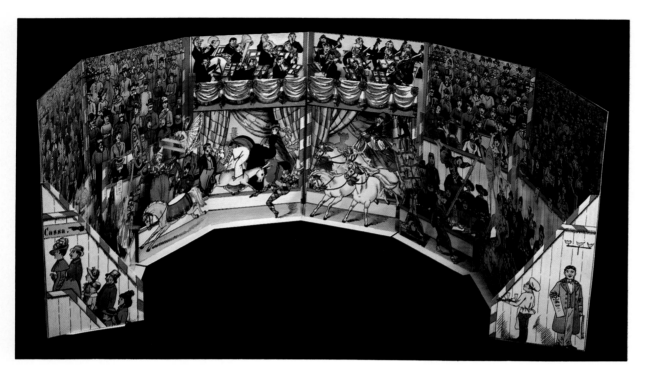

Color Illustration 31: The *International Circus* is the work of Lothar Meggendorfer, and was first published in 1887 by J.F. Schreiber. A panorama book which when opened reveals six scenes or acts. Opened it is 13in high and 52½in wide (33.0 x 133.3cm). *Photo by Len Rosenberg.*

Color Illustration 32: The "Traveling Circus" is pictured on the outskirts of a French village. Published by Pellerin & Cie. of France as scenery for his *Grand Theater Nouveau* series, c.1910. The sheet size is 16½ x 22in (41.9 x 55.9cm). *Photo by Len Rosenberg.*

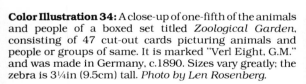

Color Illustration 33: The *American National Circus* was published by Brown, Taggard & Chase of Boston, Massachusetts, in 1858. Typical of both the early European and American circus, the trick equestrian acts were the star performances. These figures are representative of the performers of the first half of the 19th century. The elephant is 5¾in tall and 9in wide (14.6 x 22.8cm). *Collection Herbert Hosmer. Photo by Len Rosenberg.*

Color Illustration 34: A close-up of one-fifth of the animals and people of a boxed set titled *Zoological Garden*, consisting of 47 cut-out cards picturing animals and people or groups of same. It is marked "Verl Eight, G.M." and was made in Germany, c.1890. Sizes vary greatly; the zebra is 3¼in (9.5cm) tall. *Photo by Len Rosenberg.*

Color Illustration 35: An early French boxed set titled *Le Grand Jardin Des Plantes* marked "H. Duru, Editeur & Lith. Prodhonme, 89r du Temple," c.1850. Set includes 50 cut-out animals and figures, each labeled by name in French. The giraffe is 7¾in (19.7cm) tall. *Photo by Len Rosenberg.*

Color Illustration 36: The *Anamorphoscope* first appeared in 1850 in France. McLoughlin Brothers offered their version in the mid 1880s under the name *The Magic Mirror, or Wonderful Transformation*. Each card offers an elongated curved distorted picture and a circled spot to place the mirrored cylinder. By looking into the cylinderical mirror, the distorted drawing becomes a squirrel clutching at a nut. The mirrored cylinder is 4in (10.1cm) high. *Photo by Len Rosenberg.*

Color Illustration 37: The *Phenakistiscope* consists of a large card disc, slotted at equal distances along the outer edge and decorated with drawings of figures that have a slight forward movement. Placing the disc on a short shaft with a handle on a 90° angle, the viewer holds it up to a mirror, spins the disc and peers through the revolving slots to observe the rapidly moving figures. The average disc size is 9in (22.9cm) in diameter. The pictured discs are from a set published by Ackermann & Co. of London, England, c.1855. *Photo by Len Rosenberg.*

Color Illustration 38: A *Zoetrope* on the left and a *Praxinoscope* both carry a selected animated strip inside the drum. The slotted *Zoetrope* drum when spun enables the viewer to watch the action through the slots. The *Praxinoscope* provides a better view of the action by watching the mirrors. Neither of these toys are marked as to maker. The *Zoetrope* is American made, the *Praxinoscope* is possibly English, c.1900. The paper strips vary greatly in subject matter and in action. The *Praxinoscope* measures 8½in (21.6cm) in diameter. *Photo by Len Rosenberg.*

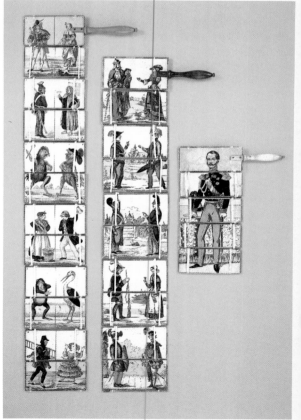

Color Illustration 39: "Jacob's Ladder" or "Flip Flop Toy" is an illusionary toy, changing pictures at the turn of a wrist. These early examples provided much amusement in the last half of the 19th century. Makers are unknown; the longest example measures 27in (68.6cm). *Photo by Len Rosenberg.*

Color Illustration 40: A trio of educational paper toys. The globe encased in the round box charts Captain James Cooks three voyages between 1768 and 1779. The two small boxes and globes and the folded strip are parts of an early game known as *The Earth and its Inhabitants*. The game in the foreground titled *Geographical Recreation or A Voyage Round the Habitable Globe*, was published by John Wallis of London, England, in 1809. *Photo by Len Rosenberg.*

Color Illustration 41: *Die Portrait Sammlung* (The Portrait Collection) is an early German rendition of metamorphoses. Each portrait card is divided into eight equal size squares. Hence all squares may be moved to form hundreds of humorous and grotesque combinations. Publisher unknown. c.1850. Each card measures 5½ x 3¾in (14.0 x 9.5cm). *Photo by Len Rosenberg.*

Color Illustration 42: A small boxed set with a theatrical theme is titled *Le Paravent ou Les Petits Acteurs*. It was printed by G. Doyen of Paris, France, in 1826. An accompanying small book introduces the de Mericort family and how this game evolved. The figures stand 3½in (8.9cm) tall and all fit into the small 4½ x 5¾ x 1¼in (11.4 x 14.6 x 3.2cm) box. *Photo by Len Rosenberg.*

Color Illustration 43: A most unusual boxed set titled *Grand Theater of Metamorphoses*. Observe the horizontal slot at the back of the stage. All the characters are swivelled at the waist, and a turn at the rear of the stage transforms a handsome youth to a dotty old man, or a young lady to a very old woman. Marked "G.W.F. & W." (G.W. Faber?) on cover. c.1860. The various double characters average 6in (15.2cm) in height. *Photo by Harry Bickelhaupt.*

Color Illustration 44: These two boxed sets are related to each other and are sometimes found in a single boxed set. *The Comic Boy* and *The Comic Girl* have the same subtitle, *Amusement With A Swinging Pendulum Figures in Many forms,* and each box is marked "G.W. Faber." Set any of the heads on the body, push slightly, and the figure will rock back and forth. Figures without head-pieces are 6¾in (17.1cm) tall. *Photo by Len Rosenberg.*

Color Illustration 45: An uncut printer's sheet before it becomes a completed boxed set of paper dolls. Titled *Les Toilettes Du Bebe*, it is marked "B. Colldert, Saussine, edt., Paris." c.1875. Notice all figures and clothing are two-sided. The sheet measures 20in high and 26in wide (50.8 x 66.0cm). *Photo by Len Rosenberg.*

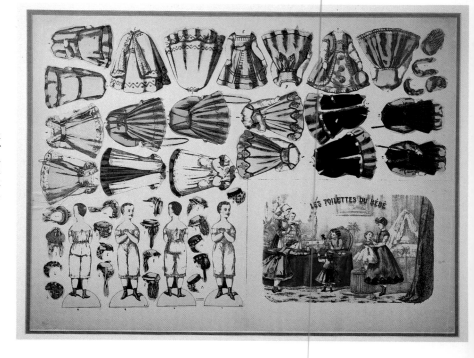

Color Illustration 46: *Bal d'Enfants* is a beautiful French toy encased in an unusual eight-sided box. Marked "de Lemercier, Benard et Cie" it possibly dates in the 1860s. The box contains a room setting with several cut-out figures and pieces of furniture. The unusual feature is the jointed figures, hung on a thread, that dance when the thread is jiggled. The room setting is 7in high and 10¼in wide (17.8 x 26.0cm). *Photo by Len Rosenberg.*

Color Illustration 47: A set of 13 fragile squares of scrap illustrating the *Kings & Queens of England, The Entire Series of 37 Rulers from William the Conqueror to Queen Victoria.* Each section measures 4½ x 6in (11.4 x 15.2cm). *Photo by Len Rosenberg.*

Color Illustration 48: *Le Parafagaramus*, is the title given to a boxed set containing a jointed tab and slot figure of a sorcerer. No markings as to maker, but appears to be French, c.1860. When assembled to the figure stands 15in (38.1cm) tall. *Photo by Len Rosenberg.*

Color Illustration 49: A grouping of colorful characters on assorted steeds. Riders are detachable; both rider and steed are two-sided, each side being entirely different in color, form and gender. Toys are unmarked. Germany, c.1885. Riders and mounts average 9in (22.8cm) in height. *Photo by Len Rosenberg.*

LEFT: Color Illustration 50: *La Dame De Paris* is strictly a novelty, a paper doll that is a high kicker. Unmarked as to maker, but kicking in Paris in the 1880s, she stands 7¾in (19.7cm) tall. *Photo by Len Rosenberg.* **RIGHT: Color Illustration 51:** Four examples of the many paper toys produced by Raphael Tuck & Sons of London, England. Those pictured date between 1900 and 1925. They vary greatly in size, the sailor boy with parrot and sailboat, sits 6⅞in (17.4cm) high. *Photo by Len Rosenberg.*

Chapter III.

GAME BOARDS

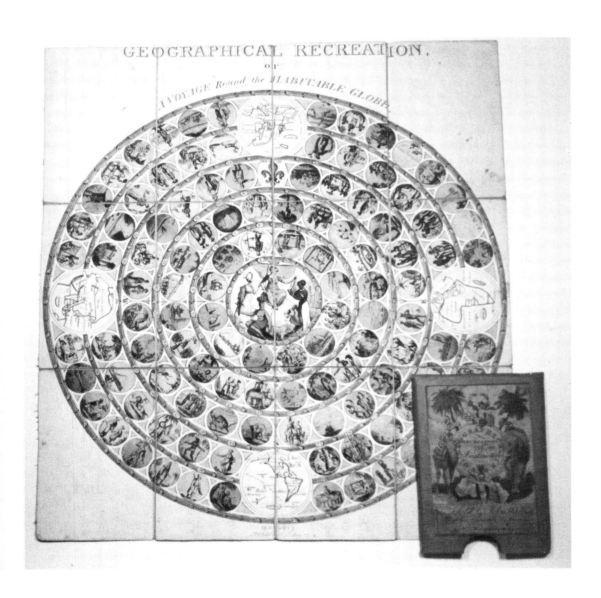

Game boards of various kinds have existed for centuries, many countries producing similar ones under different titles. The *Game of Goose*, a spiral type game with the tokens being moved inwards towards a central goal or home, is believed to have originated in Italy in the 16th century. It was brought to France, where it enjoyed several centuries of popularity. The French realized the potential of this game as a means of instruction and propaganda, and many variations of it appeared. In the 18th century, this game appeared in England and met with immediate acceptance. It again was published in many variations, but the basic principal of the game remained unchanged.

During the latter part of the 1700s, games and maps were printed on paper from engraved copper or steel plates and were later hand colored with watercolor paints. Around 1840, lithographed games began to appear. The early game papers were mounted on fine canvas or linen to prevent tearing, then folded and enclosed in a slip case. These early slip cases were made of cardboard covered with marbled paper, and a printed label was affixed to the outside. Later on, an attached folding cover took the place of the slip case. Rules of the game were either printed on the game itself or on a separate pamphlet enclosed within the game. **(Illustration 13.)**

It must be remembered that other countries, particularly France and Germany, produced huge quantities of games. George Hieronimus Bestelmeier of Nuremberg, Germany, was one of the

Illustration 13: The game of *Geographical Recreation* was published and sold by John Wallis at his Instructive Toy Warehouse, No 13 Warwick Square, London, England, in 1809. This game sheet, consisting of paper sections mounted on linen, is 22 x 20in (55.9 x 50.8cm).

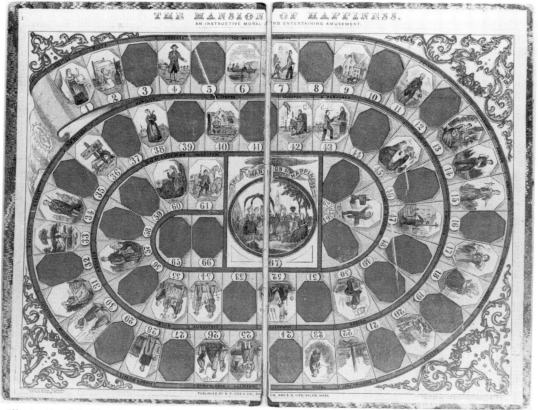

THE MANSION OF HAPPINESS.
AN INSTRUCTIVE MORAL AND ENTERTAINING AMUSEMENT.

Illustration 14: *The Mansion of Happiness,* first published by W & S.B. Ives of Salem, Massachusetts, in 1834.

creating their own variant games. All have educational or high amusement value to the children
and adults of their respective countries.

In the United States early board games were
either brought over by immigrants or imported
by shopkeepers. Imported games were for the
wealthy, and their numbers were few. Some
simple games were constructed at home by
parents who remembered board games from
their childhood. From 1800 to 1830 the importation of games and toys increased, but for the most
part these toys remained in the urban areas.
Transportation between cities and out into the
rural areas was still very limited. No doubt many
of the early printers published games in limited
quantities, but it wasn't until the 1830s that W.
S.B. Ives of Salem, Massachusetts, brought out
the *Mansion of Happiness.* **(Illustration 14)**
This was followed by a second moral game, *Game
of Pope or Pagan, or The Siege of the Stronghold
of Satan by the Christian Army.*

Another prominent American publisher of the
19th century was John McLoughlin. McLoughlin,
a Scotsman, had immigrated to this country in
1819 and quickly found a job with a company
that manufactured printing presses. This type of
work seemed to arouse a desire within him to
study the art of printing in his spare time. Late in
1827, he was in a position to purchase a hand
press and other accessories needed to become a
job printer. His interest seemed to be in children's
books, and in 1828 he produced a book of semi-
religious stories for children. Following this single
publishing venture, he merged with a competitor
by the name of Elton. Together they developed an
active business which, as time passed, became
moderately successful. About 1850 both men
decided to retire and the firm passed into the
hands of John McLoughlin Jr. He had joined the
company as a teenager, learned the trade, and at
the age of twenty-one was made a partner. The
firms name became "John McLoughlin, successor
to Elton & Company," and from that point on the
publishing house progressed rapidly. Having a
sharp eye for progress, young McLoughlin always
kept ahead of his competitors by taking advantage
of new improvements in methods of lithographic
printing. The process of printing by lithography

earliest publishers of a sales catalog from which
he sold his merchandise. An 1803 Bestelmeier
catalog features well over one thousand line
illustrations of objects for sale, among which are
hundreds of toys and an assortment of 133
games, many of which are board and card games.
When we delve back into the history of board
games, we find that there were three basic games
all originally played by adults that, over the years,
have developed into thousands of variations
played by adults and children alike. The first
basic game was playing cards, which was played
to pass the time of day and for gambling purposes.
These same two reasons exist today, and will
remain with us in the future. While playing cards
are not a part of this study, one of its variations,

the educational card game, is. The second basic
game is that of a race, that is any game board that
has a starting point and a finishing point with a
marked route in between, said route being marked
with penalties and rewards. Movement along the
route is governed by the roll of dice, the teetotum,
or a spinner. A very early example of this type of
game is *Parcheesi,* still a very popular game at the
present time. The third basic game is laid out in a
series or pattern of squares, and has an equal
number of tokens opposing one another. This is a
strategic type of game, usually requiring skill and
patience. Examples of this game are checkers and
chess. As the centuries passed, the ever increasing
variations of these three games have appeared,
each country involved having contributed by

STANDARD FOLDING GAMES.

In speaking of the marked excellence of this line of games, both in the style of the boards and in play, we can scarcely refrain from covering a page or more of our catalogue. As they cannot fail to be conspicuous among other lines of goods, we will let them speak for themselves, simply saying that each board contains three distinct games, each executed in the best style of art that we can command. The games themselves are simple, varied, and entirely new. Size of boards when opened, eighteen inches square. The implements are neat, substantial, and pleasing. Directions clear and explicit.

THE PILGRIM'S PROGRESS---(New.) Ready September 1

Three Games in one Board, viz.:

Pilgrim's Progress.   Going to Sunday School.   Tower of Babel.

Each Board separately wrapped and labeled.

THE PILGRIM'S PROGRESS

Is based upon the work of John Bunyan. The design is in the form of an eight-pointed star. The Celestial City, surrounded by the River of Death, occupies the centre of the board. At the angles and points of the star there are illustrations of the principal events in the Pilgrim's journey. The game is played with our new Indicator, and is based upon six different colors, which have been worked into it in a very pleasing manner. An illustrated synopsis of Bunyan's book accompanies the game.

GOING TO SUNDAY SCHOOL

Occupies one-half of the inside of the board. In the centre of this game there is a large clock dial, entwined with an elaborate and graceful vine of ivy. The margin of the board is handsomely laid out, and contains a number of illustrated spaces. At the four corners there are four large and handsome churches. The players move around the margin of the board, and register upon the clock dial the time occupied in so doing.

THE TOWER OF BABEL

Occupies the remaining half of the inside. This is an elaborate design, and presents the appearance of an imposing structure, with the artisans busily at work, as they might have appeared just prior to the dispersion of its builders. The game is played with the Indicator, using both colors and numbers. At one stage of the game there is confusion among the players, corresponding to that which must have taken place upon the confounding of tongues. The players change men by means of the Indicator.

VALDEVIA, or Central Park Game—New. Ready in October.

Three Games in one Board, viz.:

Valdevia.   Robin Hood's Archers.   Ten Pins.

Each Board separately wrapped and labeled.

VALDEVIA

Occupies the outside of the board, and is a bird's-eye view of   Central Park, laid out in lawns, groves, ponds, streams, bridges, &c. The players move over the boulevards, promenades, and rambles of the park. None of the boards of this series are laid out in set spaces, like most of their predecessors, and they will be found equally varied with them in play. When this board is laid out upon the table on a cold wintry evening, it cannot fail to impart a cheerful influence.

BOARD GAMES

No. 633.—INDIA
Retail 45c. Express extra

Size, 15½ x 18½ inches

This is a new and revised edition of this excellent game. The dice, cups and men are in a compartment at the side.

The board is in full colors and is very showy

No. 686.— MANSION OF HAPPINESS
Retail 45c. Express extra

Size, 15 x 22 inches

This is one of the oldest and most popular of games. It is one that conveys such good moral lessons that it is suitable for playing on Sundays as well as week days.

Put up in ¼ dozens

No. 687.—MAIL AND EXPRESS GAME
Retail 45c. Express extra

Size, 15 x 22 inches

This game is played on a handsome map of the United States. It is a very instructive game, from which a large amount of geographical and statistical information can be derived.

Put up in ¼ dozens

No. 425½.—NELLIE BLY— Fine Edition
Retail 55c. Express extra

Size, 16 x 19½ inches

This is a large edition of the famous Nelly Bly race around the world game, the merits of which have made it one of the most popular games of its class.

No. 441½.—TELEGRAPH BOY GAME
Retail 50c. Express extra

Size, 16 x 17 inches

This is an excellent game, which children can play with profit as well as pleasure, indicating, as it does, the qualities that lead to success in life.

No. 525.—FUN AT THE CIRCUS GAME
Retail 30c. Express extra

Size, 16½ x 16½ inches

This is a capital game for young children, as in playing it they can fancy they are enjoying the delights of the circus, all the features of which are depicted on the board.

Put up in ¼ dozens

Illustration 15: A page from McLoughlin Brothers' 1875-76 catalog listing some new board games. *The Pilgrim's Progress, Valdevia, or Central Park Game* and *Jerome Park Steeple Chase Game.* Each board contained three games within this grouping. Board size 18in (45.7cm) square.

Illustration 16: A page from McLoughlin Brothers' 1914 catalog. Notice the game *Mansion of Happiness* top center. Pirating of games and publishing under new designs was a common practice.

Introductory.

THE following complete Catalogue of our Manufactures and Publications is presented to the public in the most convenient and systematic form that we are able to devise for a class of goods as miscellaneous as is comprised in our list.

The alphabetical list enables any one to determine readily whether a required article is manufactured by us, and if so, refers to a full description of it in the succeeding pages, and gives the usual retail price.

The descriptive list is classified to suit various ages, thereby aiding to some extent in the selection, when it is not possible to make a personal examination, but as all goods sent by mail are liable to more or less damage, it is better to purchase of a dealer when a good fresh assortment can be selected from; but whatever orders we may receive, accompanied by the cash, will be filled promptly, and packed as securely as possible.

During an experience of several years in the manufacture and publication of home amusements, we have endeavored, with a conscientious regard for the good of the youth of our land, to exclude from our list everything liable to abuse or tending to pervert the tastes of old or young, and to admit only such as we believe to be innocently amusing, or positively instructive and elevating. We have a pride in presenting this Catalogue, the most complete and valuable collection of fireside recreations ever offered by any publisher in this or any other country; and we believe that in our attempt to build up a business very largely original with ourselves, we have also conferred a blessing on the present generation of parents, by enabling them to provide elevating and instructive recreations for their children, thereby rendering home attractive.

Being fully convinced of the value of the general principles of the Kindergarten method of instruction, we have not only published the only complete guide to this method in the English language, and manufactured a full line of the occupation material, but we have, as far as possible, incorporated the principles in various other articles.

THE KINDERGARTEN ALPHABET AND BUILDING BLOCKS are original with us, and combine the principles of Froebel in a remarkable degree. The KINDERGARTEN WEAVING and BRAIDING is another adaptation of these principles to the popular demand of the family. Among the games adapted to adults and youth, we invite special attention to the following:

POPULAR CHARACTERS FROM DICKENS.

KAKEBA; or JAPANESE BACKGAMMON, the best modern board game ever published.

MAGIC HOOPS. The best active game, for all places, and all seasons, ever invented.

AUTHORS IMPROVED.—Patented. This improvement in the old games of Authors doubles the interest of the game, while the old game can be played as well, if desired.

ROBINSON CRUSOE IMPROVED. An elegant game and very interesting.

BAMBOOZLE; or THE ENCHANTED ISLE. Original and interesting.

EVENINGS AT HOME. Judicious selections from our list, put up in fine walnut cases, for Holiday Presents.

BRADLEY'S PATENTED CROQUET. Embracing improvements for which little or nothing extra is charged, but which double the value of any set for scientific playing.

With thanks to all who have encouraged us in the past by their words and patronage, we shall endeavor in the future to merit the esteem and good wishes of all who are interested in the welfare of the youth of the present generation.

Milton Bradley & Co.

Illustration 17: The *Introductory* page to Milton Bradleys' 1873-74 catalog. Quote: "...we have endeavored, with a concientious regard for the good of the youth of our land, to exclude from our list everything liable to abuse or tending to pervert the tastes of old or young, and to admit only such as we believe to be innocently amusing, or positively instructive and elevating."

is based on the principal that grease and water will not mix. The ink is applied on the greased printing area while it is rejected on the non-printing areas that hold water. This printing process was developed by a German, Aloys Senefelder, in 1798. In experimenting, he used flat slabs of limestone found mainly in Bavaria. This type of stone had a porous texture that absorbed grease and water. He also worked with metal plates, treated to have a grained surface, as an alternative to the limestone; both worked, but the stone was the most popular with printers. The stones were used until around 1900, when commercial demands became greater than the supply of the Bavarian limestone.

Many publishing firms other than McLoughlin were using the lithographic process. Notable among the publishers was Currier & Ives of New York City, producing vast quantities of historical, current topical, and religious subjects. The lithographs at that time were printed in black outline and hand colored by women, each applying a specific color.

In the 1850s, John McLoughlin's New York City place of business, located on Division Street off Chatham Square, burned to the ground. A move to a larger location at 24 Beekman Street was soon accomplished, and in the same year his brother Edmund joined the firm. In 1858 the company name was changed to McLoughlin Brothers, and their line of published items included game cards, game boards, puzzles, novelty blocks, valentines, and paper dolls, as well as their principal product, children's books. The paper doll production increased in volume until it was near that of their children's books. **(Illustrations 15 & 16.)** Paper cut-out furniture and folding cardboard dolls' houses followed. Increased business necessitated a move to larger quarters at 30 Beekman Street, in 1864. The Civil War slowed the business down, but plans for expansion and the development of newly designed lines continued. Always aware of new improvements in printing technology, McLoughlin Brothers quickly used new ideas in color printing on all their products. They moved from hand printing and stenciling to hand painting, to lithography and on to chromolithography. In 1870 they moved to a new factory in Brooklyn, New York, said to have been the largest color printing plant in the country at the time. McLoughlin's major competition at this time was the color picture books and paper dolls imported from England and Germany. Publishers such as Warne, Tuck, Routledge and Nister, were all issuing beautiful paper products. When such imports were not protected by the United States copyright laws, McLoughlin Brothers pirated issues and published them at a lower price. By the 1890s the reliance on English and German illustrators had nearly disappeared. American artists such as Thomas Nast, Justin Howard, Henry Herrick and others appeared. McLoughlin Brothers were quick to acquire the services of these illustrators whenever possible. Nast, the political cartoonist, originated the American image of Santa Claus, illustrations of which are found in McLoughlin's edition of Clement Moore's *Visit From St. Nicholas.* George Webeler's *Rip Van Winkle* was also illustrated by Nast. Justin H. Howard, believed to be the originator of the figure of Uncle Sam, and Henry Herrick, were prolific contributors to the McLoughlin line of books. Palmer Cox, the Canadian illustrator who was the creator of the popular Brownies, illustrated several different paper items, such as jig-saw puzzles, calenders, sets of cut-out nine-pins and other toys featuring the funny little people. While the company made use of these name artists the majority of the illustrators worked anonymously.

Edmund McLoughlin retired from the firm in 1885, and John McLoughlin died in 1905. At this time the company was controlled by John's two sons, James and Charles, and remained a family company until Charle's death in 1920. It was then sold to a competitor, Milton Bradley of Springfield, Massachusetts.

Milton Bradley was born in Vienna, Maine, on November 8, 1836. At seventeen he entered the Lawrence Scientific School which later became a part of Harvard University. He remained there for three years and then moved to Hartford, Connecticut, with his parents. Still later he moved to Springfield, Massachusetts, where he worked for two or three firms as a draughtsman. Bradley then took a course in lithography in Providence,

Rhode Island. In 1860 he began doing lithographic work and during the same year published his first game, *The Checkered Game of Life.* This game had a long and successful run, and was still a good seller after the turn of the century. In 1870, Bradley opened a factory on Dewight Street in Springfield, Massachusetts, and at about that same time his father, Louis Bradley, joined him in the business. In 1882 the factory was moved to Willow Street, and the business continued to expand. At the turn of the century, the company employed over 500 people. At that time they were publishing over four hundred games and puzzles, plus other playthings. Their educational Kindergarten books and supplies gained a world-wide reputation. While Milton Bradley & Company published numerous popular games, their policy and standard of being very selective in the theme subjects of their games is exemplified in the introduction to their 1873-74 catalog. The "Introductory" is illustrated here along with a three-page alphabetical listing of games, puzzles and other playthings. **(Illustrations 17** & **18 A, B, & C.)**

In covering the history of American games, we have to mention another company that played an important part in its growth. Selchow & Righter of New York City was established in 1867, and is still a thriving business located on Long Island, New York. While this company published scores of games, they were basically toy distributors and importers. The company started at the close of the Civil War when a man called Albert B. Swift opened a small shop on John Street, east of Broadway, in New York City. His primary business was the wholesale distribution of toys and games. In his first catalog to the trade he advertised the game of *Parcheesi* along with other items. *Parcheesi* is one of the oldest toy trademarks still in existance, and was first registered in the United States patent office in 1874. In 1870 Swift sold his business to Elisha G. Selchow. Selchow appointed John H. Righter to manage the company. At a later date, he made him a full partner and the firm became Selchow & Righter. Selchow & Righter in their early advertising of the game of *Parcheesi* stated that Bayard Taylor, in his book *India, China & Japan,* mentions the game being

played in India. Taylor wrote that he viewed an outdoor playing board of great size, constructed of sheets of varying colors of marble, built on the royal palace grounds in Delhi, India. "Within these fairy precincts"/lies a garden still overrun/ with roses and jessamine vines, in the midst of which fountains are playing. There is also a court, paved with marble of various colors, so as to form a Parcheesi Board. This is a game somewhat resembling backgammon, but instead of ivory pieces, it is played by Akbar and his wives, or eunuchs with girls who passed from space to space as the moves were made." The game of *Parcheesi* has proven to be one of the great steady sellers over the years and is still produced by Selchow & Righter today.

Later, in 1889, Selchow & Righter became the sole selling agents for Charles Crandall's famous puzzle *Pigs in Clover.* This simple game became an immediate success, and was purchased and played by young and old nation-wide. Selchow & Righter was swamped with orders, and Crandall's Waverly Toy Works was hard-pressed to fill them, sometimes falling two to three weeks behind. The game consisted of a wooden disc base six inches (15cm) in diameter, with four concentric circles scribed on the top surface. Four rings of colored cardboard, three quarters of an inch (2cm) high are glued into the grooves. The outer ring is a solid wall, the inner three each having one staggered opening three quarters of an inch (2cm) wide. The center smaller ring is covered and marked "Pen." Four small balls, the pigs, are placed between the two outer rings. The object of the game is to drive the pigs from the outer enclosure, through the inner openings, into the pen by hand tilting the game itself. While everyone, sooner or later, drove the four pigs into the pen, the game became very competitive when two or more people played to see who could pen the pigs in the shortest length of time. **(Illustration 19.)**

Another prominent American game manufacturer was George Parker of Salem, Massachusetts. He started in the game business in 1883 and built it to a point where Salem was called the "Game Capital of The World." Parker, at the age of sixteen, devised a game which he called *Banking.* Working during his summer vacation, he made and saved enough money to have 500 sets of cards for his game printed. The following November he received permission to take time off from school to take a selling trip to the larger cities of eastern Massachusetts and Rhode Island. His trip proved successful, and he cleared a satisfying profit. Two other games, *Bakers Dozen* and *Famous Men*, helped the young businessman along and he was soon in a position to obtain the rights to all the games previously published by W. & S.B. Ives. Most of these games he reissued, some under new titles.

In 1887, Parker, now a young man of twenty, wanted to expand his game business but lack of capital presented a problem. He knew he could develop new games and had proven that he could sell them, so he decided to make a trip to New York City. He developed and closed a deal with a prominent wholesaler whereby he exchanged a stock of his games for an equal amount of their games and sporting goods. This line of sporting

	PAGE.	PRICE.
*Paradise of Childhood,—A Manual of Kindergarten Instruction,	23	$3 00
Parlor or Carpet Bowls,	7	2 00
Parlor Puzzle.—Cross Puzzle,	15	20
*Panoramas,—See Myrioticon and Historiscope,		
*Panorama of the Visit of Santa Claus to the Happy Children,	18	1 25
*Permutation Dissected Map of United States,	15	1 00
*Picture Tablets.—See Indestructible, etc.,		
*Popular Pastimes for Field and Fireside,	15	1 50
*Poetical Predictions,	15	25
Poetical Pot Pie,	12	40
*Popular Characters from Dickens,	6	60
Puzzle Map of North America,	20	25
*Queen's Guards,	16	25
" " Larger Edition,	16	50
*Rescue of Robinson Crusoe,	15	25
" " " " Larger Edition,	15	50
Rescue of Robinson Crusoe,—Improved,	13	1 25
Rings.—See Magic Hoops,		
*Record Dials for Bezique, etc.,—Set of Four,	9	75
*Reveries of Jemima Spinster,	12	40
Robinson Crusoe.—See Rescue of Robinson Crusoe,		
*Robbers and Giant,	15	25
*Santa Claus Puzzle.—See Chinese, etc.,		
*Sam Slick from Weathersfield to Paris,	12	40
Santa Claus Panorama, See Panorama of,		
*Scripture Game of Who Knows,	15	50
Siege Boards,	13	75
*Set and Take,	19	25
*Sequences,	19	40
*Silhouette Picture Puzzle,	20	25
Ship.—See Model Ship Puzzle,		
*Smashed-Up Locomotive,	17	75
" " " Polished Walnut Box,	17	1 25
Solitaire Boards,	13	75
*Spelling Puzzle,	19	25
Squalls.—See American Squalls,		
*Steam Fire Engine.—See Blown-up Steamer,		
The Way to Make Money.—See What Is It,		
*Uncle Raphael's Puzzle Chromos,—No. 1,	20	80
" " " No. 2,	20	50
*United States Map.—See Dissected Outline Map,		
Variety Dozens,	26	
*What is it, or The way to Make Money,	16	60
Wheel of Life.—See Zoetrope,		
*What will You Give,	16	25
*Who Knows.—See Scriptural Game of Who Knows,		
*Weaving and Braiding.—See Kindergarten Weaving and Braiding,		
*Wolf and Sheep,	18	25
	16	50
*Yacht Puzzle,	9	3 50
Zoetrope or Wheel of Life,	10	1 00
*Zoetrope Pictures,—Per Set of 12 Scenes,		
1776.—See Games of 1776,		

18 C

OPPOSITE PAGE and ABOVE: Illustration 18 A, B & C: A listing of items on page 3, 4 and 5 in Milton Bradleys' 1873-74 catalog offers a wide selection of paper toys, books and games at this early date.

Illustration 19: In 1889, Selchow & Righter became sole selling agents for Charles Crandall's puzzle game *Pigs in Clover*. An overnight success, it was played by young and old alike and kept both companies busy filling orders. Size 1⅜in (3.4cm) high by 6¼in (15.9cm) diameter.

equipment provided ideas for new games, and young Parker developed a new baseball game and games of table polo and croquet. At this time he issued a new catalog listing 125 items. Parker's brother's Charles and Edward, joined the firm and it became known as Parker Brothers. George Parker's love of history was reflected in the games his company produced. Games with Spanish American War themes appeared along with those about prominent figures of the day, such as Teddy Roosevelt and Buffalo Bill. Financial games, such as *Wall Street* and *Pit*, proved to be great sellers around 1900. Parker Brothers 1916-17 catalog featured *Pollyana*, *Rook*, *Halma* and several war games. **(Illustration 20.)** In the latter part of 1925, Parker Brothers purchased the educational card game division of the United States Playing Card Company of Cincinnati, Ohio. Later, during the depression years in 1935, they offered a new game by the name of *Monopoly* which became a lasting family favorite. The world famous game of *Monopoly* was developed and designed by Charles B. Darrow of Germantown, Pennsylvania, during the years of the great depression. In 1934 Darrow offered the game to Parker Brothers who turned it down as they felt it was too complicated, and that the play action was drawn out. Darrow published the game himself and sold 5,000 sets to a large department store in Philadelphia. Sales

POLLYANNA

REGISTERED U. S. PAT. OFFICE
PATENTED OCT. 19, 1915

THE GLAD GAME

The best new board game that has appeared in the last quarter century. Extensively advertised in the leading magazines. Pollyanna possesses splendid new features. It is known everywhere. It delights young and old and appeals strongly to the home. A perfect game for two, three or four players. Partnership games are the greatest of fun. Played upon a handsomely made, folding board illustrated in colors with Pollyanna pictures.

The curved side-tracks on which a player may travel either to escape capture or to avoid blockade are a unique feature of Pollyanna, and a great improvement over one-track games. Pollyanna's "glad there are turnouts."

POLLYANNA. Best Edition. Extra heavy board, attractive box supplied with 16 brass bound counters, four dice boxes and eight dice.   Price, $1.00

No. 102. Pollyanna. With two new double spinning indicators. No dice used.   Price, 85 cents

No. 103. Pollyanna. Popular edition, four dice boxes and four dice.   Price, 75 cents

HALMA

REGISTERED U. S. PAT. OFFICE. COPYRIGHTED U. S. A.
RE-ISSUED U. S. PAT. OFFICE JAN. 1916

HALMA is by far the most popular game of skill, excepting checkers, which is played in America. It is known everywhere. While full of skill and scientific interest, it may be lightly or skillfully played according to the age and ability of the players. Of great fascination and interest for children, it offers also opportunity for the most skillful and mentally capable of adults.

No. 104. Halma, best
Extra heavy folding board, richly bound in leatherette; with set of sixty-four large size enameled men and booklet of rules, with illustrations and examples.   Price, $1.75

No. 105. Halma
Well made folding board, with equipment of sixty-four boxwood men and booklet of rules.   Price, $1.25

No. 106. Halma
Popular edition, board bound in familiar basket pattern paper, with set of sixty-four hardwood men, and booklet.   Price, $1.00

Illustration 20: Parker Brothers of Salem, Massachusetts, offered two new board games in their 1916-17 catalog. *Pollyanna* and *Halma* enjoyed continuous popularity for a number of years.

were good and the following year Parker Brothers reconsidered and made a deal with Darrow. The game of *Monopoly* soon sold beyond Parker Brothers expectation and now, 50 years later, is still a winner. Published in 19 languages, it is licensed in 32 countries, and is played in local and national tournaments in the United States and abroad. *Monopoly* has been played on mountain tops and under water, set marathon playing records in many forms, the longest I believe is 59 days. The board has been made in various sizes by enthusiasts: the largest outdoor game board 550 by 470 feet, largest indoor gameboard 122 by 122 feet, and the smallest, a miniature, 1 inch square.

Another toy company that published game boards was the R. Bliss Manufacturing Company of Pawtucket, Rhode Island. This company was established in 1832 for the purpose of making wooden tools, principally clamps and tool handles. Wooden toys appeared as early as 1871, and from that point on the company produced a quantity of colorful lithographed paper on wood toys of various types. They also published a number of board games, a selection of titles follows, picked from four of their catalogs.

The 1889 catalog illustrates three games, all introduced that year. The *Game of Wild West*, which illustrates scouting life in the Indian country of the far west. Players started their Indian or Scout figures at certain points along a printed trail; movement was decided by the roll of dice, with points of advancement or set-backs along the way. The *Game of Detective* was quite similar, a route-type game that detectives followed, controlled by the roll of dice. Both were games of amusement and luck. The *Game of Attack*, mechanical in its action, was a game of skill which illustrated famous American battles.

The 1891 catalog illustrated the three games mentioned above plus the following; *Newsboy*, *The Dudes*, *Frog Pond*, *Game of Shopping*, *The Great Railroad*, *Minnehaha*, *The Hunting Match*, and *Noahs Ark*. Also pictured were *The Bad Boys Little Game*, *Open Sesame*, *Stanley's African Game*, and the *Game of Domino Pool*, a board game with a set of dominos which is played by matching the domino designs on the board.

In 1895 there were fewer games offered. The *Game of Arena*, *Improved Stanley in Africa*, *Improved Wild West*, *Good Luck* and *Fish Pond* were offered. A new game, *The Worlds Columbian Exposition*, was offered. This game took the participant on a trip through the grounds and buildings of the Great Exposition at Jackson Park, Chicago, Illinois. The game could be played by two to four people. Included were four dice cups, dice, fancy turned counters and a set of directions.

The 1901 catalog pictured fewer games, but all were new. Illustrated were the *Stars & Stripes*, a patriotic game played along the lines of the East Indian game of *Parcheesi*. Also *Humpty Dumpty* named after the famous clown, and the *Game of*

A.B.C., an educational game played like *Fish Pond*. Minaiture fishing poles with lines and hooks looped alphabet blocks, rather than fish, to spell out words.

Other companies producing quantities of games from the turn of the century on were the W.S. Reed Toy Company of Leominister, Massachusetts, E.I. Horsman and Samuel Gabriel Sons & Company, both of New York City, and the Peter G. Thomson Company of Cincinnati, Ohio.

It may be well to note here that copyright laws were bent in the early years, consequently the game companies published the popular games of the day in one version or another and in series. *Lotto*, *Authors*, *Dr. Busby*, *Fish Pond* and *Old Maid* are all examples of games published in multiple form. While hundreds of new games were developed in the 19th and 20th centuries, many of them did not specifically attempt to teach educational facts or moral philosophy. Games that were boringly educational did not last more than a year or two, while games that hit a happy medium between learning and amusement were popular and stayed in demand for years. On the other hand, however frivolous a game might be, it taught children to understand the rules of the game, to add up scores, and in most cases the meaning of sportsmanship and how to lose gracefully.

Before this survey of game cards, gameboards and their respective manufacturers is complete, mention should be made of an adult game that first appeared in the *Sunday New York World*, under the name "Work-Cross." The originator was Arthur Wynne, editor of the Sunday magazine section. It was an immediate success with subscribers, many of whom became addicted to the game. They sent in scores of suggested rules to be followed, and made up new word patterns trying to outwit fellow readers. The game's popularity remained at a high level with the World's readers until 1924 when the cross-word puzzles were published in book form by Simon & Schuster. During the same year, they published three more cross-word puzzle books with a total sales figure of close to a half million copies. A new series published annually has continued ever since and still is a top seller with a world-wide market.

Chapter IV.

BLOCKS & PUZZLES

Many writers state that toys in general are educational, and an equal number believe that only certain toys have educational value. Hence the interested reader realizes or comes to the conclusion that toys can be educational to varying degrees. In using toys as a teaching aid for children they become tools of education. A parent or an adult must play-teach with a child about a toy. They must tell and show the educational value within a particular toy. It is then that the pre-school child learns effectively. The amount of patience, love, and teaching that the adult puts into the play-teach process determines the amount of knowledge that the child absorbs. This is not usually a one time process, it may have to be repeated several times depending on how quickly the child comprehends what he or she hears and sees.

A.B.C. blocks are one of the first toy forms offered to a child once he leaves the crib and plays on the floor. While the majority of this type of blocks were made of wood, many were made of cardboard and covered with colorful paper. As a child progressed in learning the A.B.C.s, recognizing the forms of different letters and then grouping them into simple words, he could then put together words such as cat or boy, and associate the words with illustrations printed on the blocks. **(Illustration 21.)**

Another form of educational paper toy, the *Strip Puzzle*, was available. This was in the form of horizontal strips of cardboard covered with colored illustrations and an alphabet block letter at the end of each strip. In it's simplest form a set could be in three strips that, when correctly put together, would picture a cat with the word CAT formed down the right side of the puzzle. A more advanced form might be a *Strip Puzzle* consisting of eight pieces which, when correctly placed in order, would picture an elephant in his natural habitat and the word "ELEPHANT" spelled vertically down the right side of the assembled puzzle. These simple puzzles were enjoyed by pre-school children before and after 1900, and were published by many of the leading paper toy makers. **(Illustration 22.)**

While we have briefly mentioned the A.B.C. blocks and the *Strip Puzzles* for young children as an educational tool, we find that another type of educational toy superceded them. This was a device in the form of a jigsaw puzzle used in the school room. This puzzle made it's initial

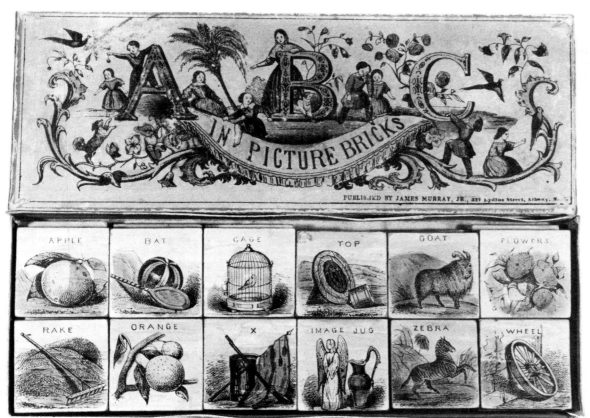

Illustration 21: *A B C In Picture Bricks*, published by James Murray, Jr. of Albany, New York, circa 1880. Box measures 3¾in (9.6cm) high, 10⅛in (25.7cm) wide and 1⅛in (2.8cm) deep.

F
O
U
N
T
A
I
N

TYLER DAVIDSON FOUNTAIN, Cincinnati, O.

Illustration 22: An example of the popular *Strip Puzzle* or *Sliced Pictures* which was an inexpensive educational paper toy made by a number of publishers. Publisher unknown. c.1910. Overall size 9 x 6in (22.8 x 15.2cm).

40 CENT SCROLL PUZZLES   50 CENT PUZZLE

No. 7045 CRISS-CROSS SPELLING SLIPS — 3 Kinds

No. 7035. CHRISTMAS TIDE SCROLL PUZZLE

No. 533. MOTHER GOOSE SCROLL PUZZLES 3 Kinds

Express charges extra

Each box contains a lettered spelling slip, with a large picture of a well-known animal upon it.

The labels are in full colors and varnished.

Put up in dozens

Size, 10¾ x 13¼ inches

These are splendid dissected-picture puzzles to amuse little children with.

The labels are in full colors and varnished.

Put up in ½ dozens

Size, 10¾ x 13 inches

These sets each contain two pictures 10 x 12 inches, of scenes from Mother Goose.

The labels are in full colors and varnished.

Put up in ½ dozens

50 CENT SCROLL PUZZLES

No. 549.—OLD SANTA CLAUS SCROLL PUZZLE

Express charges extra

No. 549½.—DOGGIE SCROLL PUZZLE

Express charges extra

No. 550.—WASHINGTON CROSSING THE DELAWARE SCROLL PUZZLE

Express charges extra

Size, 11 x 16 inches

This puzzle contains a handsome cut-up picture in full colors, and measuring 15 x 18 inches.

The labels are printed in full colors and varnished.

Put up in ½ dozens

Size, 11 x 16 inches

This puzzle contains a fine cut-up picture all in full colors and measuring 15 x 18 inches. The labels are printed in full colors and varnished.

Put up in ½ dozens

Size, 11 x 16 inches

This puzzle contains a full-color picture, 15 x 18 inches.

The labels are in full colors and varnished.

Put up in ½ dozens

Illustration 23: A page of scroll puzzles from McLoughlin Brothers' 1882 catalog. Puzzles were offered in several grades and in sizes from 6 x 8in to 18 x 26in (15.2 x 20.3 to 45.7 x 66.0cm).

appearance during the latter half of the 18th century. At first, these puzzles were simply maps mounted on thin boards and later on cardboard. They were cut into eccentric shapes and were called *Dissected Maps.* They were an educational device that was immediately accepted in the school room as well as the home. The first known publisher of the *Dissected Maps* was John Spilsbury of London, England, who was in business as early as 1763. Wallis & Son, who was mentioned as a publisher of card games, started to publish *Dissected Maps* and quickly followed with cut-out history and religious sheets which he made into puzzles. Linda Hannas in her book *The English Jigsaw Puzzle 1760 to 1890*, covers this subject completely and furnishes numerous photographs of the intriguing early puzzles. The book offers a check list of the puzzles, arranged by subject matter, publisher if known, date, size and description.

In the United States few if any picture puzzles

appeared before those mentioned in the McLoughlin Brothers catalog of 1867, where they were briefly listed as "Cut Up Pictures, a Puzzle to put together, Printed in oil colors, twelve kinds, per gross $24.00." Their 1875-76 catalog had a more descriptive listing of a greater variety. They were listed as "Dissected Picture Puzzle Blocks (Flat Blocks — Scroll Pattern)." *The Little Folks Series*, listed 72 kinds, 12 series, each consisting of six title variations within the series. The various series were offered under titles such as *The Three Little Pigs, The Old Woman Who Lived In A Shoe, Diamond & Toads, The Three Bears, Mother Goose, Old Dame Trot*, and so on. Quoting from the catalog description: "These puzzles are 6 inches wide and 8 inches long. They are dissected in a novel manner. The border pieces have a round projection on one side, and a curved recess on the other, cut in such a manner that they will lock together. The inside pieces are nearly square. This style of dissection retains the puzzle in one piece when put together. Very

durable, put up in a pasteboard box labeled with the puzzle picture." The same catalog also offered a new series for that year, the *Brilliant Series*, six kinds, two puzzles in each box. Puzzle size nine by eleven inches (22.9 x 27.9cm). An equal offering was made of wood-backed puzzles at a slightly higher price. All in all, a huge assortment of puzzles and flat blocks were offered to the trade, but it must be remembered that McLoughlin's primary business was publishing children's books, and that thousands of colorful chromolithographed illustrations were available to be mounted on cardboard and cut into puzzles. **(Illustration 23.)**

The 1882-83 McLoughlin catalog lists the above mentioned scroll puzzles plus a number of cube puzzles. The *Aunt Louisa Series* of cube puzzles consists of sets of 30 cubes, each 1¾ inches (4.5cm) square. Twenty offerings were made in this size. A second series, *Little Folk Cube Puzzles*, were made up of sets of 12 cubes. These six-sided puzzle blocks pictured such

subjects as *Robinson Crusoe, Visit of St. Nicholas, Yankee Doodle, Little Bo-Peep, Pocahantas*, and so on. **(Color Illustration 1.)** By 1900, the McLoughlin catalogs illustrated a huge assortment of scroll puzzles selling from 15¢ to 75¢. The *Locomotive Puzzle* and the *Fire Engine Puzzle*, illustrate two of the 60¢ puzzles offered at that time. **(Illustrations 24 & 25.)** The 1911 catalog pictures 85 cube block puzzles with prices ranging from 10¢ to $2.50 a set. **Illustration 26** pictures the cover of a fine set of blocks from this period, *Battleship Picture Puzzle Cubes*. It consists of a box of 20 blocks that make up pictures of six battleships of the White Fleet that participated in the Spanish American War. Pictured are the *Maine*, the *Oregon*, the *Texas*, the *New York*, the *Brooklyn*, and the *Olympia*. Each of these puzzles, when completed, offer some educational information in the form of a caption in the upper right hand corner. As an example, the *Maine* puzzle reads: "Second class battle ship. Built at Brooklyn Navy Yard 1888-1890. Her main

Illustration 24: One of McLoughlin Brothers' larger scroll puzzles, the *Locomotive Puzzle*, offered in 1900. Notice the interlocking feature of the outside or border pieces that hold the puzzle in place. 18 x 26in (45.7 x 66.0cm).

Illustration 25: The *Fire Engine Puzzle* is an example of McLoughlin Brothers' large 60¢ puzzle offered in 1900. Size 18 x 26in (45.7 x 66.0cm).

Illustration 26: The box cover illustration of a set of 20 square blocks that make up pictures of six battleships that were attached to the White Fleet that took part in the Spanish-American War. c.1900. The six-sided blocks are 2½in (6.4cm) square.

battery consists of four 10 inch and six 6 inch beech-loading rifles. The Maine was sent to Havana at the request of Consul General Lee to protect American interests. She arrived on the 25th of January 1898, and on February 15th, she was treacherously destroyed by a mine. 286 men and two officers were lost."

The 1911 catalog also illustrates two pages of "Nested A.B.C. And Picture Blocks." These nested blocks are so constructed that each one is small enough to fit inside the next larger size which is open on the top to receive it. In this way a number of graduated blocks, from five to eight, can be packed into a small area, that of the largest block. **(Illustration 27.)**

McLoughlin also issued *Dissected Maps* in several variations and sizes, maps of the United States, New York State, and the World. *The Dissected Map of the World*, measuring 16½ by 21½ inches (41.9 x 54.6cm) is rather unique in that it is two sided. On the reverse side is an early illustration of the Capitol at Washington, D.C. Another unusual set of paper covered cardboard blocks that McLoughlin Brothers produced was the *Peep Show A.B.C. Blocks*. The box cover gives a patent date of 1884, possibly this is when the

patent was applied for. The patent was issued to a Josiah Burnham Anderson of Boston, Massachusetts, on February 17, 1885. The patent copy reads in part: "This invention relates, principally, to cubical alphabet blocks for children, the aim of the invention being to render these blocks more attractive and instructive to young children. To this end my invention consists in providing the cubical block with a recess or cavity extending into it from one side, containing a suitable object, ornament or picture, and covered with glass." **(Color Illustration 2.)**

The Milton Bradley Company entered into the

Illustration 28: Milton Bradleys' *Smashed-up Locomotive* is a 53-piece scroll puzzle which, when completed, pictures the early 4-4-0 steam locomotive and eight-wheel tender pictured above. Notice that the various parts of the locomotive are named. This puzzle was offered in the 1896-97 catalog. 8¼ x 24in (21.0 x 61.0cm).

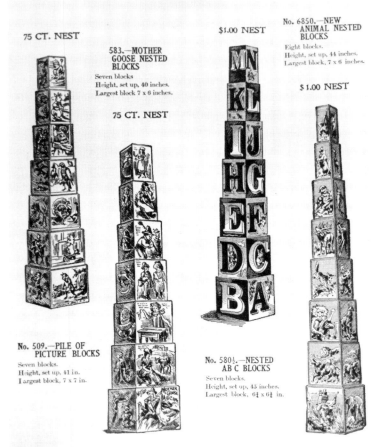

NESTED BLOCKS

75 CT. NEST

583.—MOTHER GOOSE NESTED BLOCKS
Seven blocks.
Height, set up, 40 inches.
Largest block 7 x 6 inches.

75 CT. NEST

$1.00 NEST

No. 6850.—NEW ANIMAL NESTED BLOCKS
Eight blocks.
Height, set up, 44 inches.
Largest block, 7 x 6 inches.

$1.00 NEST

No. 509.—PILE OF PICTURE BLOCKS
Seven blocks.
Height, set up, 41 in.
Largest block, 7 x 7 in.

No. 580½.—NESTED ABC BLOCKS
Seven blocks.
Height, set up, 45 inches.
Largest block, 6¼ x 6¼ in.

Illustration 27: A page from a 1911 McLoughlin Brothers' catalog offering a variety of "Nested Blocks." Notice that the blocks vary in size and in number from set to set.

puzzle and block market a bit later than McLoughlin, yet soon became a serious competitor. Their 1896-97 catalog listed: "The cheapest and best dissected map of the United States ever published. It is lithographed in five colors. Size 9 by 12 inches, price each, five cents." Also offered were dissected pictures in square sections that could be constantly shifted, thereby securing innumerable exciting combinations. *The Animated Forest, Farmyard Scenes, Wild West Show* and the *Interchangeable Combination Circus,* were all typical examples. The *Wild West Show* was made up of forty puzzle pieces so ingeniously designed that the various parts will mismatch to form an almost unlimited number of different pictures representing many of the most exciting incidents in Indian and frontier life. The *Smashed-Up Locomotive* was another outstanding puzzle featured in this catalog. This scroll puzzle illustrates a colorful early locomotive and tender constructed of 58 sections, none of which have the interlocking feature of the McLoughlin puzzles. The locomotive puzzle parts are marked on their respective pieces; head light, smoke box, steam cylinder, boiler, driving wheel, and so on. The tender is marked in a similar way. (**Illustration 28.**). It is packed in a wooden box with a hinged cover having a large paper label picturing a smashed up locomotive. Inside the cover a second label states, in part: "As some dissected pictures have a pattern picture with each box, many persons suppose this Puzzle should have one also; but as it is already known that the whole when put

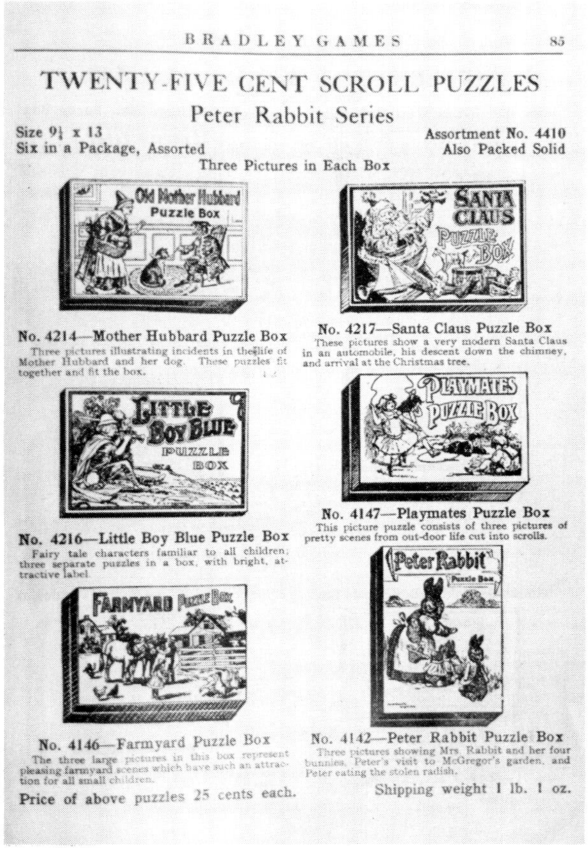

TWENTY-FIVE CENT SCROLL PUZZLES
Peter Rabbit Series

Size 9¼ x 13   Assortment No. 4410
Six in a Package, Assorted   Also Packed Solid
Three Pictures in Each Box

No. 4214—Mother Hubbard Puzzle Box
Three pictures illustrating incidents in the life of
Mother Hubbard and her dog. These puzzles fit
together and fit the box.

No. 4217—Santa Claus Puzzle Box
These pictures show a very modern Santa Claus
in an automobile, his descent down the chimney,
and arrival at the Christmas tree.

No. 4216—Little Boy Blue Puzzle Box
Fairy tale characters familiar to all children;
three separate puzzles in a box, with bright, attractive label.

No. 4147—Playmates Puzzle Box
This picture puzzle consists of three pictures of
pretty scenes from out-door life cut into scrolls.

No. 4146—Farmyard Puzzle Box
The three large pictures in this box represent
pleasing farmyard scenes which have such an attrac-
tion for all small children.

No. 4142—Peter Rabbit Puzzle Box
Three pictures showing Mrs. Rabbit and her four
bunnies, Peter's visit to McGregor's garden, and
Peter eating the stolen radish.

Price of above puzzles 25 cents each.   Shipping weight 1 lb. 1 oz.

Illustration 29: A page from Milton Bradleys' 1914 catalog showing some of their offerings of Scroll Puzzles. Each box contained three puzzles measuring 9¼ x 13in (23.5 x 33.0 cm).

together is a Locomotive, that is sufficient, and a pattern sheet would destroy much of the interest in the puzzle. Therefore, no pattern picture belongs to this Puzzle." Another Bradley puzzle of this period pictures six horse-drawn fire wagons in a line; a chief's wagon, a steam pumper, a hose carriage, a chemical wagon, a patrol wagon, and a hook and ladder wagon. The completed puzzle measures 84 inches (213cm) long and is seven inches (17.8cm) high. The name of each piece of equipment is marked along the bottom edge of the puzzle. A similar railroad puzzle pictures a

SCROLL PUZZLES—Continued
Three Pictures in Each Box
No. 4046—Our Battleships Puzzle Box

A big, new scroll puzzle with fine sepia prints of some of Uncle Sam's greatest fighting ships, made from photographs taken by the official U. S. Government photographer. These pictures were taken during the New York maneuvers last year and are remarkably clear in detail. There are three puzzle pictures showing the U. S. S. New York, U. S. Dreadnought Texas, and a modern K-1 submarine with a fine picture on the label showing the U. S. S. Louisiana under full speed.

Size, 12⅞ x 18¼.   Price, each, $1.00; shipping weight, 3 lbs. 1 oz.
Two in a package.

Illustration 30: The 1917 Milton Bradley catalog offered *Our Battleship Puzzle Box* which contained three puzzles picturing the U.S.S. New York, the U.S. Dreadnought Texas and a K-1 submarine. Box size 12⅞ x 18¼in (32.8 x 46.3cm).

complete train consisting of a steam locomotive, tender, combination mail and baggage car, smoking, parlor, sleeping, and a dining car. All sections are identified by labels, and the total puzzle is eight feet (243.8cm) long.

A 1914 Bradley catalog pictures an up to date version of a similar train called the *Twilight Express.* The puzzle was nine feet (3m) in length and priced at 50¢. A large selection of boxed puzzles with the ever-popular themes of nursery tales, historic places or personalities, farm scenes, wild animals, circus, Santa Claus, and so on, were offered in prices ranging from 12¢ to 50¢ per box. **(Illustration 29.)** A number of dissected maps were offered, one of the United States, measuring 12 by 20 inches (30.5 x 50.8cm), was cut out along state lines. The reverse side is colorfully lithographed with the flags of various nations. The range of puzzles offered in the Bradley catalogs

from 1909 to 1919 were much of the same. Exceptions were the scroll puzzles picturing some of America's battleships and submarines that appeared in the 1917 issue. **(Illustration 30.)**

Parker Brother catalogs from 1916 to 1919 were competitive and similar in size, subject matter and price, in regard to puzzles and blocks, with those of the Milton Bradley Company. However a 1917 and 1918 catalog insert listed a selection of 200 or so adult puzzles in beautiful color, taken from well-known paintings of the past. Titled *Famous Pastime Puzzles,* they ranged from 100-piece puzzles priced at $1.00 to 1200-piece puzzles priced at $12.00 each. This line proved to be a popular item as it was still listed in Parker's 1940-41 catalog. However, the later puzzles were backed with wood and the price had increased to $18.00 for the larger puzzles.

Chapter V.

PEEP SHOWS, PANORAMAS AND THE HISTORISCOPE

The peep show was a paper toy that was developed during the early 1600s and grew in size and variety of subject matter over the years. It seemed to reach the peak of popularity in England during the 1800s. **(Illustration 31.)** Traveling men carried the peep show boxes from town to city, from village to country fair, in fact anywhere a crowd might gather, so that people could be encouraged to spend a half-penny for a peak at the hidden contents within the box. Originally the peep shows took the form of nativity scenes. They were cut out of heavy cardboard with a decorated transparent background and had a small candle at the rear of the box. In the early 1800s the peepholes were equipped with glass lenses, then the number of peepholes began to multiply and the boxes were made larger. One was known to contain 26 peepholes so that a like number of people could enjoy the same show. Subject matter changed greatly, although lighting by candles still remained in vogue. The addition of action inside was provided by the proprietor pulling wires.

From the early peep show a variant developed in the mid 1800s. This consisted of a set of related cut-out views, engraved and colored, set one behind the other, and spaced to give a three-dimensional effect. These cut-out card views were attached together with two long strips of paper, folded accordian style so that the panorama could be opened out for viewing or folded flat when not in use. **(Illustration 32.)** This panorama, or peep show as it was called in England and the United States around 1900, seems to have originated in Germany around 1730. Popular in Germany, France, and the British Isles, it was made in numerous sizes. It was commonly found with one peephole on the front decorated face, but occa-

Illustration 31: Early European peep show box with a wood frame covered with brown grained paper and edged with embossed gilt paper. Contains twelve 5¾ x 7½in (14.7 x 19.1cm) paper plates illustrating game birds, insects, wild flowers, butterflys, sea life, snakes and wild life. Maker unknown. France, circa 1865. Size 6 x 8 x 13¾in (15.2 x 20.3 x 35.0cm).

sionally with three peepholes, each with it's own vista of views. The open length or depth could be any length from 24 inches (61cm) to an unwieldly 12 feet (39m). The subject theme usually covered an event of wide importance — an exhibition, a coronation, or a view of one of the wonders of the world. **(Color Illustration 3.)** A fine example of a peep show produced in the United States was a souvenir of the New York World Fair, in 1939. **(Illustration 33.)**

A small flat box with the title *Panorama* on the decorated cover contains a novel peep-type glass window which is set in front of a small green cardboard easel. The 3½ by 2½ inch (8.9 x 6.4cm) folding easel has a mirror mounted on its tilted back wall. Included in the box are 12 small hand colored landscapes of country, mountain, lake, and city scenes of Switzerland. Location captions are printed backwards so that they became legible when read in the mirror. **(Illustration 34.)**

Illustration 33: The *New York Worlds Fair* peep show extended, showing the four cut-out sections between the face and back card. Notice the connecting papers are on the top and bottom, usually they are on the sides. This peep show was copyrighted by Elizabeth Sage Adre and Warren Chappell.

Another panorama is in the form of an upright paper covered cylinder with a turned walnut base, top, and turning knob. Labeled *Panorama of the Jubilee Procession 1935*, it was drawn by Mary McNeile for Capt. J.R. Abbey, in April 1937. It was limited to 100 copies of which this in No. 30. Produced at the Chiswick Press Ltd., London, England, by Collotype and stencil-colored by hand **(Illustration 35.)** The parade procession pictures units of cavalry and horse-drawn coaches, including the Life Guards, the 9th Royal Lancers, the 4th Queen's Own Hussars, the 7th Queen's Own Hussars, the 15th and 19th Kings Royal Hussars, the Queens Bays, the 3rd Carabiniers, the 5th Innishilling Dragoon Guards, the Royal Horse Artillery (with caisson and field piece), the Sovereign's escort of Life Guards, a carriage carrying their Majesties King George V and Queen Mary, an escort of Life Guards, the Captains escort of Life Guards, a carriage carrying the Queen of Norway, the Prince of Wales, and the Duke of Gloucester. A second carriage is occupied by the Princess Royal, Princess Victoria, the Earl of Harewood, Lord Lascelles and The Hon. G. Lascelles. They are followed by an escort of Life Guards and the Captains escort of Royal Horse Guards. A carriage carrying the Duke and Duchess of York, Princess Elizabeth, Princess Margaret Rose, then a second carriage containing the Duke and Duchess of Kent, followed by an escort of Royal Horse Guards as the final group. The paper covered cylinder pictures the Royal Family and their guests standing on the balcony

Illustration 32: Faces of two peep shows. *The Great Exhibition 1851*, printed by C. Moody, Holborn, London, England, and the *New York Worlds Fair*, 1939. Copyrighted by E.S. Adre and W. Chappell, United States. The Early example measures 6¼ x 6⅞in and extends to 25in (15.9 x 17.4 x 63.5cm). The later example is 5 x 6½in and extends to 25½in (12.7 x 16.5 x 64.8cm).

Illustration 34: Box marked *Panorama* containing small peep type glass window mounted on cardboard easel with mirror on back wall. Twelve 4 x 5in (10.2 x 12.7cm) cards picturing various scenes in Switzerland. Hand printed captions are reversed so that they may be read in the mirror. Possibly produced in Switzerland, circa 1860. Box measures 4½ x 5½ x 3/4in (11.4 x 14.0 x 1.9cm).

section. A trade mark, "J.W." over "B." on the white shield, is located bottom center. Pictured on the screen is Major Baden Powell who later became the founder of the Boy Scout movement. **(Illustration 37A.)** The panorama strip illustrated 30 scenes concerning the Boer War. Starting with a troopship sailing to Africa, the landing, a view of the city and a scene of a bridge demolished by retreating Boers. Continuing views picture British troops fording rivers, battle scenes, an armored train, more battle scenes, hospital scenes, hauling of field guns over rocky terrain, Cronjé's surrender to Lord Roberts, Baden Powell, portrait of O. P. Kruger, the late President of the South Africa Republic, Field Marshall Lord Roberts V.C., Commander in Chief of the Army of South Africa, and a final scene exemplifying peace.

This panorama has a rather unusual working mechanism, the two upright reels holding the paper panorama strip have a grooved flat reel at their bases. A third grooved reel, with a hand crank on top, extends out on an arm

of the palace. Above their heads is a flowing scroll banner with the words "Panorama of The Silver Jubilee." The cylinder plus the turning knob measures 7½ inches (19.1cm) high and has a base diameter of 2⅝ inches (6.7cm).

Another form of a panorama is one constructed with a long strip of paper containing a pictorial story in color, moving horizontally from one roll to another. It was first called a diorama in Europe and later called a *Historiscope* and a *Myriopticon* in the United States. They were made in the form of a fairly flat oblong cardboard box with a large opening or screen on the front flat side. The box was covered with highly colorful decorated paper. The subject theme of the *Historiscope* was from Columbus to the Revolutionary War. The *Myriopticon* featured the Civil War. Both were manufactured by Milton Bradley. McLoughlin Brothers published a horizontal moving panorama in a larger size, framed within a theater-like front. It featured the mythical character Yankee Doodle Dandy and had a patriotic theme. Pictured is a similar panorama featuring *The Wild West Show*. **(Illustration 36.)**

A novel panorama toy of the reel type with a theme featuring the *South African Boer War* is worth studying at this point. The brilliantly colored proscenium pictures Queen Victoria at the top, with General Joubert and Lord Roberts V.C. on each side, and two soldiers on the lower

Illustration 35: The *Panorama of the Jubilee Procession 1935,* was produced by the Chiswick Press Lt. of London, England. A limited edition of 100 copies, this is number 30. The cylinder plus the turning knob measures 7½in (19.1cm) high and the 4in high panorama strip opens out to 10 feet (10.2cm x 3m).

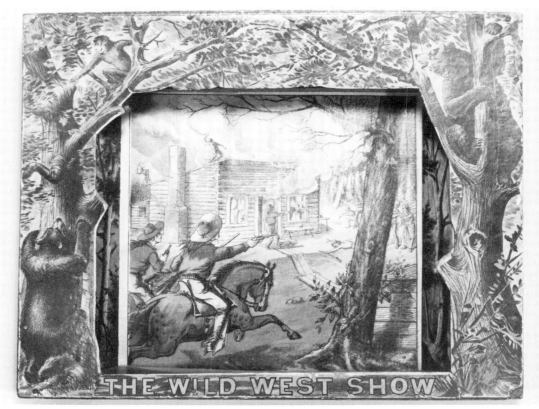

Illustration 36: McLoughlin Brothers' reel type panorama titled *The Wild West Show* features scenes depicting a Buffalo Bill character, frontier life, Indian camps, white men fighting, and a soldier firing at Indians. circa 1890. The box-like proscenium measures 10 x 12½ x 1¾in (25.4 x 31.7 x 4.4cm).

behind the box. The three grooved horizontal reels are connected by a loop of cord forming a triangle pattern. When the crank is activated, the strip pictures run from one upright reel to the other. Illumination is by a short candle, the holder of which is located in the center of the triangle, behind the opening that views the translucent picture strip. **(Illustration 37B.)**

Two unusual examples of toys utilizing the panorama principal can be found among the early patent papers. Edith E. Morrison of New York City was issued a patent for a "Moving Picture Book" on August 26, 1917. A portion of the descriptive copy reads as follows: "My invention relates to an article or toy which is

preferably constructed to possess the appearance of a book and is arranged to display a series of pictures which are carried upon a picture strip, the cover of the toy book being provided with an opening or transparent portion through which the picture may be viewed." Behind the moving screen, which is activated by a hand crank, are three extra rolls of entertaining panoramas. These rolls are easily interchangeable and contain picture themes that are instructive and entertaining. **(Illustration 38.)** The second example is a patent issued to A.M. Birdsall on March 19, 1918, which illustrates a profile drawing of a doll. Inside the rear of the head are two rollers, one

above the other, with turning pins extending outside of the head on the left side. The panorama strip is mounted on the rollers in a verticle position. A small electric bulb is mounted inside the head behind the upper lip and is wired to a battery in the doll's body. The doll's eyes are magnified and by looking closely into them and turning the knobs at the side of the head, the moving panorama comes into view. **(Illustration 39.)**

A varient form of a panorama toy is a book with the pages folded accordian style and when opened up would be several feet long, usually four to six feet (13 to 20m). One example printed in Holland in 1878 illustrates a caravan in which Willem VI traveled in 1415, escorted and protected by scores of mounted knights in armor and nearly 100 armed foot soldiers in their various regalia. This impressive military spectacle was hand colored. It authentically illustrates how royalty traveled in the 15th century, and how fighting men were dressed and equipped in that period. The panorama measures 10½ by 15 inches (26.7 x 38.1cm) closed and when opened extends to 25 feet (82m) **(Illustration 40.)** This type of folding panorama became very popular in the United Kingdom, due to the efforts of Raphael Tuck & Sons Ltd. One of their fine examples is titled *A Day in The forest* which consists of a book cover containing seven stiff panels arranged accordian style. **Illustration 41A** shows the cover picturing a boy and girl approaching a gate. The hinged gate when opened reveals four children having a picnic. As the cover is turned and the panels opened out, the six children are pictured seated around a cloth on the ground enjoying their picnic lunch. The next panel pictures a group of deer titled "Uninvited Guests." Panel three pictures the children and two dogs playing "Hide and Seek." The next panel, "In The Meadows," shows three of the children waving to a small herd of sheep and two cows. The last two panels, "Blackberry Gathers" and "The Peep Show," picture the children picking berries and two of the children kneeling behind a bush, quietly watching a family of rabbits playing. Each panel is equipped with a cut-out front section which

Illustration 37 A: A small reel-type panorama titled *South African Boer War.* Decorative proscenium with small opening revealing a strip picturing 30 scenes from the Boer War and some of the principals involved. Proscenium measures 7 x 6⅞in (17.8 x 16.8cm).

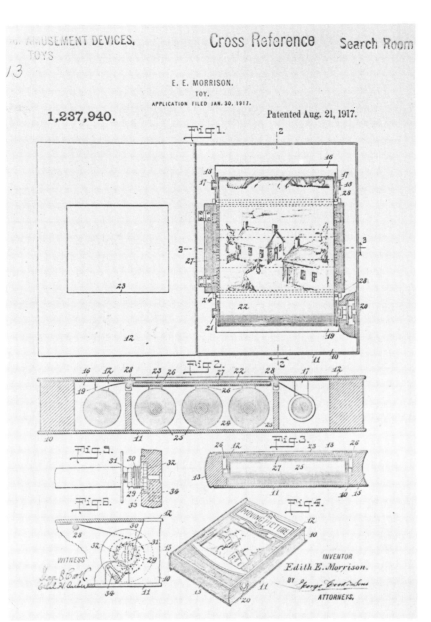

E. E. MORRISON.
TOY.
APPLICATION FILED JAN. 30, 1917.

1,237,940.   Patented Aug. 21, 1917.

INVENTOR
Edith E. Morrison.
BY George Crockdon
ATTORNEYS.

Illustration 37 B: Rear view of the Boer War panorama showing the unusual working mechanism. The crank provides movement to the strip joining the two upright reels in the rear by the triangular cord set-up. Illumination is provided by the candle in the center, behind the opening that views the translucent picture strip.

Illustration 38: Patent drawing of a "Moving Picture Book" patented by Edith E. Morrison of New York City, in 1917. A reel-type panorama in a book-like container with room for three extra interchangeable reels.

51

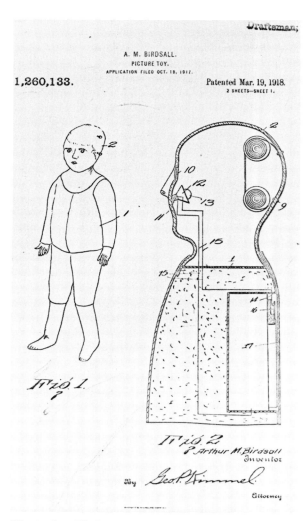

A. M. BIRDSALL.
PICTURE TOY.
APPLICATION FILED OCT. 18, 1917.

1,260,133.   Patented Mar. 19, 1918.
2 SHEETS—SHEET 1.

Draftsman;

FIG 1.

FIG 2.
Arthur M. Birdsall
Inventor

By Geo. F. Kimmel
Attorney

Illustration 39: A patent issued to A. M. Birdsall in 1918, which illustrates an unusual use of a reel type panorama inside a doll's head. It is not known if this novelty was ever manufactured.

Illustration 40: An early accordian-fold panorama from Holland illustrating a caravan in which Willem VI traveled, in 1415. Publisher unknown. Printed in Holland in 1878. Folded, the panorama measures 10½ x 15in, opened it extends to 25 feet (closed 26.7 x 38.1cm, opened 7m and 72.4cm).

lifts out on paper hinges. Folded the book measures 7½ by 9½ inches (19.1 x 24.2cm); extended it measures 56½ inches (143.5cm). **(Illustration 41 B.)**

A second example published by Tuck is a slightly different type of panorama and unfortunately is not complete. A panel and some of the cut-out characters are missing. The sections that remain will give you an idea of what a beautiful paper toy it was. The three existing colorful panels have three or four horizontal slits or pockets into which the accompanying cut-out characters may be inserted. Titled *With Father Tuck In Fairyland*, it is accompanied by some verses by Grace C. Floyed on the back cover. **(Illustration 42.)**

A later colorful panorama published by Tuck is titled *Coronation Procession Panorama*. It consists of a four-panel spread with a series of numbered horizontal slots or pockets on each decorated panel. The back of the last panel is so constructed as to have a built-in large envelope containing numerous cut-out objects that fit into the slots. Assembling directions are printed on the envelope and read as follows: "It you break the seal above, and lift up the flap, you will find an envelope in which are a number of cut-out coloured pictures. There are delightful models of the Coronation coach, horses and riders, soldiers,

decorations, and so on; also of Buckingham Palace and the Queen Victoria Memorial. These are for you to fit into their places in the large background scene of this Panorama, so making a beautiful, life-like scene of the Coronation procession as it leaves the Palace and passes along the Mall on its way to Westminster Abbey." This toy panorama is an historical record of one of the Coronation events of George VI. **(Illustration 43.)**

In the United States, the panorama became popular in the latter part of the 19th century. *Autumn Sports*, a panorama with 12 panels each measuring 12 by 8 inches (30.5 x 20.3cm), opens up to a length of 11 feet 8 inches (39m). It was published by McLoughlin Brothers around 1890. **(Illustration 44.)** Another fine example was published by Louis Prang of Boston, Massachusetts, who established his business in 1860. Often referred to as the "Father of the American Christmas Card," he published a very fine panorama about Santa Claus. **(Illustration 45.)** Prang was one of the leaders in the use of chromolithography, a process of printing with color. Experimenting had been done as early as 1837 in this field, but it did not come into wide commercial use until 1860. It then became the most widely used method of color printing up to and beyond the turn of the century. As in lithographic printing, the flat Bavarian limestones were used

each separate stone prepared by hand. The design was sketched on the stone with oily ink and then the stone was dampened with water before pulling an impression. The overlapping of the stones — sometimes as many as thirty were used — could produce a hundred or more various shades of color. The registering or positive positioning of stones was important. This was accomplished by the use of pointed brass pins, fixed to the frame, which held each stone in position. The point of each pin would penetrate the paper on the first impression and the pins on the following stone would be fixed in place. The last step in the process was to size and varnish the print. The chromolithographic technique became known as "Mechanical Painting."

Illustration 41 B: Inner panel of the panorama *A Day in the Forest*, by Raphael Tuck & Sons.

Illustration 41 A: *A Day in the Forest* is an accordian-type panorama book with a hinged gate on the cover and spring out sections on the inner panels. Published and copyrighted in 1895 by Raphael Tuck & Sons, London, England. Folded it measures 7½ x 9½in., extended it is 56½in. (19.0 x 24.2, extended 1m and 43.5cm).

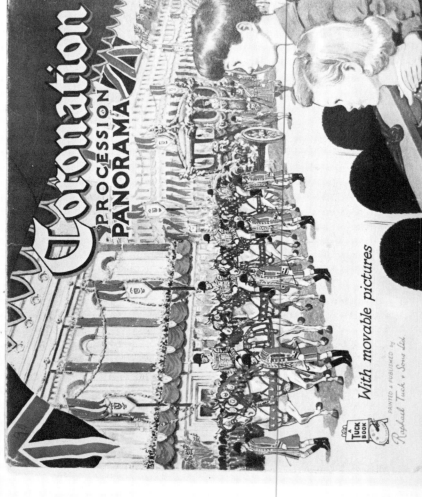

Illustration 42: *With Father Tuck in Fairyland* is an accordian-type panorama with horizontal slits cut in the highly decorated background panels. Within these slits die-cut storybook characters may be inserted to complete the overall pictures. circa 1900. Book size 10⅝ x 12in (27.0 x 30.5cm).

Illustration 43: Raphel Tuck & Sons Ltd. published the *Coronation Procession Panorama* in 1953 when Queen Elizabeth II was crowned. A four-panel, accordian-type booklet with a large envelope built into the back cover, each panel has several numbered slots in which the numbered die-cut objects from the envelope may be inserted to complete the procession. This panorama booklet is 10in high and opens to 4 feet (25.4 x 1m and 21.9cm).

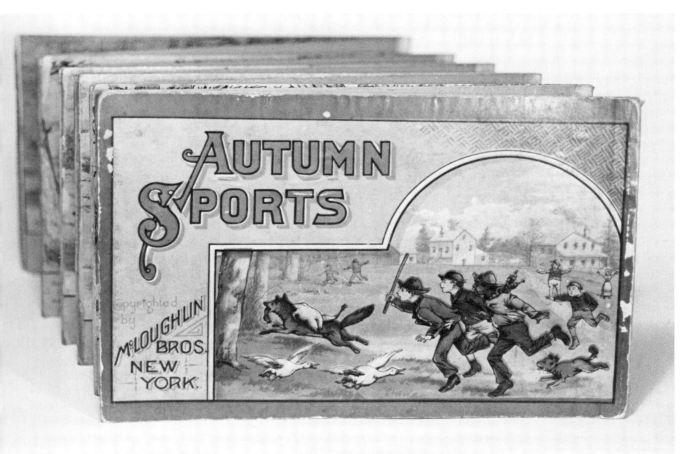

Illustration 44: *Autumn Sports* is an accordian-style panorama consisting of twelve panels. Published by McLoughlin Brothers, circa 1890. Panels picture groups of young children gathering nuts, picking apples, rolling hoops, playing marbles and enjoying the sport of archery. The panorama measures 8 x 12in closed and extends to 11 feet, 8in (20.2 x 30.5 extends to 3m and 56.5cm).

Illustration 45: A fine example of a small Christmas panorama published by Louis Prang of Boston, Massachusetts, in 1864. Titled *A Visit From St. Nicholas*, it contains 12 colorful drawings and the verses from Clement Moore's famous poem. The book measures 4⅛ x 2½in and extends to 29in (10.4 x 6.3 x 73.7cm).

Chapter VI.

TOY BOOKS WITH MOVEMENT

The action book, which is related to the panorama, is a subject of debate as to whether it is a toy or a book. Let us overlook the difference of opinion and classify it as a toy as far as this study is concerned. The earliest action books were published in the mid 16th century for the purpose of scientific instruction. The publishing of moveable books for the purpose of entertaining children did not occur until the 18th century. Action books appeared in several forms and the *Harlquinade*, a fold over sheet, seems to be the earliest form, appearing in the latter part of the 18th century. Illustrations in this type of action book would be overlayed with one or more half and quarter pages, all of which when folded one by one over the base illustration page, would change the picture at each folding. After 1850 a variety of action books appeared, among which were the following. A round illustration, cut in pie-shape slits, could be completely changed by revolving the disc and pulling a ribbon loop at the bottom edge of the circle. A similar movement was found with a square illustration having diagonal cuts at 45 degrees from corner to corner. A pull of the ribbon loop would completely change the picture. Further interesting types are the dissolving views which are cut like a venetian blind. A square or oblong picture is divided into four or five equal sections by horizontal slices or cuts. When a tab at the bottom of the page is pulled, the picture changes completely. Still others had figures of adults, children, and animals mounted on paper springs which, when the pages were fully opened, would stand out in relief from their scenic backgrounds. Another form is the action picture in which the figure's head, arms, or legs move realistically, the movements provided by a series of odd size levers constructed so that they all work together. The smaller levers connected to the main lever which is tied into, or riveted to, the back of the illustration at a near central location. This lever system is controlled by a pull-tab at the bottom of the page. The actions mentioned above are worked singularly or in combinations of two or three, and in some cases four.

Most of the early action books were published in England and Germany. In England, the *Harlquinade* or fold-over page book was the first form of moveable book — at least the first form printed with verses in the English language. **(Illustration 46. A.-D.)** It was developed in 1765 by an Englishman, Robert Sayer. Basically it consisted of a single sheet of paper folded vertically into four sections, each section having a horizontal fold at the top quarter and the lower three quarter level with vertical cuts at these folds. All surfaces were covered with illustrations and appropriate verses. At each opening of a fold the picture changes and the story verse is continued. These inexpensive folding books were very much in demand at the time, and numerous publishers produced them. Cheap paper and to many hands folding and unfolding these novelties over the years have left few survivors. Lucky is the collector who finds one intact. **(Color Illustration 4.)**

Prior to 1850 the action books published in England were primarily for adults. At this date a young Thomas Dean started a small business devoted to the publishing of children's books. The company became Dean & Bailey, later Dean & Munday, and finally in 1847 it became Dean & Son, when his son George came of age. One of the early examples of moveable books Dean published was found in a series he called *Dame Wonder's Transformations*. The idea was a simple one. On the last page of the book was a hand colored illustration of a young English lady. On the numerous preceding pages were a series of costumes and cut through each page, on the shoulder of each costume, was a hole the exact size of the face of the beautiful young lady on the last page. As one turned the pages, they saw the young lady wearing costumes from all over the world. This was actually a form of overlay book. **(Illustration 47 A & B.)** A rather rare variation of the above transformation is one whereby the figure on the last page has a moulded gutta percha face which protrudes through the holes in the preceding pages and on out to the cover of the book. **(Color Illustration 5.)**

At a later date Dean published another type of moveable book which he called *Scenic Books*. Using the folding peep show idea of cut-out cards, one behind the other, they produced scenes which consisted of three or four layers of cut-out figures and backgrounds, all laying flat within the book. When the page was opened and the loop of ribbon at the bottom of the page was pulled out, the whole scene rose up into perspective. Each layer of figures was connected to the next by a number of hidden short folded strips or hinges. The story copy was printed on the lower half of the page, which became exposed when the folded scene was lifted into position. **(Illustration 48.)** Dean published other types of moveable books, such as lever action, pop-up, and dissolving views. One unusual Dean publication titled *Seaside Fun* has a series of sailboats as flat pop-ups activated by horizontal strings from page to page that stretch and lift the sails up when each page is fully opened. **(Illustration 49.)**

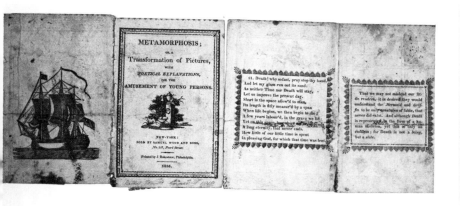

Illustration 46 A, B, C & D: An example of one of the earliest forms of a moveable book printed in the English language. The illustrations picture a *Metamorphosis*, published in 1816 by J. Rakestraw of Philadelphia, Pennsylvania. It illustrates the different folded openings and the pictorial changes that occur. Opens to 6½ x 10in (16.5 x 25.3cm). *Collection Herbert Hosmer.*

That I was an American girl,

You never did suppose;

But I am, and ever shall,

Be only plain Miss Rose.

Illustration 47 A & B: *Miss Rose,* c. 1880, an early overlay book published by E. Dunigan of New York City, is similar to an earlier example published by Dean & Son of England. Size 7½ x 5in (19.0 x 12.7cm).

Raphael Tuck (1821-1900), a German who came to Great Britain as a young man, tried one or two business positions before entering the publishing field in 1870. The business proved successful, and he gained a reputation as a fine arts publisher. All designing and necessary editorial writing was done in his London studio, while all printing was done in Germany. Among his accomplishments was the production of children's books, and a part of this was moveable books in the form of lever action, pull-outs, peep shows, panoramas, overlays, and slatted picture books. **(Illustration 50.)** Tuck's favorite subject matter seemed to lean towards illustrating groups of children and domesticated animals. **(Illustration 51.)** Raphael Tuck became a British citizen in 1875, and later was appointed publisher to Queen Victoria in recognition of his contributions to the art of fine printing. In 1882 he retired, turning the business over to his three sons, and the firm was henceforth known as Raphael Tuck

Illustration 48: *Little Red Riding Hood*, an early fold-out book published by Dean and Son, London, England. It contains a series of eight, three-tier hand colored fold-out scenes and the story of *Red Riding Hood*. c. 1860. 10 x 7⅛in (25.4 x 18.0cm).

Illustration 49: *Seaside fun* from the "Surprise Model" series published by Dean & Son, 160a Fleet Street E.C. London, England. A story about a boy and his two sisters and their visit to the seashore. Three seashore scenes are in the form of pop-ups that are activated by two horizontal strings that run from cover to cover. c.1920. 12 x 9in (30.5 x 22.8cm).

Illustration 50: *To Picture Land*, published by Raphael Tuck & Sons of London, England. A book of childrens verses with two double page fold-outs featuring a farm scene with two boys, horses and a herd of sheep, titled "Friends At The Farm" and the illustrated "Seaside Pleasures" above. Copyright 1895. 9 by 7½in, opens to 15in. (22.7 x 19.0cm., opens to 38.1cm).

Illustration 51: *Cosy Cot Farm* published by Raphael Tuck & Sons of London, England. A book of verses about children and farm animals with two double page fold-outs. "Morning at the Farm" features children, horses, donkeys, sheep and fowl. "Breakfast Time" is illustrated left. Copyright 1895. 9 x 7½in opens to 15in (22.7 x 19.0cm).

& Sons. The business continued to grow and always maintained its reputation as a producer of fine art paper products. We will read more of this great firm at a later point, as they were prominent in the publishing of other beautiful paper items.

Germany, a leader in the development of printing, had more than its share of printers and publishers of moveable books. It would take many pages to cover them all, so we will be satisfied just mentioning a few of the more prominent ones and give some pictorial evidence of their beautiful work. Wilhelm Nitzschke of Stuttgart, Schaller & Kirn of Furth, J.F. Schreiber of Stuttgart and later of Esslingen, Braum & Schneider of Munich, and Ernest Nister of Nuremberg, all produced work of excellent quality — in some cases it was magnificent. **(Illustration 52 A & B.)** Quality and depth of color was of high order and while all the movements were adequate, some were outstanding. **(Illustration 53.)** In some cases the relationship between the subject matter and the movement was at a very high level. **(Color Illustration 6.)**

Such was the work of Lothar Meggendorfer, artist and creator of movement in books. Born in Munich, Germany, in 1847, he studied art as a young man and later served on the staff of two satirical publications for several years. He started designing his novel mechanical picture books in the 1880s, utilizing nearly all the various types of action. Meggendorfer had the rare ability to

Illustration 52 A & B: A moveable page from the book *Lustige Gesellschoft*, published by Theodore Stroefer of Nürenberg, Germany. A large book of assorted verses in German and eight lattice-like pull-tab illustrations of children and animals. c.1910. The accompanying illustration pictures the owl and the sparrow in conversation. A pull of the tab changes the figures to an ostrich and penguin. 12¼ x 10in (32.4 x 25.4cm).

Haſt du bald genug geſeh'n,
Wie die Eule iſt ſo ſchön;
Zieh' und laſſe ſie verſchwinden,
Gigerln wirſt du mehr noch finden.

Haſt du bald genug geſeh'n,
Wie die Eule iſt ſo ſchön;
Zieh' und laſſe ſie verſchwinden,
Gigerln wirſt du mehr noch finden.

Illustration 53: The beautiful cover of Wilhelm Nitzschke's book which contains an assortment of eight moveable pages with various types of action. An extremely unusual example is found in **Color Illustration 6 A and B.** Nitzschke of Stuttgart, Germany, published outstanding examples of colorful illustrations with unusual movement. c.1875. 12¾ x 10in (32.4 x 25.4cm).

create a personality for the subject of his art work and, through the intricate movements he provided, bring the figure to life. **(Illustrations 54 A & B.)** His numerous books, over 60, were published principally by Braum & Schneider and J.F. Schreiber. Meggendorfer's books were printed in many editions and translated into several languages. He gained a world-wide reputation as the master for producing mechanical books. He had the four necessary qualities, that of being artistic, creative, humorous and having a mechanical talent. **(Illustrations 55 A & B.)**

Ernest Nister of Nuremberg, Germany, seems to have been one of the more prolific German publishers of moveable books. Many collectors believe that his works are among the most beautiful of all moveables, but this is a matter of personal opinion. Nister realized that there was probably a difference in taste between the children of his country and those of the English speaking countries, particularly in the written text of the books. He opened a branch in London, England, and staffed it with people skilled in translating copy and verse writing. All printing was done in the base plant in Nuremberg, Germany. Just before the turn of the century, Nister's London office made a cooperative agreement with the American book publishing firm of E.P. Dutton of New York City. Originally the Dutton firm was founded in 1852 by two brothers, in Boston, Massachusetts. One brother, Edward, bought out his brother's interest and moved the business to New York City. Dutton, in his agreement with Nister, was given exclusive rights to distribute and sell Nister books in the United States. They published several types of moveable books under this arrangement. A description of the principle of movement used in the books and some of the titles used are as follows: A rotating circle type consisting of two separate circular cards, each illustrated, cut halfway through so as to overlap, both mounted on a center axis between two pages sealed around the outermost edges. The face page has a circular viewing opening with a decorative page frame. A ribbon pull loop at the bottom of the page may be pulled around the perimeter of the circular opening to reveal the illustration on the inner card. **(Illustration 56 A & B.)** This example

Illustration 54 A & B: Lothar Meggendorfer's wonderful moveable book *Automaten Theater* was published by J. F. Schreiber of Esslingen, Germany. It contains eight pull-tab action illustrations, one of which is the humorous situation of a gentleman hunter being treed by a wild boar. When the tab is pulled, the hunter opens his mouth shouting his anger, driving his right forearm and the hand holding the gun downward, striking the butt of the rifle on the boar's head. Action is also seen at the hunter's jaw and mouth, his right elbow and wrist, and at the boar's head and tail. c.1905. 14½ x 10¼in (36.8 x 26.0cm).

Illustration 55 A & B: Another example of Lothar Meggendorfer's work is found in his *Automaten Theater* which was published by J. F. Schrieber of Esslingen, Germany. The well dressed black dandy sits at a table holding a long stemmed pipe and reading a magazine. As the tab is pulled, the action starts. The dandy lowers the tabloid, brings the pipe to his opening mouth and raises his eyes upward. In all, there are four realistic movements that bring a smile to the face of the reader. c.1905. 14½ x 10¼in (36.8 x 26.0cm).

is from one of six dissolving views from a book titled *Round About Pictures For All Little Folk.* Other examples of similar styles are titled *Dissolving Views* and *All The Way Round, Pictures & Rhymes.*

A variation of the above rotating circle principle is when the two illustrated interior circular cards are sliced into six equal pie-shaped cuts. The ribbon loop is pulled in the same manner, revealing the hidden illustration. The example pictured is from a book titled *Magic Moments,* showing an illustration of Cinderella in her coach which dissolves into a scene picturing Cinderella running down the Palace steps at midnight. **(Illustration 57 A & B.)** Other versions of this type of moveable book are titled *Something New, For Little Folk* and *Twinkling Pictures.*

Another type of moveable book that Nister utilized was that in which a two-part cut-out scene was connected by tabs to a scenic background, which sprung up when the book was opened wide. **(Illustration 58.)** This illustration accompanies a poem titled *The Nursery Train.* The book is titled *The Pets Panorama,* and contains six moveable illustrations, each accompanied by a short story or verse. Other fine examples of Nister books utilizing this particular movement are *Peeps Into Fairy Land, Peep Show Pictures,* and *What The Children Like.*

The Magic Toy Book is an interesting illusionary type which requires a bright light to complete a picture. Pictured is an oval illustration featuring a child with a half completed back-

Illustration 56 A: A moveable page from the book titled *Round About Pictures For All Little Folk,* published by Dutton & Nister, London, England, and printed in Bavaria. It contains six revolving disc pictures featuring children and / or animals. This illustration pictures young Tom on a hobby horse. c.1910. 7¾ x 7½ in (19.8 x 19.1 cm).

Illustration 56 B: The reverse of the revolving illustration shown in **Illustration 56 A.** "Little Nell in the Goat Cart." This example consists of two complete illustrated discs, one over the other, each one slit from outer edge to a center point. As the ribbon is pulled the top disc slides under the bottom disc.

LEFT: Illustration 57 A: A moveable page from a book titled *Magic Moments*, published by Dutton & Nister of New York City and London, England. It contains seven discs with highly decorative borders that picture scenes taken from children's literature. Each scene is accompanied by verses written by Clifton Bingham. This disc pictures Cinderella in the Royal Coach. c.1910. 11 x 10⅜in (28.0 x 26.3cm).

RIGHT: Illustration 57 B: The reverse of revolving illustration **57 A** pictures Cinderella running down the steps at twelve o'clock. This variant revolving picture consists of two illustrated discs, one over the other, each slit into six equal pie-shaped cuts. A pull of the ribbon loop dissolves one picture into the other.

Illustration 58: One of six action illustrations in a moveable book titled *The Pets Panorama*, published by Dutton & Nister and printed in Bavaria. Four double-page spreads have fold-out action, each accompanied by a single page of story and a second page of verse. c.1905. 9⅝ x 7¾in (24.4 x 19.7cm).

Illustration 59 A: *The Magic Toy Book,* published by Dutton & Nister, contains seven incomplete pictures, a short introductory story and seven verses, one accompanying each picture. Each illustration is backed with a second illustration drawn in reverse, which adds a feature or completes the first illustration when the page is held up to a light. c.1900. 8⅝ x 7⅞in (21.9 x 20.0cm).

Illustration 59 B: The reverse illustration of Santa peeking behind the curtain to see if the child is enjoying her Christmas toys. Santa is invisible in the original picture but when held up to a source of light he appears.

ground; on the other side of the page the incompleted background would be painted in, in reverse. When the illustration on the front page is held up to a light, the back illustration shows through, providing a complete picture. **(Illustration 59 A & B.)** The title page displays this explanatory verse: "This is the Magic Picture Book. When at each page you come to look, you'll find but half the picture there. But raise each pretty page on high, and something more you will espy; just let the light but shine behind and you will find - what you will find."

Still another moveable book by Nister was of the square venetian blind type, activated by pulling a tab at the bottom of the page. **(Illustration 60 A & B.)** This is from a book called, *Transformation Pictures & Comical Fixtures.* Other titles with similar movement include *Here & There, A Book of Transformation Pictures, Sweets From Fairy Land,* and *Pleasant Surprises.*

A lever action book provides another type used by Nister. Two illustrated squares, joined at the center, with the top illustration slit at a 45 degree angle, are encased in a paper frame with a backing. When the lever at the side of the page is pulled down, the top illustration splits, the top triangle moving upward and the bottom dropping down revealing the illustration beneath. **(Illustration 61 A & B.)** This example is from a book titled *What A Surprise, A Mechanical Book For Children.*

Another type of Nister moveable book is one that by simply opening the story page, the three-tier flat cut-out figures are pulled up by means of a tab connected to the preceding page. **(Illustra-**

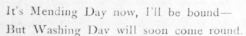

It's Mending Day now, I'll be bound—
But Washing Day will soon come round.

It's Mending Day now, I'll be bound—
But Washing Day will soon come round.

Illustration 60 A & B: *Transformation Pictures & Comical Fixtures*, features six square venetian blind-type of moveable pictures. Each illustration is accompanied by a four-part verse. Published by Dutton & Nister of New York City and London, England. This illustration is titled "Mending Day" and "Washing Day." It pictures a boy repairing a wooden doll and is the first part of a two-part transformation. By pulling the tab at the bottom of the page, the scene showing the boy mending his sister's doll is transformed to a scene picturing the sister washing the doll and its clothes, and a young friend hanging the doll clothes on a line. c.1910. 7¾ x 6⅞in (19.6 x 17.5cm).

tion 62.) *The Model Menagerie* pictures six caged wild animals, each with accompanying stories. This, and a similar volume, *Wild Animal Stories*, was published for children at an age when they could read, while most of the previously mentioned action books were geared to a preschool age.

Several action books were published in Europe for American companies. An outstanding example is a set of four individual pop-ups picturing groups of various buildings at the Worlds Columbian Exposition at Chicago, Illinois, in 1893. No. 1, pictures the Naval Exhibit, the Pier and the Fisheries Building. No. 2, shows the Casino and Pier, the Art Palace and the Dairy Building. No. 3, the Electrical Building, the Hall of Mines and the Wisconsin State Building. No. 4, pictures Ma-

chinery Hall, the Administration Building and the Forestry building. **(Illustration 63 A & B.)** Each of these fine examples are marked "Printed in Germany" and "Patented June 26, 1883."

Another outstanding example, printed in Germany, for the International News Company of New York City, is titled *Columbus Panorama, Three Pictures From American History*. This three-section fold-out, 32 inches (81.3cm) wide depicts the landing of Columbus in the New World in 1492, the Declaration of Independence, and the Emancipation of the Slaves in 1864. The center panel pictures Columbus and his jubilant crew stepping ashore, holding the standard of Queen Isabella of Spain. In the foreground is the Santa Maria at anchor, while in the background are forests, an open field or two, and an occasional

Indian observing a bit of history in the making. The left panel pictures Washington taking the oath as Commander of the Continental Army from Benjamin Franklin. Washington's soldiers stand behind him holding American flags, while members of the Continental Congress stand behind Franklin. The last panel shows Abraham Lincoln standing on a platform, waving a copy of the Emancipation Proclamation. Behind Lincoln stand Generals Grant, Sherman and Sheridan. **(Color Illustration 7.)**

Unfortunately, I have not found too many examples of French moveable books, although I have found several fine French paper toys. While my examples are limited, I do have a series of four pull-outs under the heading *Libraire Enfantine Illustrie*, published by A. Capendu of Paris, France

Two to make a prancing team;
Two to fish beside the stream.

Two to make a prancing team;
Two to fish beside the stream.

Illustration 61 A & B: *What a Surprise, A Mechanical Book for Children*, published by Dutton & Nister of New York City and London, England. It contains six transformation pictures that are moved by pulling a tab lever downward at the side of the page. As the side lever is pulled down, the top illustration, which is cut at a 45 degree angle, opens up. The top triangle, moving upward and the bottom section dropping down revealing the pictured illustration.

Illustration 62: *The Model Menagerie* consists of a series of six wild animals in cages that open outward when the pages are fully opened. Each colorful activated illustration is accompanied by two or three pages of story, text about each specific animal. Published by Dutton & Nister, c.1920. 10¾ x 14in (27.3 x 35.5cm).

Illustration 63 A & B: The cover of one of four hardcover folders titled, *World's Columbian Exposition Chicago 1893*, which when opened gives a pop-up presentation of some of the fair's buildings. Marked "Printed in Germany" and "Patented June 26, 1883." The opened pop-up displays the "Machinery Hall" in the background and moving forward, the "Administration Building," the "Illinois State Building" and the "Forestry Building" in the foreground. 10¼ x 12¼ x 10¼in opened (26.0 x 31.1 x 26.0cm).

The titles include *Cendrillon, Le Cirgue Corvi, Guignol* and *Croquemitaine.* Each is a very colorful pull-up and, when opened, consists of three cut-out cards, one behind the other, picturing characters and props, with the rear card picturing the background scenery. On the back of each toy is a printed play, each composed of three scenes and a listing of the characters involved. **(Illustration 64.)**

There are several other European examples that I have not been able to explain or picture because of the limitation of space. However, mention should be made of a series of 12 very unusual, quite large and strongly colored pop-ups called *Panascopic Model Books.* The artist is V. Kubasta, they were published by Bancroft & Company Ltd. of London, England, and printed in Czechoslovakia from 1960 to 1962. Each consists of a large three-section fold-out, a six-to eight-page story on the first section and a large colorful pop-up on the last two sections. **(Illustration 65.)** This illustrates a tribe of Indians and, strangely, nearly all are chiefs in full headdress. The other versions are equally colorful and impressive, both in design and subject matter. These are the titles: *Marco Polo, Noah's Ark, Circus Life, Farm Life, In The Jungle, Alice in Wonderland, Gulliver, The Castle Tournament, Father Christmas,* and *Christopher Columbus.* **(Color Illustration 8.)**

In the United States, McLoughlin Brothers seems to be the most prominent of the early producers of moveable books. The first McLoughlin catalog I have found that mentions moveable books was dated 1884. It lists "The Little Showman's Series" and "The Little Showmans No. 2." The latter is marked copyright 1884, while the former is unmarked. An earlier 1877 catalog does not list any moveable books. What the six years between had to offer is a question that may possibly be answered in the future. The *Little Showman's Series* consists of six books: *The Wild Beast Show, Jumbo & The Countryman, The Aquarium, The Snake Charmer, The Lion's Den,* and *Happy Family, The Lively Apes.* All are similar in construction and action, and each consists of two stiff board covers hinged at the top. By lifting the top cover up to a ninety degree position, a cage with cut-out bars opens out. In

Illustration 64: One of a series of four pull-outs titled *Librairie Enfantine Illustrie,* published by A. Capends of Paris, France. The pull-out illustrated is titled *Guignol.* On the back of the rear scene is a printed play in three scenes. c.1890. 7⅝ x 10¼ x 12¼in opened (19.3 x 26.0 x 31.1cm).

Illustration 65: A large three-panel folder with an American Indian chief on the front and back cover, no title, marked with the artist's name "V. Kubasta." Published by Bancroft & Co. Ltd. of London, England, and printed in Czechoslovakia. A short story titled *The Day of the Bison Hunt* is found inside the front page. The next two panels support a strongly colored Indian camp in pop-up form. Dated 1962. 10½ x 17¾ by 12¾in opened (26.7 x 45.1 x 32.3cm).

the *Happy Family* book, the monkies are climbing on the bars and a cut-out boy and girl are looking into the cage. A second cut-out tier consists of monkies climbing in a tree and a white poddle sitting upright on a pedestal. The background is the rear of the cage with the figures of two young children looking in. An accompanying verse is printed on the foreward half of the bottom board in the foreground.

(Illustration 66.) The *Little Showmans Series No. 2* is equally as colorful as the earlier series, but is considerably larger in size. The series consists of the four seasons: *Spring, Summer, Autumn* and *Winter.* **(Illustration 67.)**

McLoughlin's 1886 catalog lists the "Pantomine Toy Books" which consists of five books: *Aladdin or The Wonderful Lamp, Blue Beard, Puss In Boots, Cinderella*, and *Sleeping Beauty.*

Each book is made up of a colorful proscenium which frames five set scenes and nine trick changes in the form of half-and quarter-pages. This arrangement provides a combination of 14 transformations. Each edition has ten pages of accompanying story text. **(Illustration 68.)**

In 1891, McLoughlin published a new series of four open out books consisting of *Robinson Crusoe, Red Riding Hood, Cinderella*, and

Illustration 66: *The Lively Apes* is a fold-out moveable in a hard-cover folder. One of six titles found in *The Little Showman's Series* published by McLoughlin Brothers of New York City. c.1880. 11¼ x 8 x 11¼in opened (28.5 x 20.3 x 28.5cm).

Illustration 67: The cover of *The Little Showman's Series No. 2, Summer*, which features a three-tier fold-out picturing children participating in Summer activities. Published by McLoughlin Brothers of New York City, it was copyrighted in 1884. 13½ x 10½ x 13½ opened (34.2 x 26.6 x 34.2cm).

Illustration 68: The center spread from *Aladdin or The Wonderful Lamp* from the *Pantomine Toy Books* series. Published by McLoughlin Brothers of New York City. Consists of a number of full, half and quarter vertical pages. It offers 14 colorful transformation scenes along with the pages of story text. c.1885. 10 x 14¾in opened (25.4 x 37.5cm).

Beauty & The Beast. The caption within the catalog reads: "On raising the covers, the likeness to a book will end in a charming surprise. A beautiful tableaux will magically appear and figures and animals will spring into being. Each of these little shows is perfect in itself and contains descriptive verses." McLoughlin Brothers continued publishing the above action books for a period of time. Several other publishers offered action books from 1910 on, but not in any great quantity. An interesting example of this period would be *The Magic Picture Book*, a hardcover book published by G.W. Dillingham of New York City. It was a simple, but colorful transformation book, with every third page a full

illustration and every second page a vertical half illustrated page, which changed the basic illustration as the page was turned. Another novel construction fun book appeared at this time called *Fun Faces*, published by Ideal Book Builders of Chicago, Illinois. It consisted of six stiff cardboard pages, each page illustrated with two humorus and colorful heads. Each head had four oval cut-outs, the two eyes, the nose, and the mouth. Inside the cover was an envelope with series of cut-out interchange eyes, noses and mouths which fit snugly into any of the holes in the various faces. Much amusement may be had by trying to find the correct features for each of the twelve faces, and possibly more amusement

by mixing them up.

In 1933, the Blue Ribbon Press of New York City published a pop-up book called *Sleeping Beauty* which was illustrated by H.B. Lentz. It contained one pop-up which pictured a castle surrounded by a moat with a mounted knight approaching the castle. During this same year Blue Ribbon Press published a series of four pop-up books with stories and illustrations by the staff of Walt Disney Studios. *The Pop-up Mickey Mouse* and *The Pop-up Minnie Mouse*, each contained three humorous action illustrations. **(Illustrations 69 & 70.)** Two larger action toy books followed, *The Pop-up Silly Symphonies* containing stories of *Babes In The Woods*, and *King*

Illustration 69: This colorful center spread was created by the Walt Disney Studios and is one of three found in *The Pop-up Mickey Mouse* book. Published by Blue Ribbon Books of New York City, and copyrighted in 1933 by Walt Disney Enterprises. 6¾ x 13⅜ x 8¾in opened (17.1 x 34.0 x 22.2cm).

Illustration 70: The third of three double page pop-ups picturing Disney's famous characters found in *The Pop-up Minnie Mouse*. Published by Blue Ribbon Books Inc. of New York City, and copyrighted in 1933 by Walt Disney Enterprises. 6¾ x 13⅜ x 1¾ opened (22.2 x 34.0 x 4.5cm).

Neptune, and *Mickey Mouse in King Arthur's Court*. Both books contained four fantastic pop-ups. **(Illustration 71.)**

The following year Blue Ribbon Books added another novelty toy book to their line, the *Mickey Mouse Waddle Book*. It contained four Disney characters; Mickey, Minnie, Pluto the dog, and Tanglefoot the horse. Each character was printed in full color on a stiff cardboard page outlined with perforated holes so that each one could be pressed out without cutting. Then with specified folding they assumed a three dimensional stature and were ready to waddle down an enclosed runway that could be attached to the back of the book. Because of the removable parts, very few complete examples of the Waddle book still exist. This is probably one of the ultimate mechanical books for a collector to find in complete, unused condition.

In 1934, Blue Ribbon Press issued four action

books of popular childrens stories, each containing three colorful pop-ups. *The Pop-up Mother Goose* pictured Mother Goose riding on a flying goose's back, blackbirds flying out of a pie and Humpty Dumpty falling off a wall with the King's soldiers watching. **(Illustration 72.)** The next pop-up book was *Little Red Ridinghood* with moveable illustrations of Red Ridinghood waving goodby to her mother, meeting the wolf in the forest, and being surprised by the wolf in her grandmother's bed. The third book, titled *Puss In Boots*, pictured Puss showing a rabbit to the King, Puss and the mouse, and Puss watching the King's carriage passing by. The last book in this series was *Goldilocks & The Three Bears*, which contained pop-ups of Goldilocks eating from the three bowls, the bears finding Goldilocks in bed, and the scene of Goldilocks running from the bear's house.

In 1935, Pleasure Books Inc. of Chicago,

Illinois, a division of Blue Ribbon Press, issued a series of pop-up books based on several of the newspaper comic strip characters. Each book contained three outstanding pop-up illustrations. *Buck Rogers 25th Century* features Buddy and Allura in *Strange Adventures In The Spider Ship*. **(Color Illustration 9.)** The *New Adventures of Tarzan* has a terrific center fold pop-up of Tarzan attacking a crocodile. **(Color Illustration 10.)** While *Flash Gordon, The Tournament of Death*, created by Alex Raymond, contains outstanding examples of fantasy in action. One pictures Ming, the Emperor, toasting Flash and Dale; a second example features Ming standing in the Skull Chariot drawn by a pair of tigers; and finally Flash carrying a lance rides a white stallion in a jousting match with Ming's champion. **(Color Illustration 11.)** *Tim Tyler In The Jungle* presents three spectacular wild animal pop-ups with Tyler and his partner Speed in the background.

Illustration 71: One of four double page pop-ups found in the book titled *The Pop-up Silly Symphonies*, containing the stories *Babes in the Woods* and *King Neptune*. Published by Blue Ribbon Books, Inc. of New York City, and copyrighted in 1933 by Walt Disney Enterprises. 7 x 15½ x 9¾in opened (17.8 x 39.3 x 24.8cm).

Illustration 72: One of the double page pop-ups found in *The Pop-up Mother Goose* book which was illustrated by Harold B. Lentz. Published and copyrighted in 1934 by the Blue Ribbon Press of New York City. 6½ x 15¾ x 9¼in opened (16.5 x 40.0 x 23.5cm).

Illustraton 73: The first of three double page pop-ups found in *The Pop-up Tim Tyler in the Jungle*. This Blue Ribbon Press book was published by Pleasure Books, Inc. of Chicago, Illinois. It was copyrighted in 1935 by King Features Syndicate, Inc. 6¼ x 15¾ x 9¼ opened. (15.9 x 40.0 x 23.5cm).

Illustration 74: One of three double page pop-ups featuring the leading character in *The Pop-up Dick Tracy, Capture of Boris Arson.* A Blue Ribbon Press book published by Pleasure Books, Inc. of Chicago, Illinois. Artwork and story by Chester Gould, copyrighted in 1935 by the Famous Artists Syndicate. 9¼ x 15¾ x 2½in opened (23.5 x 40.0 x 6.3cm).

Illustration 75: One of three double page pop-ups featuring Harold Gray's famous characters in *Little Orphan Annie & Jumbo the Circus Elephant.* The Blue Ribbon Press Book published by Pleasure Books, Inc. of Chicago, Illinois. Copyrighted in 1935 by the Famous Artists Syndicate. 6½ x 15¾ x 9¼in opened (16.5 x 40.0 x 23.5cm).

Illustration 76: One of three double page pop-ups in a book titled *Bobby Bear.* Published by the Whitman Publishing Company of Racine, Wisconsin, and copyrighted in 1935. 7⅝ x 14½ x 2½in opened (19.3 x 36.8 x 6.3cm).

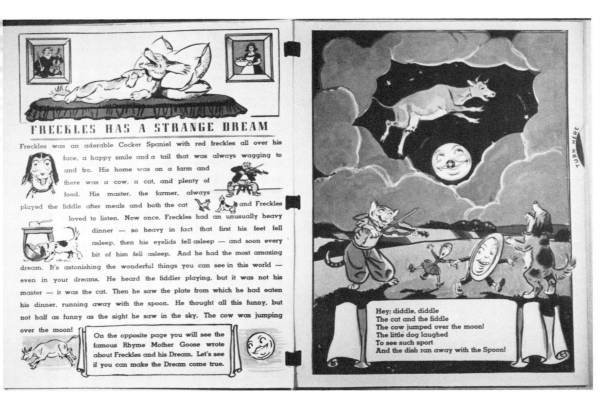

Illustration 77: Two pages from *Tony Sarg's Surprise Book*. The left page has a story about a little dog's strange dream. The right page contains a revolving disc that when turned, makes the cow jump over the moon. This humorous novelty book was published by the Jay Publishing Company of New York City, and was copyrighted in 1941 by B.F. Jay. 10¾ x 16½in (27.3 x 41.9cm).

Illustration 78: *Tony Sarg's Treasure Book* is just that, a treasury of three stories. The bulky box-like covers are unique. The sailing ship, a man calling for help and the shark in the large opening move when the disc in the small hole lower right is turned. Published by the B.F. Jay & Company of New York City in 1942. 11½ x 9½ x 2⅞in (29.2 x 24.2 x 7.3cm).

(Illustration 73.) *Dick Tracy* and *Little Orphan Annie & Jumbo, the Circus Elephant* complete the comic series. **(Illustrations 74 & 75.)** During this same year the Whitman Publishing Company of Racine, Wisconsin, noted for their paperback story books, coloring and cut-out books, issued *Bobby Bear*, a pop-up book with three action illustrations **(Illustration 76.)**

In the 1940s, the subject matter of moveable books seemed to be geared to a more youthful audience. *Tony Sarg's Surprise Book* was based on the five senses: sight, sound, smell, taste and touch. The introductory page pictures a dressed elephant standing on his hind legs holding a cut-out stage proscidium. Three children stand in front watching the show. At the outside edge of

the double page is a cut-out half circle which reveals the edge of a large turnable disc between the two pages. Turning the disc reveals a series of five pictures within the proscidium. These pictures, plus a one line title taken from various Mother Goose rhymes, preview the following pages of surprises. **(Illustration 77.)** A one-page story of *Simple Simon* is followed by a full page illustration of Simon in a long tattered coat with a patch pocket containing a real penny. The following page tells a story of *Baa Baa Black Sheep* followed by an illustration of a little boy and a sheep with a body covered with black felt. The story of *Jack & The Beanstalk* follows with a cut-out Jack climbing a slit beanstalk alongside a castle. When Jack is pushed to the top of the stalk,

the Giant's face appears in the castle window. This is followed by a story about *Misstress Mary & Her Garden*, with a second page covered with scented flowers. The next story is about a little dog that has a dream about a cow jumping over the moon, followed by a double page concealing a revolving disc. When turned, the cow jumps over the moon, the scene being revealed in an opening in the clouds. The last story tells the tale of *Old King Cole* which is followed by an illustration of a jolly fiddler holding a large base fiddle which has two rubber band strings. When plucked by youthful fingers, they go "Zoom & Zing." This novel book of surprises was copyrighted in 1941 by B.F. Jay.

A second book full of surprises was copy-

PULL

Illustration 79: One of three pull-tab moveable pages from the book *The Animated Pinocchio* by Marion Merrill. A pull of the tab brings about three movements: Pinocchio's ears become shorter; Creaky, the figure in the basket, hides; and then window curtains flip up revealing the coach driver in the window. Published by The Citadel Press of New York City. c.1945. 11 x 8½in (27.9 x 21.6cm).

Illustration 80: One of four moveable pages in the book *Rip Van Winkle*. The animations were provided by Julian Wehr. Moving the tab sideways gives a swing to the bowler's arm, moves two of the little men behind the pins and moves the peeking Rip's head up and down. Published by Stephen Day, Inc. of New York City in 1945. 8½ x 6½in (21.6 x 16.5cm).

righted the following year by the same B.F. Jay. It is titled *Tony Sarg's Treasure Book*. **(Illustration 78.)** A large box-like book measuring 11½ inches high, (29.2cm) 9½ inches (24.2cm) wide and 3 inches (7.6cm) deep consist of two box covers hinged together front and back with 22 pages in between. As you can see there are two openings or cavities on the cover. The larger opening, covered with a fine thread screen, pictures an early two-masted sailing ship and a man with his arms outstretched floundering in a rather stormy sea. The smaller opening reveals the edge of a finger turning disc that, when turned, provides action in the opening above. The sailing ship rocks back and forth, the man disappears into the water, and the heads of two sharks break the surface of the water. The interior story pages hold brief renditions of three popular classics; *Alice in Wonder-land*, *Treasure Island*, and *Rip Van Winkle*. These tales are accompanied by numerous color illustrations, several of which have movement. The back cover has two openings similar to the above described front cover. The large opening pictures a young Rip Van Winkle holding a jug of ale in his right hand. He stands in the company of several dwarfs in a wooded background. Activated by a movement similar to that of the front cover, Rip lifts the jug of ale to his mouth, while some of the dwarfs disappear behind the trees and boulders and then reappear.

In 1944, the Animated Book Company Inc., of New York City, published *The Three Little Pigs*. Illustrated and animated by Hank Hart, it contained five animated pictures activated by pull tabs, slide tabs and a rotating disc. The following year Merrill Novelty Books issued *The Animated Pinocchio*, illustrated by Marion Merrill. It featured three action pictures moved by pull tabs. **(Illustration 79.)** In the same year, 1945, *Rip Van Winkle* was published by Stephen Daye Inc., of New York City. Animated by Julian Wehr, it contained five action illustrations worked by sliding tabs. **(Illustration 80.)**

The ever popular Santa Claus theme appeared in 1950 in the form of *Visions of St. Nick*, published by Phillip Peeble, Inc., and illustrated by A.E. Bradford. This toy opened out back to back showing a series of five separate scenes; Santa's castle, Santa's workshop, Santa in sleigh with reindeer, St. Nick's visit and a tired Santa back home. Each scene is made up of two cut-out sections which project outward from the background page. **(Illustration 81.)**

Illustration 81: A novelty book that opens out forming a five point star on top and five Christmas scenes on the sides. Titled *Visions of St. Nick in Action*, it is an In Action Book Publication, published and copyrighted by Phillips Publishers, Inc. in 1950. 7 x 14½in (17.7 x 36.9cm).

Chapter VII.

THE MAGNIFICENT PAPER SOLDIER

Illustration 82: The armed guards of Louis XV. *Cuirassiers de Louis XV.* Marked: "Imageries Reunies de Jarville-Nancy 205." c.1900. 15¾ x 11½in (40.0 x 29.2cm).

In the history of paper toys, the paper soldier must be given important consideration. It is next to impossible to record the first paper soldier. Toy soldiers of other materials have existed since early Greek and Roman times. Soldiers have been "looked up to" and "down upon" by the peoples of the world, but they were always newsworthy. While the early toy soldier was handcrafted for the nobility and the wealthy, the paper soldier was published in quantity, thus lowering the cost and making them available to people of moderate means. One must remember that the early sheets were uncolored, the painting, or coloring, and the cutting out had to be done by the purchaser. Early paper sheets have been found from the mid 1740s, and by 1775 scores of printers published sets of military sheets, beautifully engraved and some hand colored. Publishers from Germany, France, Italy, England, Holland, Spain, and Austria seem to have been the most prolific producers of early paper military figures. Each country produced prints of their fighting men, their heroes, their battles, all of which instilled a feeling of patriotism within the country.

Possibly the first paper soldiers were published in Strasbourg, which is located in Alsace, a territory lying along the eastern border of France. In the early 1740s, Strasbourg was paid a visit by Louis XV, attended by an escorting company of colorfully uniformed soldiers. **(Illustration 82.)** A printer by the name of Seyfried observed the interest of the townspeople in the soldiers and decided to publish sheets picturing the honor guards in their magnificent uniforms. The idea proved to be a profitable one, and other printers followed suit. The growth in the publishing of paper soldiers was to continue for the next 200 years, and scores of publishers and engravers became involved. Among the more prominent publishers were Striedbeck, Silbermann, Fischback, and Gerhardt. J.F. Striedbeck, an Alsatian engraver, produced paper soldiers in 1780 in authentic military dress. He actually set up a manufacturing shop that printed paper soldiers exclusively. H.R. Silbermann (1801-1876) is credited with developing a method of color printing with oils. His paper soldiers reached a high level of quality as did his production, 130,000 sheets per year. Gustav Fischbach, successor to Silbermann, continued to produce very fine quality sheets from 1872 to World War I. J.H. Gerhardt, another Alsatian publisher, is recorded as the first to print paper soldiers on the front and back. **(Color Illustration 12.)**

While just a few important publishers of the paper military are mentioned here, it must be remembered that there were two to three hundred others involved in publishing these colorful sheets. All the armies of Europe were represented, early sheets consisting of rows of soldiers in dress uniforms. Later sheets depicted them in battle action, naming scenes of famous battles. **(Illustration 83.)** More recent sheets illustrated fighting men in various action positions using the more modern hand weapons, such as machine guns, grenades, and bazookas. Prior to the start of the 20th century, military uniforms were highly decorative and offered a kaleidoscope of colors. The quality and depth of color used by the printers reached a high level, as publishers and printers, prideful of their work, strove to outdo their competitors. **(Color Illustration 13.)** In the later period, the advanced development of mass production provided quantity at a lower price, but sacrificed a certain amount of quality. This, along with the use of the practical khaki uniform

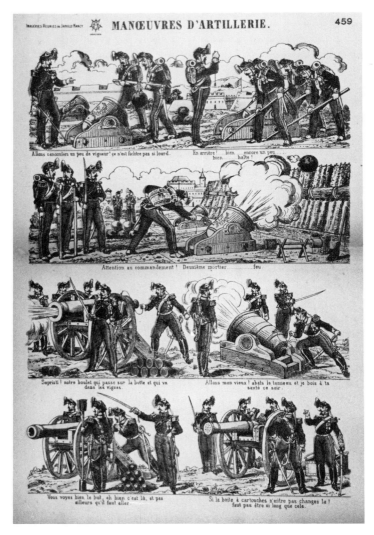

Illustration 83: The drilling of French artillerymen. Sheet marked: "Imageries Reunies de Jarville-Nancy 459." c.1890. 15¾ x 11⅝in (40.0 x 29.5cm).

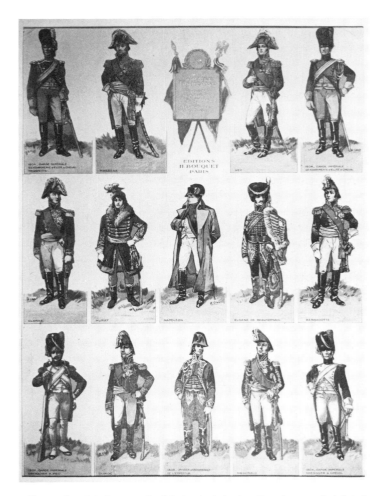

Illustration 84: Large colorful sheet picturing Napoleon and eight of his officers of the period 1790-1814. The four figures in the corners are 1804 Imperial Guards. The figures are outlined on the back of the sheet. Each outline contains information about the military campaigns and dates in which the officer took part. Published by H. Bouquet, Paris, France. c.1890. 17½ x 13½in (44.4 x 34.2cm).

that appeared during World War I, changed the magnificent paper soldier to a brown-clad fighting man of action.

Going back in time to the home of the paper soldier, Strasbough, France, we can visit the local Historical Museum which houses one of the world's best exhibits of paper soldiers. Originally published as playthings, this collection of paper military figures represents an entire period of history. The story of Napoleon's rise to a position of power in France, his numerous successful military campaigns, his years as Emperor, his fall at Waterloo, all these moments of history, along with the officers and soldiers involved, are portrayed. **(Illustration 84.)**

During these same periods many French publishers became prominent in this field. The Pellerin Family seemed to command the most attention. The Pellerin dynasty was started by Jean-Charles Pellerin (1756-1836). In 1782 he purchased a building in Epinal France, and

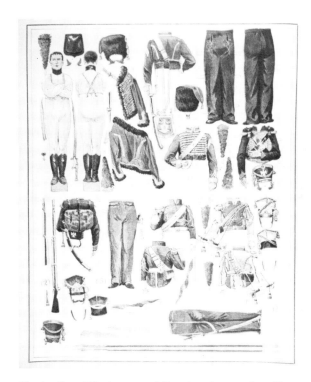

Illustration 85: A page of Napoleonic guard uniforms illustrated by Job. From the book *L'Empereur L'Imperatrice Le Garde Imperiale*, published by Hachette & Cie, Paris, France. c.1900. 10¾ x 8¼in (27.3 x 21.0cm).

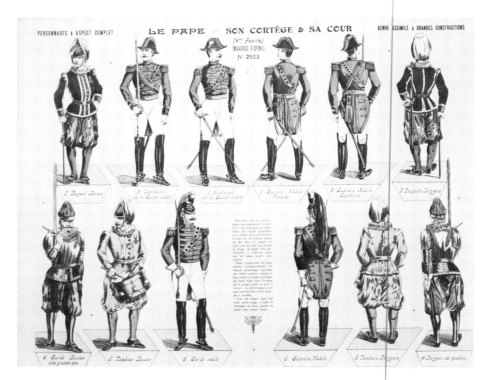

Illustration 86: A sheet picturing the various court attendants at the Vatican. Marked: *"Imagerie D'Epinal No. 2503."* c.1890. 11½in x 16in (29.2 x 40.7cm).

started a printing business. He had received his early training from his father Nicolas (1703-1773), who had learned his skills from an uncle, Dominique-Ignace Tisserand.

Napoleon and his armies became subject matter for Jean-Charles Pellerin's prints. In 1815, when Napoleon was exiled and Louis XVIII was made ruler of France, the king passed a decree that censored all images that were hostile to the new monarchy. Jean-Charles Pellerin was sentenced to four months in prison for ignoring this decree. Prior to Napoleon's downfall, Pellerin published prints of this great leader's campaigns. Pellerin was advised in these military illustrations by engravers who had formly served in the army, and who knew of the beautiful uniforms and also

the horrors of military battle. **(Illustrations 85 & 86.)**

Another important French publisher is Hachette & Co. who issued a group of hardcover books on fighting men of the past. They pictured military personalities, their various uniforms, and the fighting equipment they used. The beautiful authentically detailed color plates, with cutout figures and uniforms, were the work of the French artist Job. A. Fabre wrote the copy that accompanied each plate, providing the history of the subject matter. The first book titled *L'Empereur I Imperatrice la Garde* contained ten color plates dealing with Napoleon and the uniforms he wore. **(Illustration 87.)** A second cutout book titled *Guerrier et Grande Seigneurs*

contained 14 color plates of historical fighting men with their different hand weapons and clothing.

Most of the other European publishers of paper toys that we have mentioned printed cutout sheets of soldiers and their uniforms. They kept the public up to date with prints of their favorite troops, scenes of important battles, and the latest in field guns and other military equipment. The authenticity of the uniforms and the factual portrayal of the battle scenes are accepted as pictorial records of military history.

Some of the early German boxed construction sets of paper military objects offered in the 1803 Bestelmeier catalog contained some interesting items. No. 816 offered a large barrack, 23 inches

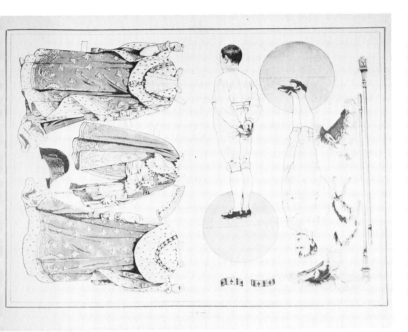

Illustration 87: Uncut page of Napoleon paper doll with coronation ceremonial robes and accessories. From *L'Empereur L'Imperatrice La Garde Imperial,* published by Hachette & Cie of Paris, France. c.1900. 10¾ x 8¼in (27.3 x 21.0cm). *Photo by Barbara Whitton Jendrick.*

Illustration 88: A boxed set of 50 assorted pieces titled in five languages, *Sebastopol, A Modern Game of Shooting by Cannon.* Manufacture unknown. Germany c.1860. The soldiers stand 3in (7.6cm) high.

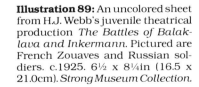

Illustration 89: An uncolored sheet from H.J. Webb's juvenile theatrical production *The Battles of Balaklava and Inkermann.* Pictured are French Zouaves and Russian soldiers. c.1925. 6½ x 8¼in (16.5 x 21.0cm). *Strong Museum Collection.*

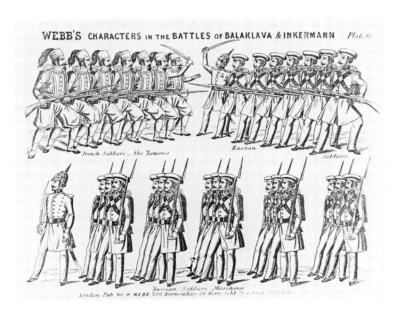

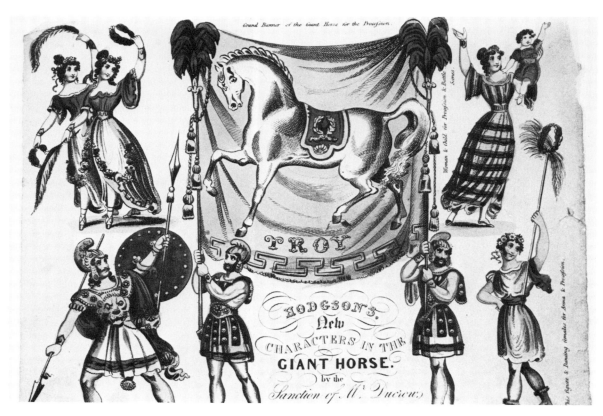

Illustration 90: The title sheet from Orlando Hodgson's juvenile drama, *The Seige of Troy or the Giant Horse.* c.1835. 6⅝ x 8⅜in (16.8 x 21.3cm). *Strong Museum Collection.*

long, 14 inches high and 18 inches wide (58.4 x 35.6 x 45.7cm), with adjoining buildings beautifully painted, and also included 34 soldiers and a Turkish band. No. 830, a fortification with doors, turrets and a drawbridge, 24 inches (61cm) square, with 20 soldiers and four cannons. No. 481, a tournament of knights, all in costumes of former times. It consists of an open space closed in by barriers. In the background is the emperor sitting on a throne. On each side of the throne are two guards and two knights in house costume. Two knights on armored horseback with lances positioned are out in front. Next to them stand shield bearers. A maiden holds a garland for the victor, and at the entrance of the barrier stands a herald with a trumpet. The set consists of 20

pieces and fits into a colorfully decorated box. No. 482 is somewhat similar to the above, consisting of a castle with 18 trees and shrubs, plus six knights and various attendants.

A later, but similar German boxed set, *The Battle of Sebastopol*, numbers 50 stand-up pieces with wooden stands. It depicts a stone fortress with towers, battlements, woven metal barricades, cannons, and soldiers in various fighting positions. All are packed in a decorated paper covered box marked in five languages. The publishers identity is lost because of wear along the bottom area of the box cover. Sebastopol (or Sevastopol) is a port on the Black Sea, located in the southwestern part of the Crimean Peninsula in Russia. The eleven month siege of the city in 1854 and

1855 was one of the major battles of the Crimean War. **(Illustration 88.)**

Many existing paper soldiers are exhibited in diorama form in museums and private collections. However, another form is found in the English toy theaters. Military productions, such as *H.J. Webb's The Battles of Balaklava & Inkerman*, billed as a military spectacle in two acts, features Scottish Highlanders, English Dragoons, Hussars, and French Zouaves. **(Illustration 89.)** *The Siege of Troy or Giant Horse of Simon* is a grand spectacle in two acts, published by Orlando Hodgson. **(Illustration 90.)** A further example is *The Battle of Waterloo*, an exciting melodrama in three acts. It consists of 12 plates of characters, mostly military, 12 scenes, and two wing sets, a total of 26 plates. **(Illustration 91.)**

The American paper soldier took a different form than it's European cousins. American publishers offered boxed sets of die-cut soldiers, usually colored lithographed paper with a cardboard backing and a small block of wood at the base to allow the figure to stand in an upright position. Exceptions to this were the early McLoughlin set of five uncut cards enclosed in a paper envelope. One card pictured a captain, fifer and two soldiers. The second set contained a drummer and three soldiers while the remaining three sets pictured five soldiers each. All were in dress uniforms of red and blue, and all had gold epaulets and buttons, crossed white chest straps, and shako headgear. **(Illustration 92.)** In 1879, McLoughlin offered boxed sets of 18 soldiers, two officers, a fifer, a drummer, and 14 infantrymen. All were die-cut and mounted on neatly turned wooden stands. A choice of the following companies were offered: 7th Regiment National Guards, 9th Regiment National Guards, 22nd Regiment National Guards, Continental Guards, Lafayette Guards, National Guards, City Guards, Irish Rifles, Old Continentals and Hawkins Zouaves. **(Illustration 93.)** These ten companies existed, in reality, in New York City at the time, and actual copies of their dress uniforms were offered in the paper soldier sets.

After 1890 the paper soldiers offered were of an international type in both infantry and cavalry form. They were sold in attractive boxed sets of 50

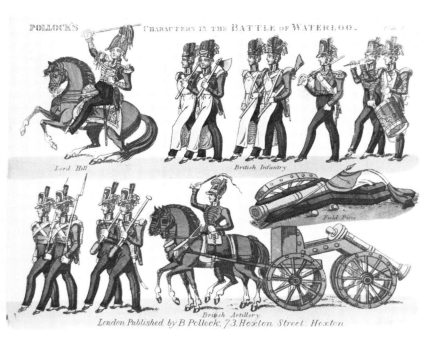

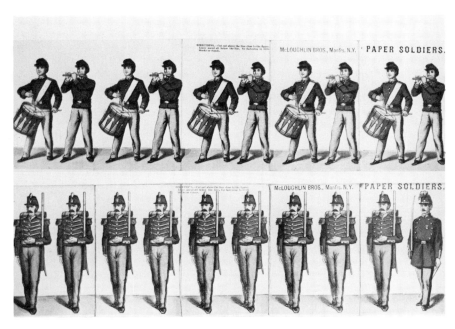

Illustration 91: A sheet of military characters from Benjamin Pollock's *The Battle of Waterloo*. It pictures Lord Hill on horseback, followed by members of the British infantry with an artillery company below. c.1920. 6½ x 8¼in (16.5 x 21.0cm). *Strong Museum Collection.*

Illustration 92: A strip picturing Civil War drummer boy and fifer in Union uniform. They wear dark blue caps and jackets with red collars and cuffs, light blue pants with red striping. The lower strip pictures Union Infantry soldiers with red headgear and jackets, yellow decorations and grey pants with red striping. Both were published by McLoughlin Brothers of New York City. c.1875. 4½ x 14½in (11.4 x 36.8cm).

Illustration 93: Strip of Union Rifles with figures in brown headgear, blue jackets with red epaulets, white cross straps and belt, light blue pants with red striping. Lower strip pictures the Old Continentals with uniforms similar to those worn in the Revolutionary War. Brown tricorn hats, red coats with yellow trim, white chest straps, grey pants and cream leggings. Published by McLoughlin Brothers, New York circa 1875. 4½ x 15¼in (11.4 x 38.7cm).

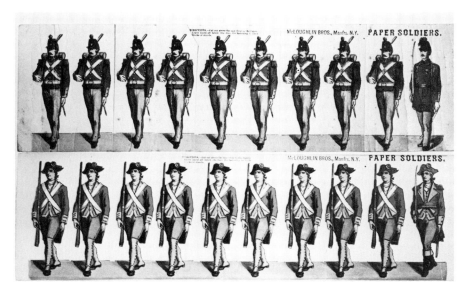

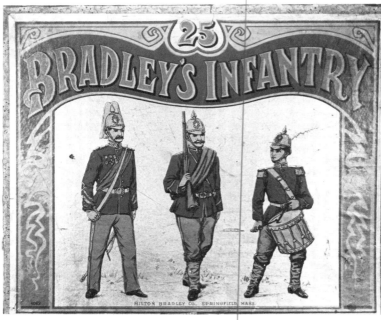

Illustration 94: The box cover of a set of 100 six-inch paper soldiers mounted on wooden stand. Includes ten different types, U.S. Regulars, Volunteers, Boers, British, and others. Published by McLoughlin Brothers of New York City, c.1910. 12¾ x 21in (32.3 x 53.3cm).

Illustration 95: Cover of original boxed set containing 23 soldiers, one officer and a bugler. The 5⅝in (14.2cm) tall soldiers are mounted on wood block stands. *Bradley's Infantry* was published by the Milton Bradley Company of Springfield, Massachusetts, c.1909. Box cover 9 x 11 x 1in (22.9 x 28.0 x 2.5cm).

or 100 soldiers **(Illustration 94.)** McLoughlin's 1914 catalog offered ten different boxed sets of soldiers representing U.S. Regulars, Volunteers, Boers, British, Rough Riders and Red Cross Nurses. In addition there were three sets of paper Boy Scout figures. **(Color Illustration 14.)**

In 1906 the Milton Bradley Company manufactured a boxed set called *At The Front* consisting of 24 cardboard soldiers and a pistol that shot wooden ammunition. A few years later they offered a boxed set of 25 cavalrymen and a second set of 25 infantrymen. **(Illustration 95.)** There is also a set called *The Siege of Port Arthur* with 24 soldiers of the Russo-Japanese War, along with two rapid-fire magazine guns mounted on swivel carriages that would shoot five wooden shells without reloading. In 1914, at the start of World War I, Bradley still offered these same boxed sets

plus some new introductions. A new type of rapid firing repeating gun that fired shells by turning a crank, brought more excitement to the young officers who manned the gun. The *Battleship Game* was another new set which included the new gun, plus a novel target in the form of a lithographed battleship. The ship was constructed of block-like sections, each section being numbered. When the ship was built up, the gun was put in action. When a smoke stack was hit, for instance, it toppled over, leaving the remainder of the ship standing. In this way the various parts of the ship were shot away until it was totally destroyed. **(Illustration 96.)** Bradley manufactured *The Sharpshooters*, a boxed set of nine 13 inch (33cm) paper soldiers, and a pop gun that shot corks. In 1918, three new boxed sets were offered representing British, French and German

troops, each set having 18 soldiers, it's countrys flag and standard, plus a repeating pistol and 30 wooden shells.

Parker Brothers, another prominent American paper toy producer, also entered into the paper soldier business. Their 1915 catalog offered two sets of giant paper soldiers, each containing ten figures and a rifle that shot rubber projectals. A third game, *The Great War*, advertised as new in 1915, consisted of four armies and four cannons, a fort, battle flags, Red Cross figures, and a large quantity of ammunition. The armies involved were British, French, German and Russian. **(Illustration 97.)** Twelve other military games were offered by Parker that same year. All consisted of paper soldiers and guns or cannons with which the figures could be shot down. Included in the same catalog was a soldier that stood two feet

NO. 4231—BATTLESHIP GAME
(New)

This game contains a new rapid fire cannon as described above and a novel target in the form of a wooden battleship made in sections, each section bearing a number. When a funnel is hit, for instance, it topples over, leaving the remainder of the battleship standing and in this way the various parts of the ship are shot away until it is wholly "destroyed."

The battleship is lithographed in colors and accompanied by a standard lithographed to represent the water, giving a realistic and attractive appearance.

Put up in strong box with attractive label as shown in illustration.

Size, 9¾ x 18¼.

One in a package.

Price, each, $1.00; shipping weight 1 lb. 12 oz.

Illustration 96: A page from a 1914 Milton Bradley catalog, picturing the *Battleship Game* which was new that year. 9¾ x 18¼in (24.8 x 46.3cm).

THE GREAT WAR
NEW 1915
THE MOST COMPLETE AND FINEST OF SOLDIER GAMES

These games are handsomely made and come with four "Armies" and four Cannon, consisting of English, German, French and Russian Troops with mounted Generals. There are four cannon, battle flags of the nations and of the Red Cross, and an extra large quantity of ammunition. There is also a "Fort" which should be used on the side operating the lesser number of troops. In two editions.

No. 25. Large size. Price, $2.00 each.

No. 26. Slightly smaller, but still a very large equipment as pictured above. Box size 23x18. Price, $1.50 each.

EUROPEAN WAR GAME SERIES
NEW 1915

GREAT VALUE FOR THE MONEY

Consists of four distinct sets. Each box includes mounted officers and men with new style cannon and ammunition.

No. 401. French Army.
No. 402. German Army.
No. 403. Russian Army.
No. 404. English Army.

Box size 19¼x9½. Price, 50 cents each.

In four styles, English, German, French and Russian.

SOLDIERS OF THE ADVANCE GUARD
NEW 1915

No. 443. This game differs from the regular edition of Advance Guard No. 44 in that the soldiers are made of extra heavy stock and sawed from that material, making a heavier and larger soldier. Comes with air rifle with attached rubber cork and nine strong troopers on horseback. Box size 19½x10½. Price, 50 cents.

Illustration 97: A page from a 1915 Parker Brothers catalog picturing war games offered that year. Parker Brothers, Inc., was, and still is located in Salem, Massachusetts. 18 x 23in (45.7 x 58.4cm) Box size.

Illustration 98 A: A card supplement offered with *The Boston Sunday Globe* on March 15, 1896. This shows views of action at the *Battle of Bunker Hill* to be cut out and assembled. 9½ x 11in (24.2 x 28.0cm). *Photo by Barbara Whitton Jendrick.*

high. The original was designed by Maxfield Parrish. It's accompanying caption read, "The head nods when a shot from the air gun (which he carries and which you may boldly take away from him) hits him fairly and squarely."

Other American publishers who issued limited numbers of paper soldier sets were Joseph E. Shaw of Philadelphia, Pennsylvania, Peter G. Thomson of Cincinnati, Ohio, and *The Boston Sunday Globe* which issued a series of colored art supplements. **(Illustrations 98 A, B & C.)** In 1897, Anson D.F. Randolf, known for his paper

dolls and paper furniture, published a 12 sheet set of Indians and structures of their village, all equipped with fold back stands. One sheet pictured marching soldiers in blue uniforms. Many fine examples of paper soldiers and their equipment appeared in magazine pages during the period of World War I. The *Delineator* offered the two following cut-out pages in 1917, a battleship along with a group of officers and crew, and a Naval airplane with pilots and their various uniforms. **(Illustrations 99 & 100.)**

Numerous paper soldiers appeared on the

American market between the two World Wars, but at the start of World War II there was a sudden increase in the amount offered. **Illustration 101** shows an example published and copyrighted by the Samuel Lowe Company of Kenosho, Wisconsin, in 1942. A ten-page booklet illustrates a die-cut punch-out navy man of a different rank on each page. The same company issued a similar book featuring army men. Another example appeared in 1942, issued by Whitman Publishing Company of Racine, Wisconsin. **(Illustration 102.)** Whitman also published an interesting

boxed set titled *30 Toy Soldiers* which consisted of 4¾ inch (12.2cm) die-cut punch-out soldiers, sailors, air force, and marine figures with attached patented stands. A later example published by Golden Press Inc. of New York City appeared in 1959. It consisted of punch-out Civil War soldiers, mostly action figures, and it featured Generals Grant, Lee and Custer. **(Illustration 103.)**

For the most part, it is obvious that there were many differences between the European paper soldiers and those of the United States. While the majority of European publishers strove for detail and accuracy in the uniforms, the Americans produced a play soldier strictly to be shot at with a wooden shell or a cork. However, one must assume that a great number of beautifully uniformed paper soldiers met their final fate by being continually knocked down with a marble, a pop gun, or some other type of shooter in the hands of a youthful European general.

Illustration 98 B: A card supplement offered with *The Boston Sunday Globe* on April 12, 1896. It pictures scenes of *Sheridan's Ride at Winchester*, for cutting out and assembling. 9½ x 11in (24.2 x 28.0cm). *Photo by Barbara Whitton Jendrick.*

Illustration 98 C: A card supplement offered with *The Boston Sunday Globe* on April 5, 1896, pictures a naval battle, *Admiral Farragut at Mobile*, to be cut out and assembled. 9½ x 11in (24.2 x 28.0cm). *Photo by Barbara Whitton Jendrick.*

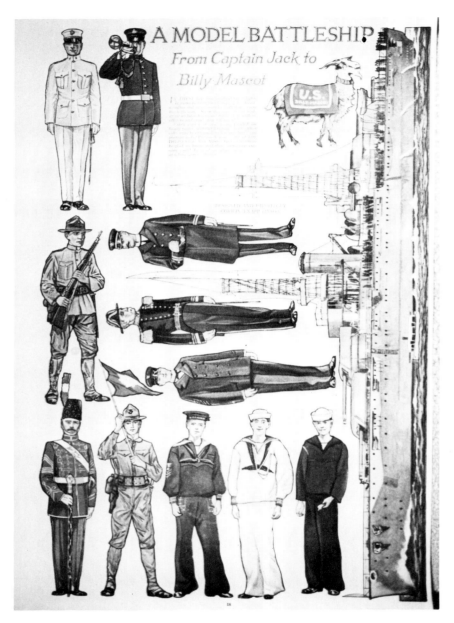

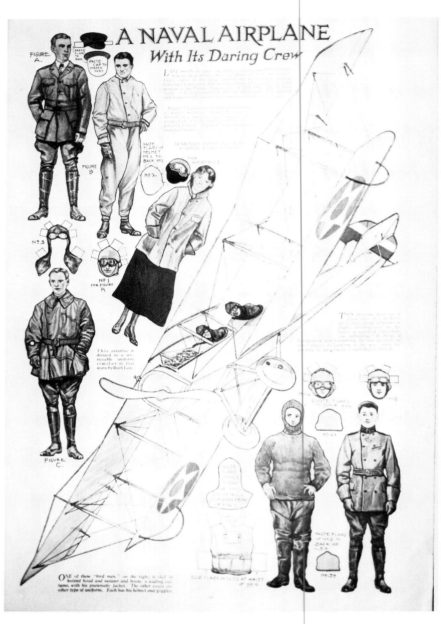

Illustration 99: A page from the *Delineator* magazine dated September 1917. The notice offers extra copies of the page printed on heavy paper, without printing on the back, for five cents. 16 x 10½in (40.6 x 26.7cm).

Illustration 100: A page from the *Delineator* magazine dated November 1917. A World War I vintage plane and the men and equipment used to fly it. 16 x 10½in (40.6 x 26.7cm).

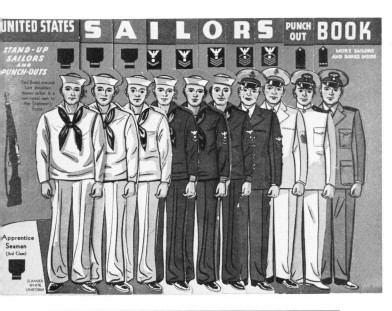

Illustration 101: A ten-page die-cut book with a sailor of low rank on the left. As each page is opened the sailor gains a new rank. Published and copyrighted in 1942 by Samuel Lowe Company of Kenosha, Wisconsin. 9⅛ x 11¾in (23.0 x 29.8cm).

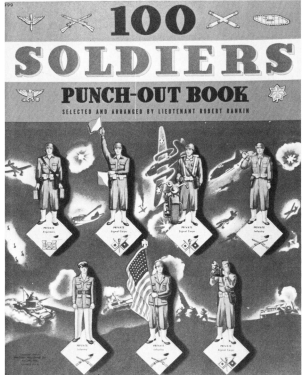

Illustration 102: The cover of a five-page booklet containing action figures of World War II American soldiers. Published and copyrighted by Whitman Publishing Company of Racine, Wisconsin, in 1942. 14⅛ x 11¼in (36.1 x 28.6cm).

Illustration 103: The cover of a six-page booklet containing punch-out soldiers of the Civil War. Published and copyrighted by Golden Press, Inc. of New York City, in 1959. 13 x 7⅜in (33.0 x 18.7cm).

Chapter VIII.

THE PAPER DOLL

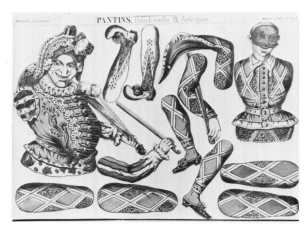

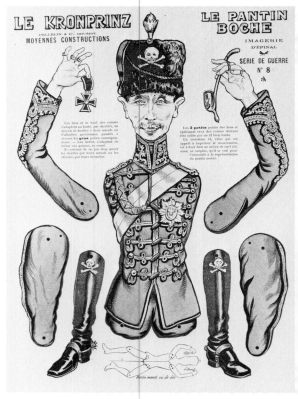

LEFT: Illustration 104: A pantin representation of an early *Pierrette* by Pellerin of Epinal, France. When assembled there is movement at the shoulders, hips and knees at the pull of a cord. c.1850. 15¾ x 11½in (40.1 x 29.2cm). *Photo by Barbara Whitton Jendrick.*

BELOW: Illustration 105: *Polichinelle & Arlequin* in the form of Pantins. This sheet was published by Pellerin of Epinal, France. The *Polichinelle* is unusual in that only one arm will move when assembled. c.1850. 11¾ x 15½in (29.9 x 39.4cm). *Photo by Barbara Whitton Jendrick.*

RIGHT: Illustration 106: *Le Kronprinz* (The Crown Prince), a pantin ridiculing the Kaiser to be. Published by Pellerin of Epinal, France. c.1900. 15¾ x 11¾in (40.1 x 29.9cm).

The paper doll has an early ancestry, reaching back centuries beyond the point where they were introduced as playthings for children. In ancient China it was the custom for a paper image or a representation of a deceased person to be burned at the funeral service as a means of purifying the body before the spirit left it. This custom was practiced during the time of Confucius, 475 B.C.

In Japan, small cut-out figures known as *Katashiro* have been used in cleansing ceremonies since the year 900. The *Katashiro* symbolizes the human form, and is purchased from a priest at the believer's shrine. It is taken home and on it the believer paints the characters making up his name, his birth date, and his or her sex. He breaths on the figure and then rubs it over his body, transferring any diseases or impurities to the *Katashiro*. It is then returned to the shrine where the priest disposes of it in a mass religious ceremony.

The French Pantins of the 17th and 18th centuries are another form of paper doll. Usually published on a sheet in six parts — the head, torso, arms and legs, it was sometimes found in a

Illustration 107: *Poupées À Habiller*, a paper fashion doll with gown and four headpieces that were in style in 1855. Sheet lithographed by Oliver-Pinot, Epinal, France. 11 x 16in (27.9 x 40.6cm).

Illustration 108: *Petit Costumier*, fashions for the young lady, the latest in afternoon dress with an assortment of four head pieces. A two-sided paper doll published by Pellerin of Epinal, France. c.1875. 12 x 17½in (30.5 x 44.5cm).

highly decorated form and consisted of other cutout parts depending on the complexity of the subject. The sheet was mounted on cardboard, the various parts appropriately painted and cut out. The head and limbs were fastened to the torso with light cords and, at a later date, metal fasteners were used. A coordinating string fastened at the back and connected to all moving parts could be pulled, causing the arms and legs to move in a dancing fashion. **(Illustration 104)** The French author Barbier in his *Journal of 1747* stated: "These silly things engrossed the attention of all Paris, amusing everyone to such an extent that you could not go into any house in January 1747 without finding a Pantin hanging by the mantel-piece. Pantins were given as presents to all the women and girls and the rage for them was so great at the beginning of the year that all shops were filled with them for New Years gifts. This foolishness passed from Paris into the provinces and soon there were no homes of fashion without Pantins from Paris. As everybody

Illustration 109: Contents of a boxed set titled *Les Travestissemens De La Poupee*. Paper doll and costumes are beautifully decorated front and back. Costumes include Paris dresses and seven Provincial dresses with matching head pieces. Publisher unknown, France, c.1845. Figure stands 10⅜in (26.3cm) tall.

Illustration 110 A - R: A fine early rare set of paper dolls featuring *Napoleon* and the outfits he wore during some of the high points of his career between 1769 and 1821. Publisher unknown. France, c.1830. Figure of *Napoleon* stands 8¼in (21.0cm) high. *Collection Jan Banneck. Photo by Barbara Whitton Jendrick.*

had Pantins of large or small size, the craze became excessive and finally collapsed." The Pantin belongs in the family of the Jumping Jack; it was a toy played with in ancient Egypt, and rediscovered in 18th century France. It traveled to Germany where it was called the "Hamplemann." Finally the toy appeared in England where it received its present name "Jumping Jack." In these various developments this popular toy was made of materials other than painted cardboard. **(Illustrations 105 & 106.)**

The commercial paper doll, as we know it today is recorded as an English invention. In 1790, an eight inch (20.3cm), one-sided paper doll with six changeable pieces of paper clothing was put on the market. The idea was a popular one and soon spread to Germany and France. The French publishing family of Pellerin had produced many of the earlier Pantins and now issued several sheets of these new paper dolls. The sheets included changes of clothing of the latest styles, beautiful headdresses, stylish wigs, and other accessories that a lady of that time might wear. **(Illustrations 107 & 108.)**

An interesting French boxed set is titled *Les Travestissemens De La Poupée.* The box cover is pea-green in color, the outer edge and lip is covered with a wide heavily embossed tape with a thin gilt strip on each side. The tan center panel pictures five beautifully costumed ladies, one possibly dressed in the latest Paris fashion, and four in elaborate Provincial dress. The box measures 12 inches (30.5cm) long, 6½ inches (16.5cm) wide and 1¼ inches (3.2cm) deep. The set includes a 10⅜ inch (26.3cm) paper female figure in an under garment, printed front and back. Her changes of costumes include a Paris fashion dress and seven very colorful Provincial costumes, along with an appropriate headdress for each costume. All are printed front and back. The publisher of this beautiful set is unknown, but judging from the style of the costumes it may date in the 1840s. **(Illustration 109.)**

An extremely fine early and rare set features Napoleon and outfits that he wore during highlights of his career, between 1769 and 1821.

Illustration 111: Paper dolls, and one card of a series that followed, picturing fashion dresses and head pieces that appeared in the French magazine *La Poupée Modèle.* The fashion card is marked "Jan. 15, 1864." 7⅜ x 11in (18.7 x 27.9cm).

(Illustration 110.) A translation of the events is as follows:

(1779) Uniform of the school of Brienne.
(1798) Named General in Chief of the expedition to Egypt, dressed in blue embroidered with gold, tricolored sash with gold fringe, hat with tricolored plumes, boots with tops.
(1802) 1st Consul for life (the 2nd August) dressed in red, embroidered in gold, hat without plumes, riding boots.
(1804) Napoleon emperor (the 18th May) imperial cloak, civil and imperial crowns.

(1805) Battle of Austerlitz (the 2nd December) grey great coat, dressed in green with white lapels, riding boots, small hat.
(1815) Arrived at St. Helena (the 13th October) dressed as a guardsman, silk stockings, buckled shoes.
(1820) Napoleon seemed to have recovered his health thanks to a more active life and to gardening which he owed to the faithfulness of his doctor.
(1821) Death of Napoleon (5th May)

Another fine series of paper dolls was published as a supplement to the French magazine *La Poupée Modèle,* in the late 1800s. The doll

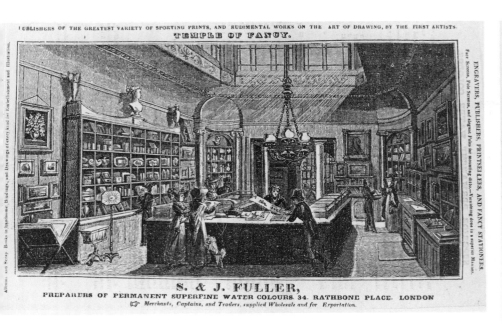

TEMPLE OF FANCY.

S. & J. FULLER,
PREPARERS OF PERMANENT SUPERFINE WATER COLOURS. 34. RATHBONE PLACE. LONDON
Merchants, Captains, and Traders, supplied Wholesale and for Exportation.

Illustration 112: The interior of the shop *Temple of Fancy* operated by S. & J. Fuller, stationers and booksellers. Publishers of the *History and Adventures of Little Henry* and other similar children's books which utilized the single moveable head and the slit at the neck of the various costumes. c.1810.

sheet consisted of four similar female figures, front and back views, all with circular stands. Notice that the hair is center parted and drawn close to the head with a bun at the back. **(Illustration 111.)** The accompanying three sheets picture the young ladies dresses in the latest Paris designs, related wigs and headpieces. Each card measures 11 by 7¼ inches (27.9 x 18.5cm) and is attractively colored. Another series of supplements was offered in 1911 featuring fashions of that period.

In England, where the first known paper doll was published, others soon followed. One of the early publishers, S. & J. Fuller, operated a retail establishment dealing in paper products. Their shop was known as the Temple of Fancy and was situated at Rathbone Place in London, England. **(Illustration 112.)** In 1810, the Fullers offered a small book containing a moral story with a number of hand colored illustrations. Each illus-

Illustration 113: S. & J. Fuller's rendition of the juvenile classic, *Cinderella.* A small book measuring 5 x 4⅛in (12.7 x 10.5cm). Contains the story in verse along with six color inserts of cut out costumes, each with a slot at the neckline in which the single head could be inserted at will as a child read through the story. England, dated 1819.

Illustrations 114 - 117: Boxed sets of paper dolls by the British publisher, Raphael Tuck, c.1895. The four dolls vary in size from 9 to 9½in (22.9 x 24.2cm) tall. *Photo by Barbara Whitton Jendrick.*

tration pictured a young boy in different costumes, all missing the boy's head, but each with a horizontal cut at the neck line to accept the neck tab of a single doll's head. The single head was moved from illustration to illustration as the reader followed the story. Titled *The History & Adventures of Little Henry*, it was the first of a series of similar books that became popular during this period of time.

The History of Little Fanny also appeared in 1810, while *Frank Feignwell's Attempts to Amuse His Friends*, the *History of Little Ellen Or The Naughty Girl Reclaimed* and *Young Albert, the Roscius*, appeared the following year. In 1812, *Phoebe, the Cottage Maid* and *Hubert, the Cottage Boy* were introduced. These were followed by *Cinderella or The Little Glass Slipper* (**Illustration 113.**) the *History of Lauretta, or The Little Savoyard*, and *Lucinda the Orphan, or The Costumes*. Some of these tiny paper doll books were republished two or three times in later years, particularly *Little Fanny* and *Little Henry*. In 1811, the Fullers published what is now one of the most sought after paper dolls, *The Protean Figure or Metamorphic Costumes*. This 8¼ inch (21cm) male doll has 12 costumes, each with its own accessories. Each costume, plus appropriate accessories, is enclosed in it's own envelope and a 13th envelope held a colorful scenic background with a slit at the bottom into which the feet of the doll could be inserted. All envelopes were contained in a book-like cover which fit into a slip case.

Another prominent paper toy publisher in Great Britain was the firm of Raphael Tuck & Sons Ltd., which was established in 1866. Raphael Tuck was born in East Prussia in 1821. In 1848 he married Ernestine Lessner, and in the years following they reared seven children. At the start of the Prusso-Danish & Austrian War of 1864-1866, Tuck felt it was time to move his family to a more peaceful climate and, in 1865, he moved to London, England. A year later he and Ernestine opened a small shop selling pictures and frames. The business progressed and they soon entered the field of publishing. In 1870 their three sons entered the business and soon were making worthwhile contributions to its growth. They

Illustration 118: An uncut German sheet showing six named paper dolls, each with an assortment of clothing and accessories. Notice the variety of styles in the costumes. Published by F. Hoth of Stuttgart, Germany, c.1890. Sheet size 13½ x 17in (34.3 x 43.2cm).

Illustration 119: A German boxed set titled *Little Rose*, obviously made for export as well as for little German girls. No markings as to publisher or printer, c.1860. Doll stands 5¼in (13.4cm) tall.

published their first Christmas cards in 1871, expanding their line of fine art prints and colored scrap sheets. 1880 marked the origin of the famous Raphael Tuck "Easel & Palette" trade mark. In 1881, Raphael retired and a partnership was formed by the sons, Adolph, Hermen and Gustave. The firm grew rapidly during the last 20 years of the 19th century, opening up branches in Paris, France, and New York City. In 1893, the company was granted the Royal Warrant of Appointment by Queen Victoria. Their beautifully colored paper dolls are eargerly sought after by today's collectors. **Illustrations 114** through **117** picture a few of the many examples that they published.

As the public interest in paper dolls increased, the publishers broadened their field. Sheets picturing paper room settings followed, complete with furniture, colored and ready to be cut out and placed in the settings with paper dolls. As mentioned previously, German publishers had entered the field, meeting and possibly surpassing the quality of the work of their competitors in England and France. **(Illustration 118.)** During the first half of the 19th century they were offering richly colored dolls, sometimes with as many as eight changes of dress, all packed in a slip case. **(Illustration 119.)** This was followed by sets containing two paper dolls, each having eight elaborate dresses printed front and back.

An assortment of wigs, beautiful handbags, and other feminine accessories were included in this set. These items were packed in colorful paper covered cardboard boxes trimmed with embossed gilt edging. **(Illustration 120.)** The boxes were usually titled in three to five languages, for export purposes. They were as beautiful in color and design as their contents. Again the depth and brilliance of color, highlighted by a shiny transparent coating, was remarkable. **(Color Illustration 15.)**

A most unusual and beautiful set of paper dolls consisting of 16 mythological figures is our next example. Enclosed in an early cardboard folder it contained a 72-page soft cover book, the title page of which describes the contents of the set. The book is printed in two languages, German on all the left-hand pages and French on the opposite right-hand pages. The double title page reads: "A Conversation on Mythology for Young People, with 16 figures and four scenes. Vienna, Publisher H.F. Muller, 1841." Very briefly, the lengthy contents gives an explanation of the scenes: No. 1, describes the secondary gods of the sky. No. 2, the secondary gods of the air and earth. No. 3, the secondary gods of the seas. No. 4, the secondary gods of the underworld. (**Color Illustration 16.**)

The Greeks worshiped the gods of mythology and later the Romans adopted them as part of their beliefs, translating the Greek names into Latin. Below is a listing of the 16 figures with both the Greek and Roman names.

Greek	Roman		Greek	Roman	
Zeus	Jupiter	The supreme god, patron of the Roman State.	Hera	Juno	Goddess of the Pantheon, patroness of marriage.
Ares	Mars	God of war.	Athena	Minerva	Goddess of wisdom, invention, the arts and martial prowess.
Apollo	Apollo	God of the sun, prophecy, music, medicine and poetry.	Artemis	Diana	Goddess of chastity, hunting and the moon.
Hades	Plato	God of the dead, ruler of the underworld.	Aphrodite	Venus	Goddess of love and beauty.
Hercules	Hercules	God of strength.			
Poseidon	Neptune	God of the sea.	Demeter	Ceres	Goddess of agriculture.
Dionysus	Bacchus	God of grapes and wine.			
Hermes	Mercury	God of travel, commerce & thievery.	Amphitrite	Amphitrite	Goddess of the sea
			Persephona	Proserpina	Goddess of the underworld.
				Pomona	Goddess of fruit trees.

Illustration 120: A boxed set, *The Little Girls Doll, Dressed in the Most Pleasing Costumes.* The title is listed in German, English, French and Italian on the box cover. The cover is also marked with the initials G.W.F. for G.W. Faber of Germany. The figure of the little girl stands 6¾in (17.2cm) tall.

Illustration 121: One of the early American boxed sets, *Fanny Gray,* published by Crosby, Nichols & Company of Boston, Massachusetts, in 1854. The artwork was produced in oil colors by S.W. Chandler & Brother, Boston, Massachusetts. The box measures 8¼ x 6¾in (21.0 x 17.2 x 2.5cm).

Illustration 122: *Miss Hattie* was published by Clark Austin & Smith of New York City. One of a series of only ten paper dolls published by this company in 1857 and 1858. The paper doll figure is 3¾in (9.6cm) tall. *Collection Herbert Hosmer.*

The first known American paper doll commercially published was issued by J. Belcher of Boston, Massachusetts, in 1812. It is very similar to, and bears the same title as, Fuller's *The History & Adventures of Little Henry*. Another early American example is a boxed set of costumes accompanied by a separate head with a neck tab. Published in 1854 by Crosby, Nichols & Company of Boston, Massachusetts, it is titled *Fanny Gray, a History of Her Life*. It is boxed in an off-white cardboard box with a cover decorated in gilt, red, and deep blue curlicue designs of leaves and flowers. The box measures 8¼ x 6¾ x 1 inch (21 x 17.2 x 2.5cm). **(Illustration 121.)** An earlier *Fanny Gray* had been published in England, and still another *Fanny Gray & Her Transformations* was published by Dean & Son following the Crosby Nichols rendition. It became obvious that pirating among publishers was a fairly common practice at this period of time.

In the latter part of the 1850s, Brown, Taggart & Chase of Boston, Massachusetts, issued a line of full bodied paper dolls and dresses in paper envelopes. All are lithographed and copyrighted by J.G. Chandler. **(Color Illustration 17.)** In 1857 and 1858, Clarke, Austin & Smith of New York City, published a series of ten paper dolls with outfits. They were offered in decorated envelopes titled *The Girls Delight*. Other important paper doll publishers, were Degen, Estes & Company of Boston, Massachusetts, **(Illustrations 122 & 123 A & B.)**, the Chromatic Printing Company of Philadelphia, Pennsylvania, **(Color Illustration 18)**, Peter G. Thomson of Cincinnati, Ohio, **(Illustration 125 A & B)**, and Frederick A. Stokes Company and J. Ottmann Lithograph Company, both of New York City. **(Illustration 126)**.

While all the above published a limited production of paper dolls, the firm of McLoughlin Brothers was the leader in this field. Their paper

Illustration 123 A & B: *Jennie June*, published by Degen Estes & Company of Boston, Massachusetts. **A** illustrates a split envelope showing the front title and the rear listing. **B** pictures the uncut doll card and the front and back views of a dress and head piece, c.1860. Paper doll is 5in (12.7cm) tall. *Photo by Barbara Whitton Jendrick.*

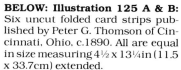

RIGHT: Illustration 124: Two uncut paper dolls on folded card strips. Published by the Chromatic Printing Company of Philadelphia, Pennsylvania, c.1875. *My Dear Mama* measures 3⅛ x 11⅜in (7.9 x 28.8cm) extended. *Lucy,* with the separate cutout figure is 4½ x 12⅛in (10.9 x 30.8cm) extended. The doll is 3¾in (9.6cm) tall.

BELOW: Illustration 125 A & B: Six uncut folded card strips published by Peter G. Thomson of Cincinnati, Ohio, c.1890. All are equal in size measuring 4½ x 13¼in (11.5 x 33.7cm) extended.

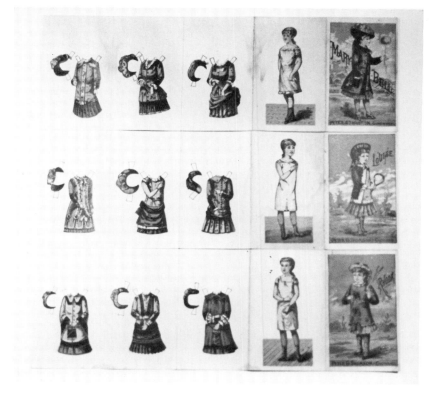

doll production was probably greater than that of all it's American competitors combined. It was McLoughlin's practice to keep pace with the development of printing technology, and all new methods were applied to their paper doll production. They issued scores of paper dolls, with assorted outfits, ranging in size from 2¼ inches (5.8cm) **(Color Illustration 19.)** Most were offered as uncut sheets, folded and inserted in an envelope which was decorated on the face and had printed listings of other offerings on the back. Paper furniture sheets or cards featuring parlor sets, drawing rooms, and bedroom sets were also printed. **(Illustration 127 A & B.)**

In the 1864-1870 period, when McLoughlin's place of business was located at 30 Beekman Street, they published an unusual Little Red riding Hood paper doll. The set consisted of an envelope, a 7¾ inch (19.8cm) figure of Red Riding Hood, a dress, a cloak, two bonnets, a wolf, a bed, the head, shoulders and arms of Grandma, and the head and upper body of the wolf. The one piece missing is the small bouquet of flowers. Inside the envelope are the directions for cutting out and assembling the toy and the story of *Little Red Riding Hood*. The following step-by-step directions will give the reader an idea of how the various parts are assembled and utilized, as a young child reads through the story and acts out the various scenes with the paper figures. I quote from the directions:

"The Plan — Take a sharp pair of scissors and cut neatly around the figure for it to stand on.

The Dress — Cut around the dress, leaving the back and front together by folding at the shoulder. Cut out the space between the shoulders to admit the head of the figure. Match the front and back carefully; then gum or paste the edges at the sides of the skirt, so as to keep it in place.

"The Cloak is to fit over the dress — The back and front of the cloak are joined together by the tabs at the shoulder — tabs may be at the bottom.

"The Hoods are to be cut out neatly and be matched perfectly, and fastened together by the tabs — cut out the space in front, for the face. The tab below on one of the hoods is to insert under the cloak at the neck.

"The Bed — Follow the line around the bed in cutting it out — cut a slit directly under the pillow, long enough to admit the tab under the head of the old woman and the wolf, when they are in bed; the arms should appear as if laying in the corner of the bed — In order to make the bed stand up firmly, it would be well to gum it on a piece of pasteboard, except just where you insert the wolf and old woman.

"The Wolf and Old Woman — Cut around the old woman and the wolf leaving the tabs. Cut up each end of the tabs to the line that divides them from the figure at the top.

"The Wolf — Cut around the back and front of the wolf — match well and fasten together.

"The Bouquet — Is to be held in the hand of the cloak, a slit must be cut between the thumb and the forefinger to receive it.

"And now having cut all out and ready, consult the story of Little Red Riding Hood. You can carry your little figures through all the scenes portrayed in it, and while away many otherwise tedious hours, by exercising your ingenuity with Little Red Riding Hood." **(Color Illustration 20.)**

In an 1875 catalog, McLoughlin offered many of the previously mentioned dolls plus a new introduction. French-type paper dolls, bridal parties, and storybook characters such as Little Red Riding Hood **(Illustration 128)**, Little Bo-peep, Topsie and Humpty Dumpty! **(Illustration 129 & 130).** Barnum's world famous midgets, Tom Thumb, Mrs. Tom Thumb, Commodore Nutt, and Minnie Warren appeared as paper dolls along with their appropriate costumes.

The ever popular Gibson Girl is well represented in the paper doll titled *Fluffy Ruffles*. The ideal typical girl of the early 1900s is pictured with her sport outfit, an evening dress, a Summer tea gown, a Fall suit, and a fur trimmed Winter coat. This five-piece set was published by J. Ottmann Lithograph Company of New York City. **(Illustration 131.)**

In the early 1900s, the Dennison manufacturing Company issued boxed sets containing paper doll figures, tissue and crepe paper, paper lace and gilt braiding, plus instructions and ideas for making dresses. The jointed dolls, in the form of babies, young children, girls, and women were made up in embossed form by Littauer & Bauer of Germany. **(Illustration 132.)** A boxed set titled *Dennison's Crepe & Tissue Paper Doll Outfit, No. 33* was produced in 1915. The set includes three jointed embossed paper dolls, two young girls and a small child, three sheets of white crepe paper 17 by 20 inches (43.2 x 50.8cm) covered with an array of colorful dresses, suits, coats and hats, and an assortment of white die-cut blanks to be used as backing for the above clothing when it was cut out. Also included was an assortment of

Illustration 126: The *Teddy Bear Paper Doll* was published by the J. Ottmann Litho. Company of New York City. The bear figure was equipped with four suits: Automobile, Baseball, Walking, Yachting Suit and a Dressing Gown, c.1912. All were offered in a heavy brown 8 x 11in (20.3 x 27.9cm) envelope.

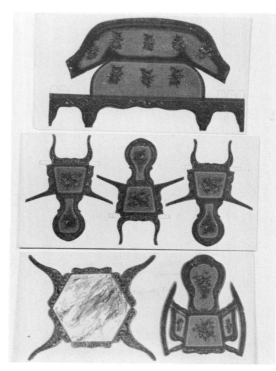

Illustraiton 127 A & B: A the envelope and directions sheet and **B** the Parlor cutout furniture sheet, was published by McLoughlin Brothers of New York City, c.1860. Envelope measures 3⅝ x 6⅞in (9.2 x 17.4cm).

colored crepe paper sheets, a rainbow of crepe paper ribbons, several strips of white paper lace, gilt and silver embossed strips for decorating purposes, a packet of assorted colored buttons, and a tube of art paste. An eight-page booklet titled *Dennison's Fashions For Dolls* and a four page folder titled *Dennison's Patterns And Directions For Making Doll Costumes* was included. The box measures 14 by 8¼ inches and is 3/4 of an inch deep (35.6 x 21 x 2cm). **(Illustration 133.)**

Parker Brother's *Improved Paper Doll Outfit*, copyrighted in 1917, is very similar to that of the Dennison set mentioned above. It has three jointed figures, an older girl, a young girl, and a small boy. The white sheets of crepe paper are printed with colorful articles of clothing, and seven rolls of different colored crepe paper and

numerous crepe ribbon strips are included. Also included are die-cut white backings for the clothing and a tube of Kindergarten paste. **(Illustration 134.)** The box measures 10¾ x 16 inches and is 1¼ inches deep (27.4 x 40.6 x 3.2cm). The American Toy Works of New York City issued a similar set titled *Paper Doll Outfit, Dresses & Hats*, but it did not have the quality of the sets published by Dennison and Parker Brothers.

This is probably a good place to mention that there was a deep interest in home-made paper dolls in both Europe and the United States. Particularly in the early years, many young ladies with some degree of artistic ability drew and cut out a doll figure and designed and cut out paper dresses. A good illustration is an early and unusual Pantin-type paper doll with moveable limbs. The art work on the face and hair is very fine and

well done, while the cut-out torso and limbs are rather crude and out of proportion. It may be that a skillful mother made the head and a child made the body. On close inspection one may see that each hand has a thumb and six fingers. The rose-colored cloth dress is sewn on the body and is decorated with pink ribbons and black lace trim, with white lace filling in the V neckline. **(Illustration 135.)** Those with limited ability cut lady figures out of magazines and created paper dresses for them. Many pleasant hours were spent drawing, cutting, and painting a paper doll family and their extensive wardrobes. It is recorded that adult women with artistic talent would create a paper doll in their own likeness, and then design numerous outfits that they felt would be becoming to them. An example of this might be a charming set from England consisting of a four inch (10.2cm) doll in a long white undergarment with nine dresses, including a nun's habit, along with seven fancy hats or bonnets. While the doll and her various dresses are well done, the variety of styles in the headgear are outstanding. Three narrow cross strips behind each dress secures the dress to the doll figure. All pieces are enclosed in a plain, very worn envelope inscribed "Emelia's Dresses for the year 1787." This seems a very early date, yet the writing is distinct. **(Illustration 136.)**

A further interesting early example of a hand-drawn and colored European paper doll, although it was commercially sold, was found in a worn marbleized cardboard folder. Its contents included a well drawn profile of a lady figure in underclothes along with an 11-piece wardrobe that makes up six complete outfits and six matching headpieces. The design, art work, and colors are superb. Included with the set is a pink covered booklet with eight yellow pages, each page supplied with a handwritten identification label on a pink crossband in which the doll and her various outfits may be inserted and held secure. The booklet measures 8 by 4¾ inches (20.3 x 12.2cm). Printed on the back cover of the booklet is an upright oval, sparsely decorated with roses, the interior of the oval containing the words "La Pouppee anglaise, a diverses modes,

Habillemens Coifures A port D'habits." Below the oval in a hanging half garland of roses are the German words "In finden bei J. L. Stahl, Nuremburg." Unfortunately these words are printed in Old German script and are rather hard to make out. The inside of the back cover gives directions in German for assembling the doll. The grey and tan folder measures 8⅛ by 5 inches (20.6 x 12.7cm) and is marked "Englische Puppe," a term that preceded the words paper doll. (**Color Illustration 21.**)

In the United States the making of handmade paper dolls became a popular pastime from 1850 on. In 1856, Anson D.F. Randolph of New York City published a small book titled *Paper Dolls and How to Make Them.* Consisting of 20 pages of text, it was written for little girls, explaining the fun and pleasure of making paper dolls. It explained the materials needed, the tools required, and the making of the dolls and their simple accessories. This was followed by a series of eight plates picturing simple and easy to make paper dolls, paper babies, and their clothing. These plates were in the form of line drawings, to be filled in with suggested colors. The following year Randolph published a new edition, improved and enlarged. The first 20 pages and the eight color plates were identical to those in the first edition. The enlarged edition presented two additional pattern plates, a little girl with three dresses and a broad brim flower covered hat, and a boy figure in a walking position with three sets of clothing with hats to match. (**Illustration 137.**) Advertised on the inside cover of this little book was a listing of 14 books for children published by Randolph. Also advertised was "The Paper Doll Family with a complete wardrobe, ready for use. Done up in a small neat wrapper, price fifty cents." Another partial quote from the advertisement reads as follows: "The advent of the Paper Doll Family will be hailed with delight by all little girls. The figures are executed on cardboard, the dresses on paper and by simply cutting them out, are ready for use. The dolls are natural in form and figure from father to the wee baby. The dresses are nicely colored and constitute a full handsome wardrobe."

The first of many paper dolls to appear in an American magazine were found in the November 1859 issue of *Godey's Lady's Magazine.* It offered a page consisting of four little girls and two boys in black and white. A second page pictured costumes in color for each of the figures. In 1866, Frank Leslie's *Lady's Magazine* issued a paper doll with six dresses and several changes of hair styles. In 1895 the *Boston Herald* newspaper issued two paper dolls on stiff card, as supplements in their Sunday edition. Later they offered 38 costume plates, one each Sunday, that were interchangeable. The purpose of these supplements was three-fold: to show the current fashions, sell dress patterns and to offer paper dolls to little girls and indirectly sell more papers. (**Illustration 138 A - D.**)

Other Sunday newspapers seeing the appeal of these weekly cut-out supplements, offered their own contributions on all sorts of subjects from paper dolls, to war scenes, to theaters, to transportation vehicles, and so on. You will find scattered examples throughout this book. Coming back to paper dolls, here are a few later examples found in other Sunday papers. A series titled *Polly's Paper Playmates* was issued by *The Boston Post.* (**Illustration 139.**) The *Worcester Sunday Spy* had a series on characters found in Mother Goose and other juvenile literature. The

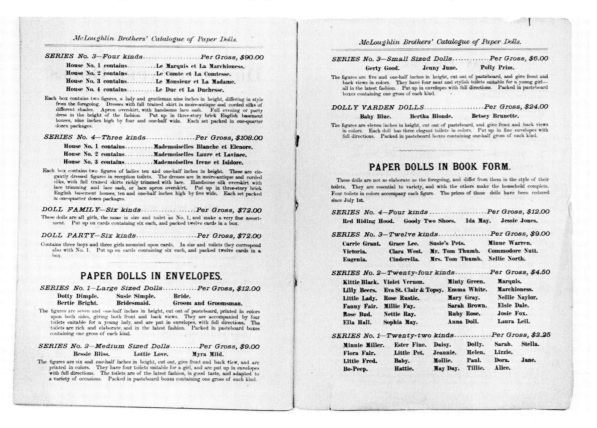

Illustration 128: Pages from an 1875 McLoughlin Brothers catalog listing their French style dolls, and their paper dolls in envelopes and in book form.

Illustration 129: Two uncut strips of small McLoughlin paper dolls that retailed for a penny each. The *Humpty Dumpty* paper doll was named after the famous clown of the period. *Little Bo-Peep* was a popular character from the Mother Goose stories. Both are c.1875. *Humpty Dumpty* is 4in (10.2cm) tall. While *Little Bo-Peep* is 4¼in (10.9cm) tall. *Photo by Barbara Whitton Jendrick.*

Illustration 130: Two uncut folded strips of penny paper dolls depicting black characters. Published by McLoughlin Brothers, c.1875. The *Dinah Varden* figure is 4⅛in (10.5cm) tall while the *Pompey Varden* measures 4¾in (12.2cm) tall.

FLUFFY RUFFLES

PAPER DOLL

WALLACE MORGAN

PUBLISHED BY J. OTTMANN LITH.CO. NEW YORK
COPYRIGHT 1907 BY THE NEW YORK HERALD CO.

Illustration 131: The *Fluffy Ruffles Paper Doll* was published by J. Ottmann Litho. Company of New York City and copyrighted in 1907 by the New York Herald Company. The paper doll stands 10½in (26.7cm) tall. *Collections Jan Banneck. Photo by Barbara Whitton Jendrick.*

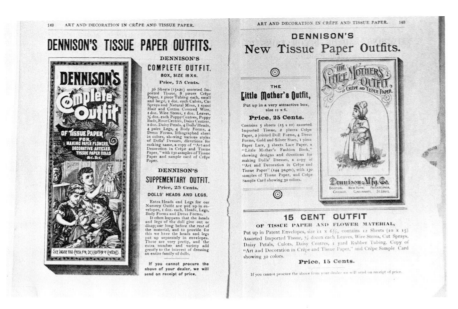

Illustration 132: Two pages from an early Dennison catalog picturing boxed sets of jointed paper dolls with crepe and tissue paper, and paper lace and ribbons used to make the doll dresses. c.1900.

Illustration 133: A Dennison boxed set of paper dolls with colored paper, decorations and other necessary materials with which dresses could be made. c.1915. The Box measures 14 x 8¼ x 3/4in (35.6 x 21.0 x 2.0cm).

PARKER BROTHERS'
PAPER DOLL OUTFIT

A DOLL OUTFIT DE LUXE

These sets come with a carefully selected assortment of beautifully colored tissue crepe and plain tissue papers for fancy and plain costumes,—with paper lace for edgings and insertions, with trimmings, dress forms, etc., and with a tube of best quality paste. With pictures in color showing a dozen specimen costumes, Middy Suit, Party Dress, Rompers, School Dress, Sweater Suit, etc. With each set come dolls with movable arms and legs, beautifully lithographed. **No Paper Doll Outfit quite compares with this. Rightly named "The Doll Outfit De Luxe."**

No. 810. IMPROVED PAPER DOLL OUTFIT. Large fine set with deep double-deck box, and large quantity of material. Price **$1.50.**

No. 807. IMPROVED PAPER DOLL OUTFIT. Box size 16x10½. Price **$1.25.**

No. 806. IMPROVED PAPER DOLL OUTFIT. Popular Dollar Edition. Box size 16x10. Price **$1.00.**

No. 804. IMPROVED PAPER DOLL OUTFIT. Box size 14x9¾. Price **75 cts.**

No. 803. IMPROVED PAPER DOLL OUTFIT. Box size 13½x9. Price **50 cts.**

Illustration 134: *Parker Brothers' Improved Paper Doll Outfit* was copyrighted in 1917. Illustrated is a page from a Parker Brothers' catalog of that year. The outfits offered were similar to those offered by the Dennison Company.

example pictured shows a boy's and girl's head and shoulders printed on one side only, while the suit and dress have a front and back. A fold at the shoulder line, and a cut at the neck line allows the heads of the dolls to be pushed up through the neck line opening. **(Illustration 140.)** An uncut *Art Supplement* issued by *The Springfield Sunday Union* amusingly pictures animals posing and wearing clothes in the manner of human beings. The bear becomes a fisherman and the rabbit a doctor — not a new idea having been done scores of time before, but always amusing to children. **(Illustration 141.)**

After 1900, paper dolls appeared frequently in many of the more popular magazines as each publication tried to out-do their competitor. These publications became the major source of paper dolls for the youthful collector, many of them being produced in series from month to month, some for three or four months, others covering several years. While time and space are not available in this study to cover all that were published, we will select a few examples that were popular at the time and are still sought after by today's collector.

In the April 1909 issue of the *Pictorial Review* magazine, an interesting and amusing paper doll appeared called *Ted E. Bear.* This standing bear figure was supplied with a paper outfit consisting of a pith helmet and a striped suit. Wearing glasses, the bear has facial characteristics similar to those of Teddy Roosevelt. In 1909, former President Roosevelt and his party toured the wilds of Africa. A day by day account of the trip appeared in the newspapers, and numerous articles appeared in the magazines of the time. "Ted E. Bear," the paper doll, appeared along with a story of his trip to, and arrival in, Africa titled *Great Excitement in The Dark Continent,* tells about a character named "Jocko Chimpanzee" who befriends "Ted E. Bear." Jocko also appears in the form of a paper doll along with his clothing and various accessories. **(Illustration 142.)** These stories are wrtten in letter form to the editor of the *Pictorial Review* by Ted E. Bear. A footnote

Illustration 135: A handmade paper doll with a nice bit of detail on the head and a poorly proportioned body with moveable limbs. The rose colored cloth dress is sewn on the body and is decorated with ribbons and lace. The doll is 8¾in (22.3cm) tall. c.1840.

Illustration 136: A very early English handmade paper doll titled and dated, *Emelia's Dresses for the Year 1787.* The set is artistically done in pencil and water colors. The doll stands 4⅛in (10.5cm) tall.

Illustration 137: A page from the enlarged edition of Anson Randolph's book, *Paper Dolls and How to Make Them.* Published in 1857, it featured two additional plates, one of a little girl paper doll with three dresses and a flower covered bonnet, and the plate illustrated above.

Illustration 138 A - D: In 1895, the *Boston Sunday Herald* issued two paper dolls on stiff card as supplements to their Sunday newspaper. Illustrated is one of the dolls and three of the 38 costume plates that followed, one each Sunday. The doll is 10½in (26.7cm) tall. *Photo by Barbara Whitton Jendrick.*

appears at the end of the second letter "Look out for Rubber, the Fat Giraffe, in the June number of the *Pictorial Review.*"

The "Lettie Lane" paper doll, created by Sheila Young, appeared in the *Ladies Home Journal* from 1908 to 1915. This magazine also published "Betty Bonnet" by the same artist from 1915 to 1918. Rose O'Neill's "Kewpies" appeared in the *Woman's Home Companion* in 1912 and 1913. **(Illustration 143.)** The "Dolly Dingle" series started in 1916 and ended in 1933. Grace Drayton drew Dolly and her friends which appeared in *Pictorial Review.* Many other magazines published serialized paper doll characters in less volume but all are eagerly sought by the present day collector. This type of magazine paper doll is possibly the most available of all paper dolls as they were published in huge quantities, some of

the magazines having a circulation of over a hundred thousand.

An interesting and rather rare group of paper dolls, each issued in a large cardboard portfolio, appeared during the 1909-1918 period. Some consisted of the same dolls found in some of the magazines mentioned above. *Paper Dolls of the World* consisted of six sheets of paper dolls to be cut out, showing the costumes of all nations, with the flag or emblem of each. The contents were designed by Cushman Parker, published and copyrighted in 1909 by George W. Jacobs & Company of Philadelphia, Pennsylvania. The portfolio measures 14 by 9½ inches (35.6 x 48.3cm). **(Illustration 144.)** *Dorothy Dimple and Her Friends*, by the same artist (Parker) consisted of six sheets of paper dolls with many additional dresses, hats, fancy costumes, dolls, toys, and

animals. **(Illustration 145.)** The "Betty Bonnet" portfolios came in three series of six sheets each. They were drawn by Sheila Young, published by Jacobs, and copyrighted in 1915 by the Curtis Publishing Company. The first series consisted of *Betty Bonnet, Betty's Brother Billy, Betty's Little Sister and Her Nurse, Betty's Best Friend, Betty's Brother Bob,* and *Betty's College Sister.* The second series was made up of *Betty's Boarding School Sister, Betty's Friend Dorothy, Betty's Father and Mother, Betty's Twin Cousins, Betty's Next-Door Neighbor,* and *Betty's Dearest Dolls.* The third series consisted of *Betty's Married Sister, Betty's Little Niece, Betty's Sister's Baby, Betty's Camp Fire Cousin, Betty's Christmas Party* and *Betty's Sister's Son.* The "Betty Bonnet" portfolio measures 16½ by 11½ inches (41.9 x 29.2cm). **(Illustration 146.)** A third grouping,

POLLY'S PAPER PLAYMATES.
POLLY'S COUSIN JANET.

SUPPLEMENT TO THE BOSTON PO:
SUNDAY OCTOBER 23ᴿᴰ, 19

Next week we shall present Polly's Brother at School.

BOBBY SHAFTOE. LITTLE MISS ETTICOTE.

SUPPLEMENT OF THE WORCESTER SUNDAY SPY.

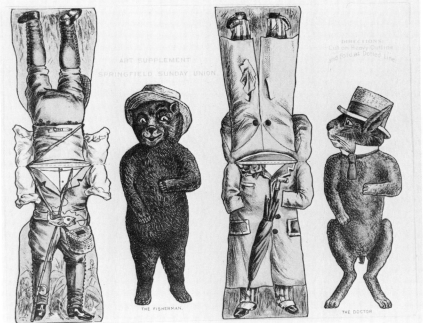

ART SUPPLEMENT
SPRINGFIELD SUNDAY UNION.

DIRECTIONS:
Cut on Heavy Outline
and fold at Dotted Line.

THE FISHERMAN.   THE DOCTOR.

ABOVE: Illustration 139: *Polly's Paper Playmates* appeared in a series as supplements in *The Boston Post* Sunday newspaper, in 1910. The illustrated sheet is titled "Polly's Cousin Janet"; next week's supplement was to present "Polly's Brother at School."

RIGHT: Illustration 141: An example of an amusing supplement issued by *The Springfield Sunday Union*, c.1910. Animals posing and wearing clothes in the manner of human beings. *Photo by Barbara Whitton Jendrick.*

ABOVE: Illustration 140: Side-by-side paper dolls, *Bobby Shaftoe* and *Little Miss Etticote*, appear as a supplement card in the *Worcester Sunday Spy*. A fold at the costumes shoulder line and a cut at the neck line allows the heads to be pushed up through the neck openings, completing the dolls. c.1910. *Photo by Barbara Whitton Jendrick.*

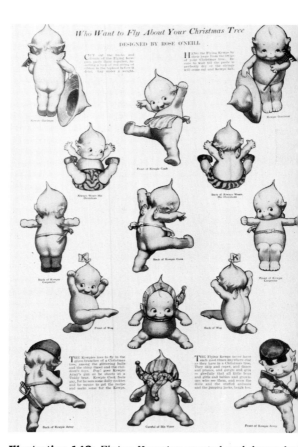

Illustration 142: *Ted E. Bear, and Central Africa,* an episode of his adventures in Africa which more or less paralleled Theodore Roosevelt's travels on the same continent. The text appeared in letter form along with dressed animal characters that could be cut out. This adventuresome letter, along with a page of cut-outs, appeared in the *Pictorial Review* magazine of May 1909.

Illustration 143: *Flying Kewpies,* created and drawn by Rose O'Neill, appeared in the *Womans Home Companion* magazine in 1912 and 1913. *Kewpie* items are presently copyrighted by Jesco, Inc. *Photo by Barbara Whitton Jendrick.*

titled "Kitty Clover" was drawn by Sheila Young, published by Jacobs & Company, and, copyrighted by the Curtis Publishing Company in 1917. Issued in two series, the first series offered *Kitty Clover's Patriotic Party, Kitty's Grandparents Now & Long Ago, Kitty's Big Brother, Kitty's College Cousins, Kitty's Halloween Party,* and *Kitty Clover's Army & Navy Cousins.* The second series consisted of *Kitty Clover's New Years Callers, Kitty's Valentine, Kitty's Rainy Day Party, Kitty Goes to a Wedding* in three parts: the Bride, the Bridegroom, and the Page and the Flower Girl. These two portfolios measure

6½ by 11½ inches (41.9 x 29.2cm) each. **(Illustration 147.)**

A "Lettie Lane" group was offered in three series, drawn by Sheila Young and published by Jacobs. The first series consisted of: *Lettie Lane, One of Lettie's Dolls, Lettie's Brother, Lettie's Grandmother, Lettie's Sister as a Bride,* and *Lettie's Baby Sister with Her Nurse.* The second series was made up of sheets titled: *Lettie's Father, Lettie's Mother, Lettie's Twin Brother & Sister, Lettie's Lady Doll, Lettie's Best Friend,* and *Lettie's Doll's Party.* The third series covered Lettie's Sister's Wedding, which consisted of the following: *The Bridegroom, The Minister and Best Man, The Maid of Honor, The Bridesmaids, Some Wedding Guests* and *The Youngest Guest.* These portfolios were the same size as those of "Betty Bonnet."

A later group published by Jacobs and copyrighted in 1918 was titled "Polly Pitcher." The dolls and costumes were designed by Lillian Caussey. They were printed on paper heavy enough to allow the dolls to stand up. There were four sheets of beautiful dresses, all in the latest styles. Polly is able to change her hair ribbon so that it will match her various outfits. The first series contained *Polly Pitcher and Her Playmates,* while the second series consisted of *Polly's Cousins: Betty, Beatrice and Bobby.* The "Polly Pitcher" portfolio measures 14 by 9½ inches (35.6 x 24.2cm). **(Illustration 148.)**

In the mid 1920s Hollywood Dollies Inc. of New York City issued a series of movie actresses and

Illustration 144: The portfolio cover of *Paper Dolls of the World,* which contains six sheets of dolls and costumes from various parts of the globe. Published in 1909 by the George W. Jacobs & Company of Philadelphia, Pennsylvania. The portfolio measures 14 x 9½in (35.6 x 24.2cm). *Collection Mrs. Stanley A. Weeks.*

Illustration 145: *Dorothy Dimple & Her Friends,* the cover of a portfolio containing six sheets of paper dolls, dresses, toys and animals drawn by Cushman Parker. Published by George W. Jacobs & Company of Philadelphia, Pennsylvania. Copyrighted by The Bodley Press Associates of Springfield, Massachusetts. c.1912. The portfolio measures 16½ x 11½in (41.9 x 29.2cm). *Collection Mrs. Stanley A. Weeks.*

Illustration 146: *Betty Bonnet, Her Family & Friends,* was one of three portfolios, each containing six sheets of dolls, costumes and accessories. Published by George W. Jacobs & Company and copyrighted by the Curtis Publishing Company in 1915. Portfolio size 16½ x 11½in (41.9 x 29.2cm). *Collection Mrs. Stanley A. Weeks.*

KITTY CLOVER
Cut-Out Paper Dolls
Designed by SHEILA YOUNG

SECOND SERIES
Published by GEORGE W. JACOBS & CO., Philadelphia

Cut Out Paper Dolls for the Little Folk

Polly Pitcher and Her Playmates
Second Series
Dolls and Costumes Designed by
LILLIAN CAUSEY

Hours and Hours of Fun Cutting out the Many Beautiful
Dresses, Coats, Hats and Changeable Hair Ribbons
PHILADELPHIA
GEORGE W. JACOBS & CO.
PUBLISHERS

Illustration 147: *Kitty Clover* was designed by Sheila Young. The illustration pictures one of two portfolios, each containing six sheets. Published by George W. Jacobs & Company and copyrighted by the Curtis Publishing Company in 1917. Portfolio size 16½ x 11½in (41.9 x 29.2cm). *Collection Mrs. Stanley A. Weeks.*

Illustration 148: *Polly Pitcher & Her Playmates* was one of two portfolios of Polly paper dolls designed by Lillian Caussey. Each portfolio contains four sheets. Published by Jacobs & Company and copyrighted in 1918. Portfolio measures 14 x 9½in (35.6 x 24.2cm). *Collection Mrs. Stanley A. Weeks.*

actors paper dolls. Famous movie personalities of the period were pictured along with the costumes they wore in their starring roles. Some fascinating examples are found in **Illustrations 149 -151.**

In the early 1940s, movie star paper doll books were offered in great variety. The glamorus stars came with an assortment of beautiful gowns they wore in their starring roles. These offerings were eagerly purchased as soon as they appeared on the Woolworth and Kresge shelves. Such film personalities as Sonja Henie, Clark Gable, Deanna Durbin, Rita Hayworth, Lana Turner, Alice Faye and Shirley Temple among others, were popular. **(Illustrations 152 & 153.)** During the 1940-1943 period many World War II paper doll books appeared. The *American Nurse, Harry the Soldier, Dick the Sailor* and *Tom the Aviator* were paper dolls with a military theme. Other examples followed: *Wacs & Waves, Paper Dolls in Uniforms of the U.S.A., Bride & Groom Military Wedding Party* and *Victory Paper Dolls.* By 1944, the shortage of paper and man power became very apparent, and fewer paper doll books were published.

During the 1950s, the military and movie personalities were replaced by television stars such as Fess Parker, Pat Boone and Elizabeth Montgomery among others.

In 1917, Parker Brothers, the game publishing company of Salem, Massachusetts, issued a four page flyer of new paper dolls. Thirteen dolls were pictured in color, the figures having moveable arms and legs somewhat similar to those offered by Dennison. Parker offered an assortment of crepe and tissue paper for both plain and fancy costumes along with paper lace, decorative trimmings, forms, patterns, and instructions **(Illustration 154.)** In their 1918-19 catalog they devoted the back cover and a full interior page to their paper dolls. **(Illustration 155.)**

Milton Bradley, another game publisher previously mentioned, also entered the paper doll field. Their 1896-97 catalog offered a group of paper dolls along with paper furniture that could be cut out and placed within a provided room setting. Titled *A Home For Paper Dolls*, it was offered in three sizes: Home No. 1, contained six rooms, price 50 cents; Home No. 2, contained ten rooms, price $1.00; and Home No. 3, contained 14 rooms and two lawns, price $1.50. The same catalog offered *The Doll's Bazar* sets in three sizes. Each assortment included heads, bodies, limbs, parasols, fans, laces, gilt trim, and a variety of fancy paper suitable to put together a number of paper dolls and their costumes. **(Illustration 156 A & B.)**

Bradley introduced "Magic Mary," a novelty type paper doll, in 1950. Made up with a concealed magnet which held the dresses firmly in place, it did away with tabs and permitted a quick change of costume. Later in the same year, three other playmates joined "Magic Mary", each with 15 different dress cut-outs. Two other new offerings were "Two-Gun Pete" and "Bronco Bess," each supplied with an assortment of western clothing and equipment.

Illustrations 149 - 151: Hollywood Dollies Inc. of New York City issued a series of famous movie personality paper dolls with costumes they wore in their films. c.1925. These uncut sheets measure 10¼ x 13¼in (26.1 x 33.7cm).

Space does not allow full coverage of the paper doll field, since the supply over the past years was enormous. Scores and scores of paper dolls appeared in magazines and newspapers during the 1900-1935 period. Hundreds of inexpensive booklets appeared in the 1930-1970 period. The paper dolls mentioned in this chapter are but a few of the many thousands published since the first English paper doll in 1790. For those interested in further study of these intriguing paper figures, sources of informatin may be found in the bibliography at the end of this book.

Illustration 152: The *Alice Faye* paper doll book is one of scores that appeared in the 1940s glamorizing movie stars in paper doll form. This example was published and copyrighted by the Merrill Publishing Company of Chicago, Illinois. *Photo by Barbara Whitton Jendrick.*

Illustration 153: *Shirley Temple* appeared in paper doll form before and after 1940. A popular child star with the public and publishers alike. Scores of *Shirley Temple* paper dolls appeared on the market. *Collection Helen Jo Payne. Photo by Barbara Whitton Jendrick.*

Illustration 155: The upper half of the back cover of the 1918-19 Parker Brothers catalog which emphasized their marketing push for paper doll products for those years.

Illustration 154: The cover of a four-page folder in full color that was issued by Parker Brothers, Inc. of Salem, Massachusetts. It illustrates various types of paper clothing that could be made from Parker products. c.1917. Folder size opened, 9 x 12in (22.9 x 30.5cm).

A HOME FOR PAPER DOLLS.

The material that we offer for this fascinating occupation consists of sheets of cardboard on which are printed interior views of the various rooms in the house. The owner of the unoccupied "house" furnishes each room by cutting out pictures of furniture and people from catalogues, illustrated papers, fashion books, etc., and pasting them on the sheets, thus making pictures showing the rooms completely furnished and occupied.

The illustration at the head of the page is an exact representation of a nursery actually furnished by a little girl. It represents one of the rooms in "A Home for Paper Dolls," after it has been furnished by pasting in the "cut out" pictures of furniture and people.

As a manual training occupation or "busy work" "A Home for Paper Dolls" exceeds in interest anything ever before offered. The little girls take as much pleasure in exchanging especially desirable pictures of which they happen to have an overstock as do the boys in trading rare stamps for their stamp albums.

While the furniture and people are usually pasted in more or less securely the people are sometimes movable. In this illustration the baby is to be just tucked under the clothes of the crib. Some owners of the sheets may prefer to color the rooms. If a part of a picture is colored all the objects that are pasted on should be colored, in order not to destroy the effect. This suggestion, however, does not apply to lawn pictures which are printed in subdued colors. Complete instruction embodied in a circular and also in the story of "Emma's Christmas Present" accompanies each "Home."

Home No. 1, contains six rooms. In portfolio.
                    Price, each, 50 cents; postage, 15 cents.
Home No. 2, contains ten rooms. In box.
                    Price, each, $1.00; postage, 30 cents.
Home No. 3, contains fourteen rooms and two lawns. In elegant box.
                    Price, each, $1.50; postage, 60 cents.

RIGHT AND FACING PAGE: Illustration 156 A & B: The 1896-97 Milton Bradley catalog offered three Homes For Paper Dolls and three boxed sets titled *The Dolls Bazar*. **A** illustrates a cardboard room setting in which a child would cut out people figures and furniture from magazines and paste them on the room sheet. **B** illustrates *The Dolls Bazar* sets made up of an assortment of paper doll heads, bodies, limbs, accessories, colored paper and ornaments with which dresses could be constructed.

THE DOLLS BAZAR.

The idea of this treasure-box originated in the discouraging attempts of some little girls to pick up suitable material—from printing offices, box shops and stationary stores—for the proper construction and decoration of their paper dolls. It is designed to furnish a complete outfit of material for making and dressing a great variety of paper dolls, thus cultivating the faculties for design and manual construction to a greater degree than has heretofore resulted from the miscellaneous and unaided efforts of the little folks. The assortment includes heads, arms, legs, outlines of bodies, parasols, fans, portemonnaies, shopping bags, laces, gilt ornaments and a great variety of fancy paper suited to the wants of the profession.

The Dolls' Bazar is put up in a large and beautiful box, with explicit directions for all the desirable combinations. No. 2 contains about half the material found in No. 1 and No. 3 about one-half of No. 2.

								Price.	Postage.
No. 1, each,	.	.	.	.	.	.	.	$1.00	$0.25
No. 2, "	.	.	.	.	.	.	.	.50	.15
No. 3, "	.	.	.	.	.	.	.	.25	.09

JENNY WREN'S PAPER DOLLS.

The material provided in each envelope includes a colored sheet of heads, arms and legs, a cardboard body and papers for fashioning a suitable dress for her ladyship. She comes well equipped, or in other words, each envelope contains careful directions for making and dressing the doll with the material furnished, so that there need be no undue maternal solicitude regarding what she shall wear.　　　　Price, per envelope, 6 cents.

GIRLS' COMBINATION.

This is a valuable collection from three of the best-selling articles on our

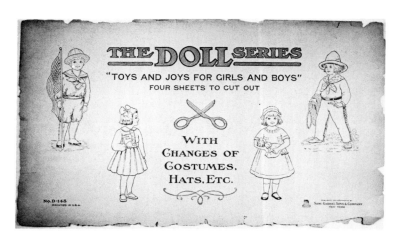

Illustration 157 A - E: The envelope and four sheets of a set published by Sam'l Gabriel Sons & Company of New York City, c.1920. Sheet size 10 x 17½in (25.4 x 44.5cm).

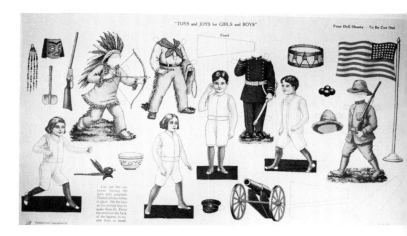

Chapter IX

CARDBOARD DOLLS' HOUSES, ROOM SETTINGS & THEIR FURNISHINGS

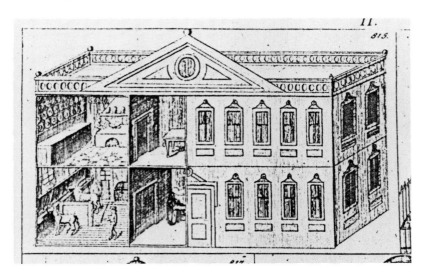
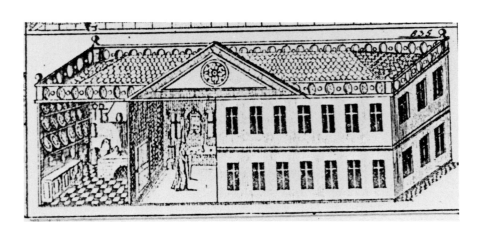

Illustration 158 A & B: Two examples of cardboard Dolls' Houses found in the 1803 Bestelmeier catalog from Germany. **A:** Notice the stable on the first floor, a common room in a well-to-do home of the period. **B:** Observe the one-story interior of the house while the exterior has two stories.

Some of the earliest examples of paper house construction sets are illustrated and described in the 1800-1803 Bestelmeier catalog, for example; "No. 695. A transparent Garden to put together. The house as well as the trees, pyramids, hedges, statues, flowers, etc. are cut out of cardboard and beautifully painted in a natural way. Everything is chiseled out and covered with a colored transparent material. There are 12 small lights with a set (alcohol pots or candles?) to illuminate it at night. At daytime you can put this garden against the sun." Another set listed was a "Large Picture Gallery with 30 nice pictures and various figures." **(Illustration 158 A & B.)**

In the last quarter of the 19th century the French publisher Pellerin issued sheets of houses, chateaus and so forth, to be cut out and assembled. They also issued sheets of room settings with all the necessary furniture to be cut out to complete a furnished room. A fine example, complete with furnishings and six figures, is titled *Salon, No. 189.* This construction sheet provides a room shell consisting of three walls, a rug-covered floor base, and a ceiling. The furnishings consist of a settee, two chairs, an oval table, an upright piano, a fireplace, a chandelier, a clock, and several candelabras. Five adult figures, three women and two men, and a young girl, are

included on the sheet. The Salon is decorated in pale green, pink, and tan with a touch of cream, brown, blue, gold, and a few touches of red. **(Illustration 159.)** This uncut sheet measures 19¼ by 15½ inches (49 x 39.4cm). The shell of the Salon when assembled is 9¾ inches (24.9cm) wide, 6⅝ inches (16.8cm) high and 3 inches (7.6cm) deep. Rather small, but it creates a feeling of grandeur in detail, color and arrangement. A second example titled *Chamber A Coucher No. 192* contains the furniture and accessories for a bed chamber. This uncut sheet consists of a bed, a dresser with mirror, a pedestal table, and a marble top chest of drawers, all in tan and brown

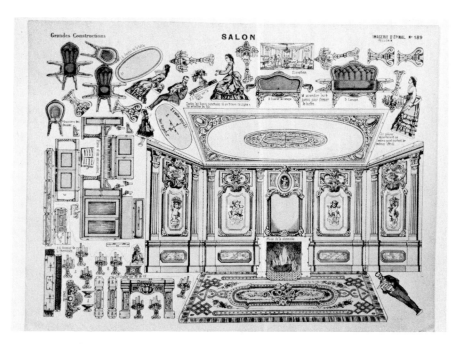

Illustration 159: A fantastic sheet that makes up into an elaborate room setting 5½in high, 9¾in wide and 2½in deep. It has three walls, a ceiling and a floor. Decorative furniture, accessories and six figures combine to make it a compact and realistic setting of a *Salon* of the 1870 period. A Grandes constructions sheet No. 189, by Pellerin of Epinal, France. Sheet size 15⅜ x 19¼in (39.0 x 49.0cm).

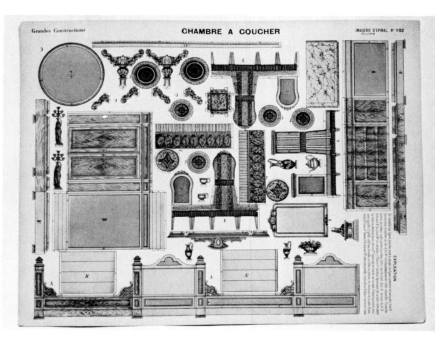

Illustration 160: *Chambre A Coucher,* an uncut sheet of bedroom furniture consisting of a well grained bed and two chests, an elaborately carved pedestal table, three chairs with upholstered seats and backs, and several decorative accessories. A Grandes Constructions sheet No. 192, by Pellerin of Epinal France, c.1880. Sheet size 15⅜ x 19¼in (39.0 x 49.0cm).

grained wood. Also three chairs upholstered in blue, red, green and gold, and several accessories such as a mantel clock, figural candelabras, decorative vases, and a bowl of flowers. The uncut sheet measures 19¼ by 15½ inches (49 x 39.4cm). **(Illustration 160.)**

A further interesting but different example of a Pellerin room setting is that of a French school room labeled *Ecole No. 196.* The room shell consists of a back and two side walls, a ceiling and a floor. The three tan-colored walls are covered with maps, graphics, tableaux, a blackboard, and a hanging shelf of books. When assembled the room has a proscenium-like front, the two side walls are faced with upright panels illustrating objects of learning and a large yellow sign board along the top with the words "Ecole Primaire."

The seated figure of a stern faced teacher with an open book in one hand and a pointer stick in his left hand, looks over his class from the left. The class consists of eight boys seated behind desks while five boys stand. One unfortunate student, who is positioned on his knees, wears a dunce cap with horns. Accessories include the teacher's desk, student desks and benches, and a blackboard on an easel. The uncut sheet measures 19¼ by 15½ inches (49 x 39.4cm). The assembled schoolroom is 10⅞ inches (27.6cm) wide, 5½ inches (14cm) high and 3½ inches (8.9cm) deep. These three examples are from scores of various room settings that the Pellerins published over the years. Each example had it's own interesting feature making them all equally appealing. **(Illustration 161).**

Another source of patterns for constructing cut-out paper furniture was found in the *Journal De Petites Filles.* Known as *La Poupée Modèle,* these patterns, on thin pink transparent paper, were bound in the magazine, one fold-out each month. For the most part the patterns were for children's clothes showing the latest fashions, yet often a pattern for paper furniture appeared. Directions for cutting out, methods of assembling and coloring were included. Certainly not as simple as cutting out and assembling the colored Pellerin sheets. These required work and dedication, transferring the tissue thin pattern to a cardboard sheet, carefully cutting it out, assembling it correctly and realistically painting and decorating in detail. However, young French children eagerly awaited the arrival of *La Poupée*

Modèle each month, so that they could start work on a pattern sheet. **(Illustration 162.)**

The same magazine, *Journal des Petites Filles*, later offered highly colored uncut cards illustrating elaborate furniture to be cut out and assembled. A fine example is found in **Illustration 163 A & B**, a highly decorated grand piano of rosewood with heavy gilt trim and colorfully painted panels. Two exquisitely dressed females are included on the card. These decorative cards came as a supplement to the magazine and were lithographed by F. Appel of Paris, France.

During this same period the German publishers were offering an assortment of construction sheets to their young model builders. One large uncut sheet marked "C. Trinker's Kleiner Architekt No. XXI," offers an assortment of colorful furniture. It consists of a marble-faced fireplace, a blue, red and tan rug, a dining table, four chairs with upholstered seats and backrests, two arm chairs and a sofa with similar upholstery, a corner what-not-shelf, a pair of vases, a pair of oil lamps with sphere globes, and a mantel clock. All wood surfaces are tan with a mahogany grained surface, while table and chair legs and backrest frames are highly carved. The upholstery has a broad vertical stripe pattern of white and blue, the white stripe decorated with a chain of red flowers and green foliage. **(Illustration 164.)** This large sheet measures 23½ by 17 inches (59.7 x 43.2cm).

Another fine example is Lothar Meggendorfer's *Puppenhaus*, an unusual grouping of a row of rooms and settings consisting of five units. Folded book-like in its cardboard slip case, this toy measures 8¾ inches (22.3cm) wide, 10¾ inches (27.4cm) high and 1 inch (2.5cm) deep. Opened and set up it is 52 inches (132cm) wide. Units 1 and 5 are exterior scenes with two walls and a triangular base; units 2 to 4 are interior rooms with two side walls, a back wall and a floor. All 5 units are connected by hinged doors. Unit 1 pictures an early open automóbile with six figures, two of which have fold-out movement, a woman carrying a tray of food and a man with a bicycle. The background is a street scene with a house in the background and the entrance to a shop on

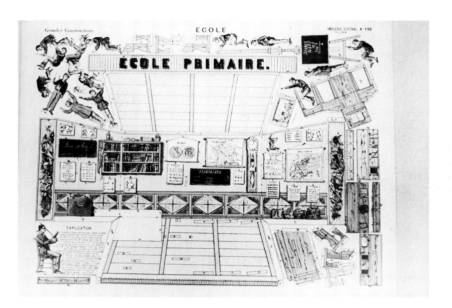

Illustration 161: *Ecole Primaire*, an uncut sheet of a typical French schoolroom. A compact room setting measuring 5½in high, 9in wide and 3½in deep when cut and assembled. It is inhabited by a schoolmaster and 14 male students, desks and blackboards, an an array of charts, maps and shelved books on the walls. A *Grandes Constructions* sheet N. 196 by Pellerin of Epinal, France, c.1900. Sheet size 15⅜ x 19¼in (39.0 x 49.0cm).

Illustration 162: An example of Dolls' House furniture patterns printed on pink tissue paper and bound into the *Journal de Petites Filles*. Observe the drawings of the finished chairs in the upper and lower right hand corners, also the date, May 1879.

the right. **(Illustration 165 A - E.)** Unit 2 is the inside of a shop with the proprietor and his wife waiting on a woman with a small boy, and to add a bit of Meggendorfer's humor, a dog pulling a string of sausages out of a basket which is sitting on the floor. The store counter, the four figures, the dog, and a rack holding a barrel, fold out when opened. Unit 3 is a sitting room which contains a fold-out table, a chair bench and a piano, along with a seated woman reading a book, and a seated girl holding a child in her lap. A piano stool appears to be missing. Unit 4 is a kitchen scene with a fold out upright cabinet, a large tiled stove, and the figures of a mother and daughter with a cat. The last unit is an outdoor scene showing a woman feeding chickens and birds, a small child on a stick horse, and a dog watching the birds. A fence, the figures, dog, birds and chickens fold out. This panorama of scenes was published by J.F. Schreiber of Esslingen, Germany.

Another example of Schreiber's work is an uncut sheet of a suite of parlor furniture. It features matched grained woodwork with finely carved decorative patterns. The pieces consist of an upright piano carrying the label "Lipp & Cie.," who a prominent piano manufacturer in Stuttgart, Germany, an oval table, an elaborate marble top sideboard, and a blue tufted upholstered sofa and matching chair. Both sofa and chair feature beautifully carved legs and backrest frames. The sheet is marked "J.F.S. iE, Mod. Cart No. 6.," and measures 17 by 14¼ inches (43.2 x 36.3cm); and dates in the mid 1860s. **(Illustration 166.)**

The publishing house of J.F. Schreiber has been mentioned in previous chapters and the name will reappear in the chapters that follow. The founder of this German firm, Jacob Ferdinand Schreiber, was born in 1809. As a child he lost his parents at an early age and was placed in an orphanage. He was later placed in a foster home where he was ill-treated and undernourished to the extent that he was placed in a hospital. During his long stay in the hospital, he amused himself by drawing. Hospital officials, impressed with his artistic ability, induced patrons to provide him with funds to receive professional art instructions. He later attended a Stuttgart, Germany, business school where he took courses in art and lithography. In his early twenties he moved to Essligen, Germany, and advertised himself as an instructor of lithography and drawing. He later married the daughter of a man of means in Essligen, received a large dowery, and started his own publishing company. The business progressed rapidly and the company went on to publish an assortment of beautiful paper products, a few of which are mentioned and illustrated in this study.

A third country that produced noteable paper toys was England. We have offered examples of their early card and board games, their peep shows, paper theaters, soldiers, and some of their interesting moveable books. While they actually published the first paper doll, they did not produce many of the early paper houses associated with paper dolls. The most popular type of paper dolls'

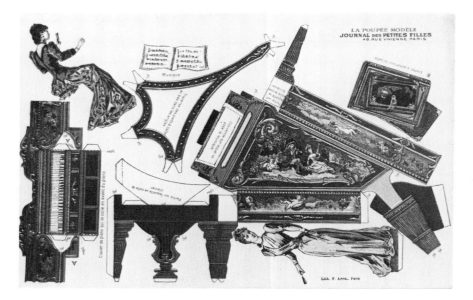

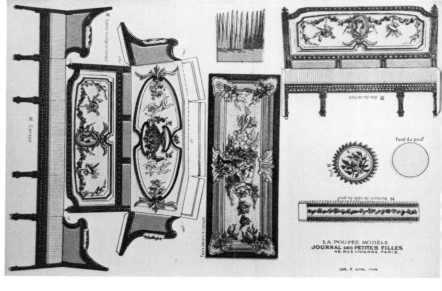

Illustration 163 A & B: Two fine examples of furniture cards from the *La Poupée Modèle* series found in the *Journal des Petites Filles*. **A:** Two female figures and an exquisitely painted grand piano. **B:** a highly decorated sofa, c.1890. Card size 7¼ x 10¾in (18.5 x 27.4cm).

house seemed to be in book form, where the book cover or an early page in the book was the facade of the house and the following pages pictured the various rooms. In some cases, some of the furniture would fold out when a page was opened; in others there might be one or more horizontal slits in a room where a paper doll or paper furniture might be inserted. Of course there were exceptions to these forms.

In 1880, an English publishing firm by the name of Griffith & Farran, whose address was listed as "Corner of St. Pauls Churchyard, London," offered a book titled *The Girl's Own Toy Maker*. Written by E. Landells and his daughter Alice Landells, it offered plans and instructions for making paper and cardboard toys, dolls' house furniture, how to dress paper dolls, puzzles, etc. In one chapter plans and instructions for building a simple cardboard house was presented along with furniture and accessories to furnish it. **(Illustration 167.)** This book was reprinted in the United States by E.P. Dutton & Company later in the same year.

A large book-like folder containing a series of rooms appeared on the English market around 1900. Titled *The Goodchild Family at Home*, it consisted of three large interior folders representing three floors of rooms in a typical English house. **(Illustration 168 A & B.)** Each folder or floor has a central hall and a room on either side. The ground floor contains a dining room and a kitchen, the second floor a parlor and a nursery, while the top floor has two bedrooms. Each of the folders has a separate backing hinged at the top so that it will stand like a tent. Each floor, consisting of a hall and two rooms, measures 24 inches (61cm) wide and is 11½ inches (29.2cm) high. Each room is drawn in perspective with furnishings both in the background and foreground. Some are slit in appropriate areas so that a paper family figure may be inserted, such as in a chair, in front of a piano, in a bed or on a hobby horse. **(Illustration 168.)** Unfortunately the piece pictured is in poor condition, soiled, and the paper figures of some of the family members are lost. This toy was designed and patented by Anna Hays and published by John Walker & Company,

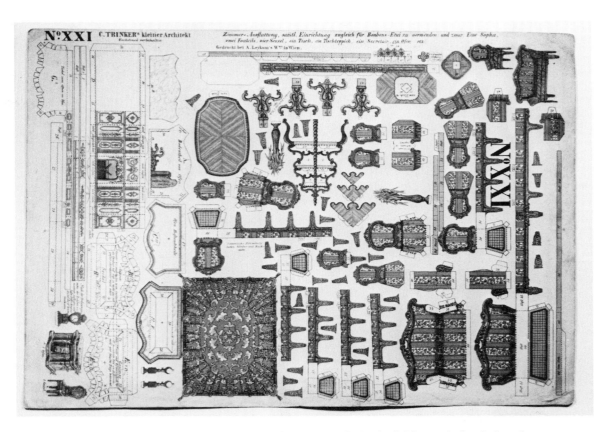

Illustration 164: Furniture construction sheet marked *No. XXI, C. Trinker's Kleiner Architekt*. It makes up into a marble fireplace, chairs, sofa, table, what-not shelf and lamps. Germany, c.1900. Sheet size 17 x 23½in (43.2 x 59.7cm).

Farrington House, Warwick Lane, E.C., London, England.

Raphael Tuck, one of Britain's leading publishers of paper toys, and certainly their outstanding producer of paper dolls, published *The Doll's House*. This was a book-like house containing six fold-out rooms. The highly colored cover represented the red brick front of a house with an entrance door that opened and closed. Inside, as we turn the pages, we find a parlor, dining room, kitchen, sitting room, bedroom, and a nursery. Each room is equipped with fold-out hinged figures of members of the household, along with various pieces of furniture. **(Illustration 169.)**

Johnson Brothers, Harborne Ltd., later known as Chad Valley, offered a paper construction set, *The Card House & Fort Builder*, in 1913. This set consisted of an assortment of various size colored cards with clips to join them together. A year later they offered a second set, the *Bridge Builder*, with an improved type of clip to fasten the cards together.

In 1921 a unique type of dolls' house book, *My Dolly's Home*, appeared. It was designed by Doris Davey and published by Simpkins, Marshall, Hamilton, Kent & Company Ltd., London, England. This 28-page hardbound book has a large envelope fastened to the inside front cover that contains paper figures, domestic animals, and an eight-page booklet titled *Biddies Adventure, The*

A

B

126

D

E

ABOVE AND OPPOSITE PAGE: Illustration 165 A - E: Lothar Meggendorfer's *Puppenhaus*, a panorama fold-out of five connecting units. **A** pictures the entrance unit with opening door to **B**, the shop where the proprietor and his wife wait on customers. **C** pictures a sitting room with door at right opening to **D**, the kitchen with door on the right opening to a rear yard **E** Germany, c.1895. Open panorama is 10¾in high and 52in wide (27.4 x 1m 32.1cm).

Story of My Dolly's Home. All illustrations are on double open pages measuring 23 inches (58.4cm) wide and 8½ inches (21.6cm) high. The first open spread pictures a high stone wall with a wide die-cut cast iron double gate. Turning the page reveals the back side of the gate and a landscaped lawn featuring a flowing fountain. A turn to the next page reveals the facade of a house which has an opening front entrance. Another turn and the reader is in the hallway, then in succession, a parlor, a dining room, a library, a hall with stairway to the second floor. This follows with three bedrooms, a nursery or playroom, a bathroom, then a stairway down to the rear hall, then a kitchen, then out the rear door to a vegetable garden. This is followed by pages of five outdoor views at the rear fo the house — a fence with a colorful flower border, a tennis court, a green-

house, a carriage house, an apple orchard in bloom, and finally a fenced in field with a horse, and two houses and a church on the distant horizon. Throughout the book, the rooms are colorfully illustrated with appropriate furniture, doors between the rooms that open and close, cabinet doors that open revealing the contents inside, all of which provided additional interest and play value. Little girls would spend hours playing with this toy, reading and acting out the story script and maneuvering the nine paper dolls, the dog, and the cat, through the rooms of the house and into the various outside areas.

In the United States paper doll furniture appeared before the paper dolls' houses. In the chapter on paper dolls mention was made that Anson D.F. Randolph had published two small books on making paper dolls. In 1857 he pub-

lished *Paper Dolls Furniture*, written by Mrs. C.B. Allair. This 63-page book contained seven chapters telling how to make paper furniture to fill several rooms. Drawings of the furniture and full size patterns for each piece were included. All objects were uncolored, but detailed coloring instructions were given. Chapter I covers the reasons for writing the book, materials required, and suggestions given with regard to neatness while at work. Chapter II covers kitchen furniture consisting of four chairs, a settle table, a plain table, and a clothes horse. Chapter III consists of dining room furniture made up of a dining table, a butler's tray, six chairs, a high chair and a clock. Chapter IV covers parlor furniture consisting of a *Tête-á-Tête*, a lounge (**Illustration 170 A & B.**) a pier table with oval mirror, a picture, a rocking chair, four mahogany chairs, a patchwork chair, a

Illustration 166: An uncut sheet of parlor furniture by J.F. Schreiber of Easlingen, Germany, c.1865. Notice the matched grained wood panels and the carving of the legs and backrest frames of the chairs. Sheet size is 14¼ x 17in (36.3 x 43.2cm). *Strong Museum Collection. Photo by Tom Weber and Mike Radke.*

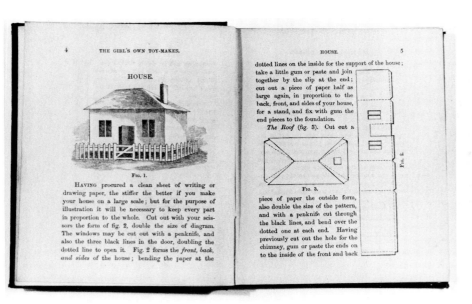

Illustration 167: Two pages from a book titled *The Girls Own Toy Maker*, published by Griffith & Farran of London, England, in 1880. It contains directions, drawings and patterns for constructing several paper toys.

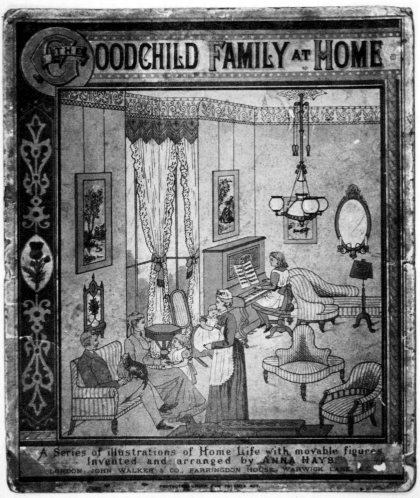

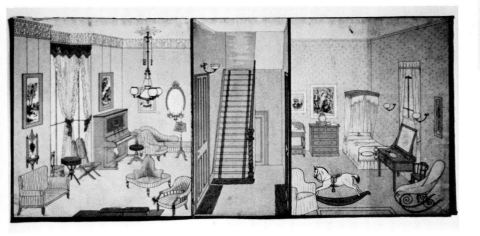

ABOVE AND LEFT: Illustration 168 A & B: *The Goodchild Family at Home* is in the form of a hardcover folder containing three large interior folders representing three floors of an English home. Each floor consists of a hall with a room on either side. It measures 11½in high and 24in wide (29.2 x 61.0cm). Each room is drawn in perspective with furnishings. Horizontal slits are found in the furniture so that members of the family may be inserted. **A** pictures cover of the exterior folder, while **B** features a parlor and a nursery. Published by John Walker & Company, London, England, c.1910.

Illustration 169: *The Dolls' House* is in the form of an accordian-type panorama. Illustrated is the cover and one of the six interior panels, each of which has fold-out figures. Published by Raphael Tuck & Sons, London, England, c.1910. The opened panorama is 7½in high and 56¼in wide (19.1 x 1m 42.9cm).

workbasket table, two foot-stools, a pair of figurines for a mantel shelf, and a vase with flowers. Chapter V covers the bedroom furniture consisting of a bed, a crib, a washstand, a bureau with a mirror, a towel rack, a rocking chair, and two plain chairs. Chapter VI includes the furnishings for a servants room; a cot-bed, a table, a washstand, a looking glass, and two chairs. Chapter VII, the final chapter, consists of a single page stating, in essence, that the author hopes the young reader and builder has enjoyed building the various furniture projects, and that she hopes in the future to offer a design for a five-room house in which this furniture may be housed.

A facsimile of the contents of the above book, along with the paper furniture patterns, was published in London, England, by Griffith & Farrar. The title and title page was changed to red; *How to Make Doll Furniture & Furnish A Doll's House, With Seventy Illustrations.* The author's name was omitted along with the date of publication.

One of the earliest paper dolls' houses published in the United States appears to be the work of G.W. Cottrell of Boston, Massachusetts. This paper house was patented by Emily S. Russell of Plymouth, Massachusetts, on July 7, 1868. **(Illustration 171.)** A quote from some of the paragraphs in the patent copy that accompanied the patent drawing, describes the house adequately:

"The invention relates to the construction of a toy designed particularly for the use of little girls in playing house with dolls, and consists primarily in a toy-house or a representation of a house, made of pasteboard or equivalent thin material, having swing doors and blinds (window shutters), each of which when open, shows, in the background, a representation of a hall, drawing room, chamber or other apartment, while, when closed it has the natural appearance of doors or windows closed by ordinary doors or blinds.

"The invention also consists in making such a toy of two sheets, placed together and united at opposite edges, the doors and windows being made in the outer sheet (which represents the outside of the house), and the pictures of the rooms being painted or printed upon the inner sheet, opposite the doors and windows, this construction allowing paper dolls to be slipped in between the sheets, and to be thus moved from room to room within the house.

"The invention also consists in combining with such a house a paper doll or dolls, with means for moving such a doll from room to room without directly touching it.

"It will be obvious that a toy thus made will conduce to the quiet amusement of children old enough to play with dolls, and especially to the diversion of little girls playing together, having great attractions for many children over any toy houses and furniture requiring building or setting up."

In an 1867 distributors catalog issued by Wm. H. Hill, Jr. & Company of Boston, Massachusetts, there is a long listing of paper products published by McLoughlin Brothers. Included in this listing are offerings of paper furniture in the form of a parlor, drawing room, and bedroom suites, selling wholesale at $12.00 per gross. Two other bedroom and parlor sets in a smaller size were offered at $7.50 per gross. Three dolls' houses were offered on this same list, all titled *Beautiful Play House.* One consisted of two rooms and a parlor at $4.00 a dozen; a second consisted of one room, a parlor and an outside room at $6.00 per dozen; and a third, two rooms, a parlor and a bedroom at $8.00 per dozen. Unfortunately this catalog is in the form of a brief list offering very little description and no illustrations.

The 1875-76 McLoughlin Brothers catalog contained 44 pages of which five pages listed paper dolls, paper furniture, and a paper house. The dolls' house was a two-story lithographed paper on wood house, 18 inches (45.7cm) high and 11 inches (27.9cm) wide. The upper room

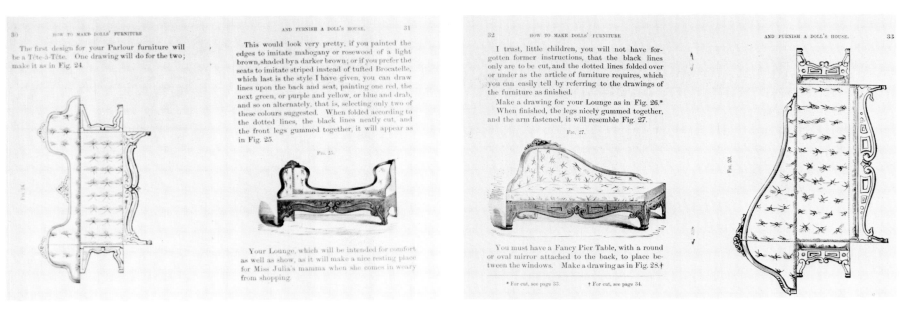

The first design for your Parlour furniture will be a Tête-á-Tête. One drawing will do for the two; make it as in Fig. 24.

This would look very pretty, if you painted the edges to imitate mahogany or rosewood of a light brown, shaded by a darker brown; or if you prefer the seats to imitate striped instead of tufted Brocatelle, which last is the style I have given, you can draw lines upon the back and seat, painting one red, the next green, or purple and yellow, or blue and drab, and so on alternately, that is, selecting only two of these colours suggested. When folded according to the dotted lines, the black lines neatly cut, and the front legs gummed together, it will appear as in Fig. 25.

Your Lounge, which will be intended for comfort as well as show, as it will make a nice resting place for Miss Julia's mamma when she comes in weary from shopping.

I trust, little children, you will not have forgotten former instructions, that the black lines only are to be cut, and the dotted lines folded over or under as the article of furniture requires, which you can easily tell by referring to the drawings of the furniture as finished.

Make a drawing for your Lounge as in Fig. 26.*
When finished, the legs nicely gummed together, and the arm fastened, it will resemble Fig. 27.

You must have a Fancy Pier Table, with a round or oval mirror attached to the back, to place between the windows. Make a drawing as in Fig. 28.†

* For cut, see page 33.   † For cut, see page 34.

Illustration 170 A & B: Four pages from *Paper Dolls Furniture*, an instruction book published by Anson D.F. Randolph, in 1857. **A** shows a pattern for a "Tête-á-Tête," a drawing of the finished piece and directions on construction procedure. **B** shows a pattern for a "Lounge," a drawing of the finished piece and construction directions.

was designed as a bedroom, the lower room as a parlor. The interior of both rooms is covered with colorful lithographed paper offering fine detail and lavish decoration. It was offered in knocked down condition with full directions for assembling. While this is not a paper house, it was sometimes used to house paper dolls and paper furniture. This same 1875 catalog offered paper dolls with tissue dresses, and others with silk dresses. Notice in **Illustration 172** under silk dresses, series 1 and 2, each set is put up in a pasteboard box, presenting the appearance of a three story brick city dwelling. **(Illustration 173.)** The 1875 offering of paper furniture consisted of two sizes of parlor sets and bedroom sets, and a single set of a drawing room in the larger size. The parlor set consisted of 11 pieces of furniture; six chairs, two fancy rockers, two sofas in maroon damask, and a marble top table. The bedroom set contained ten pieces: four chairs, two ottomans, a

marble top wash stand, a bureau, a table, and a bed. The drawing room set was made up of nine pieces consisting of four chairs, two fancy rockers, a sofa in maroon brocatelle, a marble top table, and a piano. The 1879-80 McLoughlin catalog offered similar sets with no new additions.

McLoughlin's 1882 catalog is more impressive than the earlier catalogs mentioned above. The emphasis was on their games, which were listed on 23 pages. A listing of paper dolls appears on one page with a dolls' house mentioned at the bottom of the same page. **(Illustration 174.)** The 1886 catalog illustrates the above mentioned house as "No. 262, Paper Doll House, Retail $1.00 each." The same catalog lists over 60 paper dolls and soldiers at 1¢ each, six paper dolls and two sets of paper furniture at 6¢ each, 15 paper dolls, three sets of furniture, two sets of Little Folk's Menagerie consisting of over 30 animals each, and two Buffalo Bill sets consisting of numerous

horses, buffalos, Indians, and frontiersmen at 15¢ each. Also listed were six kinds of paper dolls at 20¢ each, and four kinds with silk dresses at 30¢ each.

There is a question as to when McLoughlin's first folding dolls' house appeared on the market. A cardboard house seems to have appeared in the mid 1880s. This beauty had two rooms, one over the other, capped with a peaked roof and a chimney, and had an open front. A three-fold house, when the back and side walls were opened up and placed in position, the hinged floors dropped into place. The front cornice, peaked at top and curved below, the center folded roof and the chimney were then secured in place. The completed house measures 18 inches (45.7cm) high, 12 inches (30.5cm) wide and 9½ inches (24.2cm) deep. Decorated inside and out with highly colored lithographed paper, it has extremely fine detail. The parlor floor is covered

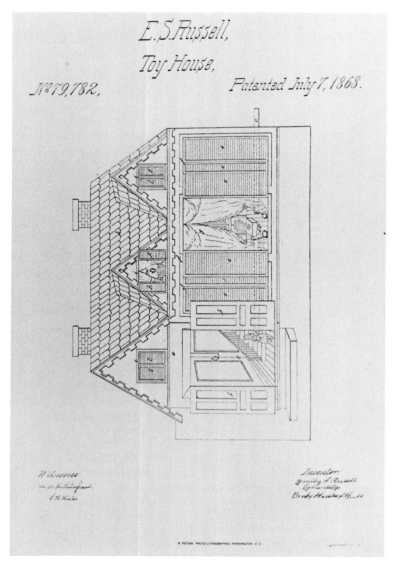

E. S. Russell,
Toy House,
Nº79,782,
Patented July 7, 1868.

Illustration 171: The patent drawing of a paper house developed by Emily S. Russell of Plymouth, Massachusetts, in 1868. Constructed of two sheets of cardboard, one over the other, the tops and bottoms joined, the ends left open. The top card pictures the exterior front of the house with open windows and a door. The interior rooms are printed on the undercard. The feet of 2 or 3 paper dolls are attached to a long card strip and placed between the two cards, enabling a child to move the dolls from windows to door and back again by pulling or pushing the end of the ridged strip.

with a beautiful green rug with an elaborate center design and a multi-colored border. The back wall supports a marble-faced fireplace with a ceiling-high gilt frame mirror above it. The fireplace is flanked by large windows hung with lace curtains and lavender draperies. The paneled side walls are embellished with fine gilt decorations. The second floor bedroom has a blue, gold, and white figured carpet. The back wall features a fireplace between two curtained windows. The walls are covered with a striped wall-paper and hung with gilt framed pictures. **(Illustration 175.)**

McLoughlin's second folding house, or rather folding group of rooms, was equally as lavish in color and detail as the house mentioned earlier. This paper toy was patented by Eleanor Mc-Culloch Smith of Baltimore, Maryland, on January 30, 1894, and assigned to McLoughlin Brothers. The patent copy reads in part:

"This invention relates to the class of folding toys, which are usually constructed from thin stiff material such as paper board and the object is to provide a toy which will stimulate a house interior with partitions between the rooms, carpeted floors, etc.

"The leading feature is the series of partitions between the rooms, preferably four, radiating from a common hinging point so that they may be folded together like the leaves of a book when not in use.

"Another feature is the hinging to the lower edge of each partition of a floor piece which simulates the completed floor of the room."

The unit is made up of four rooms, a parlor, dining room, kitchen and bedroom. The floor of the parlor is covered with a cream-colored rug with a diagonal rose pattern supplemented with blue corn flowers and a scroll patterned border in brown and cream. The walls are papered with a yellow-cream background with a soft blue fleur de lis-type pattern. One wall has a fireplace decorated in a Grecian theme that extends upward to the ceiling. A large built-in mirror is set over the mantel. The fine detail of the vases on the mantel and the brass fire irons in front of the tiled firebox of the fireplace, is remarkable. The second wall

DRESSED PAPER DOLLS.

These are a new feature in the Doll Line, and make attractive and salable gifts. In the different series, the figures vary in size, and in the style and beauty of the toilet. These are made of fine imported papers, in imitation of moire-antique and corded silks, elaborately trimmed in imitation with lace, and are only excelled by the original fabrics. The dresses have full plaited skirts with slight trains.

DOLLS WITH TISSUE DRESSES.

SERIES No. 1..*Per Gross, $24.00*

    Three kinds...............**Baby. Brunette. Blonde.**

The figures are eleven inches in height, made of pasteboard, and give front and back views. The dresses are made of tissue paper tastefully trimmed, with sash. Put up in pasteboard boxes containing one dozen each, and packed six dozen in a package.

DOLLS WITH SILK DRESSES.

SERIES No. 0..*Per Gross, $12.00*

Each box contains twelve dolls, same in size and toilet as No. 1. This series is assorted, and enables dealers to meet the demand for single dolls.

SERIES No. 1—Three kinds................*Per Gross, $24.00*

    House No. 1 contains....................Rosie and Charlie.
    House No. 2 contains...................Lillie and Harrie.
    House No. 3 contains...................Susie and Willie.

Each box contains two dolls, a girl and a boy, mounted upon separate standards. They represent two well-dressed children about ten years old. The dresses of the girls vary with each figure, and are in imitation of silk, trimmed with lace, and in the latest style. Each set is put up in a pasteboard box, presenting the appearance of a three-story brick English basement house. Put up in pasteboard boxes containing one dozen sets each, and packed assorted gross cases.

SERIES No. 2—Three kinds................*Per Gross, $72.00*

    House No. 1 contains......Mademoiselles Madeliene and Jeannette.
    House No. 2 contains.....Mademoiselles Fanchon and Louise.
    House No. 3 contains......Mademoiselles Nannette and Hortense.

Each box contains two fashionably dressed dolls, seven and one-half inches high, drawing-room dresses, full plaited, with slight train, made in imitation of moire-antique and corded silks, trimmed with lace; also handsome lace sash. Put up in three-story brick English basement houses, seven and one-half inches high by three wide. Each set packed in quarter dozen packages.

Illustration 172: A page from a 1875-76 McLoughlin Brothers catalog that introduced a new line of paper dolls, some with tissue dresses, others with silk dresses trimmed with imitation lace. Also, a new line of novelty packaging in the form of a cardboard box with a lithographed cover to represent the front of a three-story red brick city house.

Illustration 173: Two of the 1875-1876 McLoughlin paper dolls and the box they came in. The cover is set upright so that you may appreciate the fine lithography. The box measures 6 1/8 x 3 1/16 x 2in (15.5 x 7.7 x 5.1cm).

PENNY PAPER DOLLS.

These are about four inches in height, and consist of a figure with three suits, printed in colors upon stiff paper. They embrace a variety of subjects, with dresses suited to each kind, and are folded and put up in pasteboard boxes containing one assorted gross each. Packed in twelve gross packages.

MULLIGAN GUARD SERIES—Three kinds..Retail 1ct. each.
Mulligan Guard. The Baby. Madame Pompadour.

HUMPTY DUMPTY SERIES—Three kinds..Retail 1ct. each.
Humpty Dumpty. Dame Trot. Little Bo-Peep.

LITTLE DOLLY VARDEN SERIES—6 kinds. Retail 1ct. each.
Pompey Varden—(colored.) Dinah Varden—(colored.) Little Dolly Varden.
Tom Thumb's Baby. Clara Louise Kellogg. Charley Varden.

GEM SERIES—Six kinds........................Retail 1ct. each.
Amelia. Emily. Isabella. Julia. Martha. Josie.

COMIC SERIES—Three kinds..................Retail 1ct. each.
Tabby (cat.) Fido—(dog.) Jocko.—(monkey.)

TOM THUMB SERIES—Six kinds.............Retail 1ct. each.
Minnie Warren and Willie. Florence and Alecia. Mr. and Mrs. Tom Tumb.
Eva St. Clair and Toysy. Maud and Louise. Fanny and Pink.

PAPER SOLDIER SERIES—Six kinds........Retail 1ct. each.
Continentals. Union Rifles. Highlanders. Brass Band. Zouaves. Infantry.
Each set consists of a company of twelve soldiers, printed in colors upon stiff paper.

PAPER DOLLS IN BOOK FORM.

These dolls are not as elaborate as the foregoing, and differ from them in the style of their toilets. They are essential to variety, and with the others make the household complete. Four toilets in colors accompany each figure. The prices of these dolls have been reduced since July 1st.

SERIES No. 4—Four kinds............   *15 cts. each*
Red Riding Hood. Goody Two Shoes. Ida May. Jessie Jones.

SERIES No. 3—Twelve kinds......   *12 cts. each.*
Commodore Nut. Mr. Tom. Thumb. Mrs. Tom Thumb. Carrie Grant. Eugenia. Victoria.
Minne Warren. Nellie North. Clara West. Cinderella. Susie's Pets. Grace Lee.

SERIES No. 2—Twenty-four kinds.   *6 cts. each.*
Kittie Black. Ella Hall. Nettie Ray. Sarah Brown. Nellie Naylor.
Lilly Beers. Violet Vernon. Sophia May. Ruby Rose. Elsie Dale.
Little Lady. Eva and Topsy. Minty Green. Anna Doll. Josie Fox.
Fanny Fair. Rose Rustic. Emma White. Marquis. Laura Leil.
Rose Bud. Millie Fay. Mary Gray. Marchioness.

SERIES No. 1—Twenty-two kinds...   *3 cts. each.*
Minnie Miller. Ester Fine. Jeannie. Dolly. Tillie. Dora. Baby.
Flora Fair. Little Pet. Mollie. Helen. Sarah. Alice. Jane. Daisy.
Little Fred. Bo-Peep. May Day. Paul. Lizzie. Stella. Hattie.

PAPER DOLL HOUSE. $1.50 ea.

This is a two-story wooden house eighteen inches high, and eleven inches wide, made in imitation of brick, with slanting tiled roof, chimney, &c. The floor of each story is furnished with a pattern carpet, and the walls are handsomely papered. The upper story is designed for a bedroom, and the lower story for a parlor. The separate parts of the house are completely put up in a neat box, with full directions for putting together.

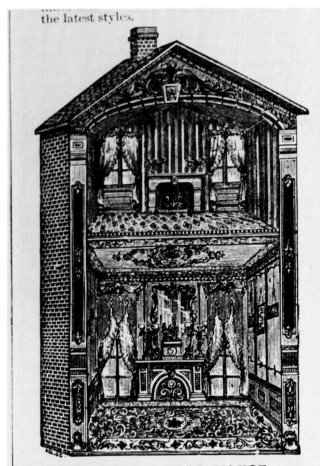

the latest styles.

No. 262.—PAPER DOLL HOUSE.
Retail $1.00 each.

This is a two-story house, eighteen inches high, and eleven inches wide, made in imitation of brick, with slanting tiled roof, chimney, etc. The floor of each story is furnished with a pattern carpet, and the walls are handsomely papered. The upper story is designed for a bed-room, and the lower story for a parlor. We give an illustration of this house on this page.

Illustration 174: A page from the 1882 McLoughlin Brothers catalog gives one an idea of the variety and quantity of paper dolls offered at that time. Observe the number of paper dolls and soldiers offered at a penny each.

Illustration 175: This illustration of the *Paper Doll House No. 262* appeared in the McLoughlin Brothers 1886 catalog. A three-fold cardboard house, when the back side walls and front facade were opened up, the two hinged floors dropped into place. The center fold roof and the chimney are then secured in place.

Illustration 176: *The Parlor,* one of four rooms in McLoughlin Brothers open dolls' house. This paper and cardboard toy was patented by Eleanor McCulloch Smith of Baltimore, Maryland, in 1894, and assigned to McLoughlin Brothers. The room measures 12 x 12 x 12in (30.5 x 30.5 x 30.5cm). *Collection Herbert Hosmer.*

Illustration 177: *The Dining Room,* the second of four rooms in McLoughlin Brothers open dolls' house. The exquisite detail offered by McLoughlin's color lithography is outstanding. c.1895. This room measures 12 x 12 x 12in (30.5 x 30.5 x 30.5cm). *Collection Herbert Hosmer.*

features an open arch leading to the dining room, with full lavender draperies tied back with gold cords. **(Illustration 176.)** The dining room floor is grained brown and tan with a parquet design around the outer edge. A colorful square rug with a diamond pattern in the center dominates the floor. A large fireplace with a double mantel which is covered with ornamental china objects, and topped with a deer head, is centered on the second wall. To the left of the fireplace is a doorway to the kitchen, on the other side is a built-in cabinet. **(Illustration 177.)** The kitchen floor is covered with a checkered linoleum. A coal stove is recessed in a yellow brick chimney that extends up to the ceiling. A copper hot water boiler stands alongside the chimney. An iron sink

stands alongside the boiler, a counter cabinet is located at the far side of the chimney. The second kitchen wall supports a double washtub working surface tops, a large upright cabinet and an exit door. The detail of the lithographed wood graining, the cooking utensils, the faucets, cabinet hardware, and the feather duster hanging on the wall, is outstanding. **(Illustration 178.)** The fourth room, the bedroom, has a floor carpet with a diagonal pattern of red and blue flowers on a cream background. The walls are covered with a soft blue diamond-shaped pattern on a cream background. One wall features a small fireplace with a detailed firebox and blue tiles facing on each side. A framed landscape hangs over the fireplace with portraits of a man and woman on

either side. The second wall has two doorways with small foot mats at their base, and centered between the doors is a "Home Sweet Home" sampler. **(Illustration 179.)**

A 1909 McLoughlin catalog illustrates and briefly describes two folding dolls' houses, the *New Folding Doll House* **(Illustration 180.)** and a bungalow-style version of a later *Dolly's Play House.* From the way the copy alongside the illustration reads, these two houses may have been offered at an earlier date. The *New Folding Doll House* is a two-story house with a shallow peaked roof. The exterior is red brick with grey stone quoins in a toothed pattern. The house sits on a grey cut stone foundation. Six steps lead up to a double front door which is framed by double colonettes supporting a shallow triangular green roof. On either side of the entranceway are double windows. Above the front door is a triple window flanked on either side by a single window. All woodwork, window frames, colonettes, steps, and baseboard are off-white. All windows are two paned, with a blue window shade behind the upper half and split white curtains in the lower half. Each window is topped with a transom made up of pink and green leaded glass in an elongated diamond pattern. Each window frame is topped with a shallow green triangular roof. Window structures follow the same style on the sides and the back of the house. The back of the house is equipped with a half porch. The house is

finished with a red tile roof. A novel feature of this house is that the facade is hinged at the base and, when opened, reveals the interior and a beautiful formal garden with a central pool. The two highly colored rooms are typical of Victorian rooms of the 1880-1900 period. Floor coverings are shown in strong colors and bold designs; window seats are covered with cushions; overpowering mantels over the fireplaces are topped with large mirrors; lace curtains hang to the floor framed with long deep colored draperies hanging from decorated boxed valances; and pictures covering all wall space contribute to a feeling of turn-of-the-century clutter.

This *New Folding Doll House*, the folding four

room unit, and the earlier *Dolly's Play House*, are three superior examples of American lithographic printing. The depth and variety of color and design is outstanding. The second folding house in the 1909 catalog was a bungalow-type titled *Dolly's Play House*, a name used on an earlier two-story house. It consisted of two rooms placed side by side, a peaked roof with two dormers, and a single chimney. The front folds down revealing the interior and adding a colorful formal garden to the front of the house. The house is 17 inches (43.2cm) wide, 7½ inches (19.1cm) high to the ridge of the roof and is 11 inches (27.9cm) deep. **(Color Illustration 22.)** The same 1909 catalog lists six "Model Books" containing objects to be

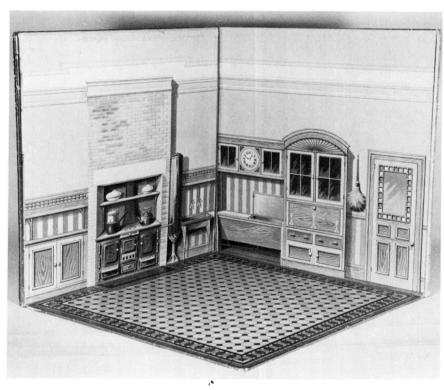

Illustration 178: *The Kitchen* of McLoughlin Brothers open Dolls' House is typical of those found in city homes of the period. c.1895. The Kitchen measures 12 x 12 x 12in (30.5 x 30.5 x 30.5cm). *Collection Herbert Hosmer.*

Illustration 179: *The Bedroom*, the fourth room in McLoughlin Brothers open dolls' house features the best means of combating cold weather, a coal burning fireplace. Notice the floor mats at the base of each door and the traditional "Home Sweet Home" sampler. c.1895. Room size 12 x 12 x 12 (30.5 x 30.5 x 30.5cm). *Collection Herbert Hosmer.*

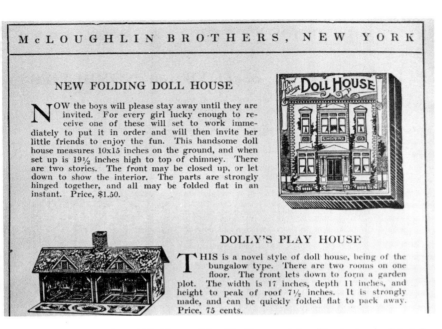

NEW FOLDING DOLL HOUSE

NOW the boys will please stay away until they are invited. For every girl lucky enough to receive one of these will set to work immediately to put it in order and will then invite her little friends to enjoy the fun. This handsome doll house measures 10x15 inches on the ground, and when set up is 19½ inches high to top of chimney. There are two stories. The front may be closed up, or let down to show the interior. The parts are strongly hinged together, and all may be folded flat in an instant. Price, $1.50.

DOLLY'S PLAY HOUSE

THIS is a novel style of doll house, being of the bungalow type. There are two rooms on one floor. The front lets down to form a garden plot. The width is 17 inches, depth 11 inches, and height to peak of roof 7½ inches. It is strongly made, and can be quickly folded flat to pack away. Price, 75 cents.

Illustration 180: The 1909 McLoughlin Brothers catalog illustrates and briefly describes the above two folding dolls' houses. *The New Folding Doll House* pictured in its box and *Dolly's Play House*, a bungalow, pictured erected.

Illustration 181: A Dunham Coconut Dining Room set of furniture, cutout, folded and glued. Uncut sheets of paper furniture, enough for four rooms, were obtained from the Dunham Coconut Company upon proof of purchase of their product. c.1900. The furniture is scaled at one inch to a foot. *Strong Museum Collection.*

cut out and pasted together. The titles in the series are as follows: *Dolls, Doll Houses, Furniture, Soldiers, Animals* and *Trains*.

Going back to the first decade of the 20th century there were four groups of colorful furniture that could be obtained through the mail from the Dunham Coconut Company. Dunham's coconut could be purchased in half pound packets which were packed in a wooden box measuring 29 inches (73.7cm) long, 11¾ inches (29.9cm) wide and 7½ inches (19.1cm) deep. The outside walls of the crate are paper covered and marked with windows and a pattern of brick siding. Instructions on the back of the box explained how to carefully lift off the front lid. Inside the box were three dividers or floors, dividing the upright box into four rooms, one above the other. Each room was realistically decorated with lithographed paper creating a kitchen, dining room,

parlor and bedroom. A cake trade-mark label on each packet of coconut could be returned to Dunham, they in turn would send back a die-cut piece of printed cardboard furniture in a flat form, ready to be folded and assembled. Printed on the back of each piece of furniture was a list of the other available pieces, each numbered for ordering ease. To obtain the twenty-odd pieces of available furniture, a family had to order quite a bit of coconut. **(Illustration 181.)**

Several other companies offered dolls' houses of paper and cardboard. The Lettie Lane red brick house was published for use with a paper doll of the same name. Lettie Lane and the doll house were illustrated by Sheila Young. The house is a three-sided two-story house with a red brick exterior and a grey shingle pitched front roof with red brick chimneys at each end. The front of the house has a door and five windows, and each side

has four windows. The house measures 15 inches (38.1cm) high, 11⅜ inches (28.8cm) wide and 10 inches (25.4cm) deep. It was published by the George W. Jacobs & Company of Philadelphia, Pennsylvania, and was copyrighted in 1909. **(Illustrtion 182.)**

The R. Bliss Manufacturing Company of Pawtucket, Rhode Island, produced several colorful folding dolls' houses. These are not nearly as well-known as their collectible lithographed paper on wood houses. The folding houses were made of cardboard, hinged with cloth, and covered with lithographed paper. On March 12, 1895, Vincent W. Wilson of Pawtucket, Rhode Island, was issued a patent for a folding cardboard dolls' house. This patent was assigned to the R. Bliss Company on the same date. The patent was the basis for the folding houses that Bliss produced later. The Bliss folding house appeared in their 1911

Illustration 182: *The Lettie Lane Red Brick Doll House* was published exclusively for the *Lettie Lane* paper doll and her family. Published by George W. Jacobs & Company of Philadelphia, Pennsylvania, and copyrighted in 1909. The house is 15in high, 11⅜in wide and 10in deep (38.1 x 28.8 x 25.4cm).

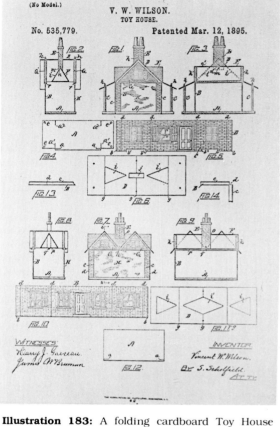

Illustration 183: A folding cardboard Toy House patented by Vincent W. Wilson of Pawtucket, Rhode Island, in 1895. The patent was assigned to the R. Bliss Company of the same city. The Bliss 1901 catalog did not offer a folding dolls' house, while the 1911 catalog offered four models. Whether any were offered between 1902 and 1910 is not known.

catalog, but did not appear in the 1901 catalog. Whether they appeared between 1902 and 1910 is a question. Their 1911 catalog offered four models, each with two stories and a peaked roof with a chimney. All four were similar in size, style, and color to their duplicated lithographed paper on wood houses. The smallest was 11 inches (27.9cm) high, 7½ inches (19.1cm) wide and 4½ inches (11.5cm) deep. The largest stood 19¼ inches (49cm) high, 13 inches (33cm) wide and 9 inches (22.9cm) deep. **(Illustration 183.)**

In 1914, magazines were offering folding cardboard dolls' houses as an inducement to subscribe to their publication. *Woman's World*, published in Chicago, Illinois, offered a "Collapsible Doll House" with a two-year subscription for the sum of $1.00. The house measured 17 inches (43.2cm) high, 17¼ inches (43.9cm) wide and 12 inches (30.5cm) deep. A quote from the description reads as follows: "Here is a Doll House that will please every child. It is made of heavy cardboard, lithographed in beautiful colors. Each of

the doors swing open and shut, the front windows are transparent. It is substantial, and when put together is rigid and as fine a Doll House as anyone would want." **(Illustration 184.)** A competing magazine, *The American Woman* of Augusta, Maine, featured a full-page color advertisement offering "Dolly's Home." **Illustration 185** pictures the upper half of the page illustrating the dolls' house. A partial quote from the rather lengthy copy follows: "May it not only fill your hearts with joy but may it sow the seeds of

Illustration 184: A *Collapsible Doll House* was offered in a 1914 issue of *Woman' World* magazine of Chicago, Illinois, as an inducement to subscribe to their publication. The house featured opening and closing doors, and transparent front windows. The erected house measured 17 x 17¼ x 12in (43.2 x 43.9 x 30.5cm).

Illustration 185: *Dolly's Home*, a folding cardboard house with six 6½in (16.5cm) paper dolls, each with three costumes and various household accessories. A total of 111 pieces, it was offered as an inducement to take two subscriptions to a magazine. Offer made by *The American Woman Magazine* of Augusta, Maine, c.1915.

love for home and all the delights of home making that in time will grow into those very qualities that make for the right kind of American citizenship." Also, "It is made of heavy cardstock in natural colors, bright red brickwork, with green tile roof and snow white woodwork and trimmings. The grounds are all laid out with beautiful flower beds and walks, while vines climb over the large swinging windows. It comes folded but is all ready to easily set up and to welcome your dollies at once. But this is not all, to go with this beautiful home we have added six 6½ inch (16.5cm) dolls with three complete costumes a piece and a number of accessories and toys." Finally, "Our offer, if you will send us two subscriptions to the *American Woman* at 50¢ each, we will send subscriber this magazine for one year, and will send you, prepaid, the doll house, six dolls and 111 piece outfit."

Two unusual cut-out booklets were published by Reilly & Britton Company of Chicago, Illinois — *Dolly Blossom's Bungalow* and *Dolly's Breakfast.* Both were designed by Will Pente and copyrighted in 1917 by the publisher. The front and back covers of *Dolly Blossom's Bungalow* is double folded thereby forming the four sides of the house. **(Illustration 186.)** One of a series called *Fold-A-Way-Toys*, with detailed instructions and graphics was offered on an inside page. Stiff paper pages, 9 by 12 inches (22.9 x 30.5cm) offered colorful interior furnishings, paper dolls and exterior features such as walks, flowering shrubs and trees, animals, and so on. All these items are printed double and fold at the top center, providing a front and a back. These same figures are equipped with a patented lock position standing base.

The second booklet, *Dolly's Breakfast,* is most unusual in its offering. It pictures a double page decorated tablecloth and a child-size china service with breakfast foods, ready for a make believe breakfast. All are double printed to show front and back and are equipped with the lock position stand that holds each piece in an upright position. **Illustration 187** pictures a coffee pot, a dish of cereal, and a bowl of fruit. The back inside cover of both booklets advertised other Fold-A-Way edi-

Illustration 186: *Dolly Blossom's Bungalow,* in booklet form, was published by the Reilly & Britton Company of Chicago, Illinois, and copyrighted in 1917. The front and back covers are double folded, thereby forming the four sides of the house. Stiff interior pages, 9 x 12in (22.9 x 30.5cm) offered the roof, chimney, paper dolls and furnishings.

tions: the *Story of Little Black Sambo* with cut-out of Sambo, his parents, and their jungle home, and a companion book titled *Peter Rabbit*, which offered uncut pages of Mr. McGregor and his garden along with Mopsy, Flopsy, Cotton Tail and Peter. A delightful and intensely interesting study in toy making, children could cut them out and assemble them, then could put them through all the escapades described in the original story.

A further example, *The Dick-Built House*, was manufactured by Hobard Rapon of Philadelphia, Pennsylvania, who received a patent for it on August 2, 1921. It consisted of a die-cut three-room first floor with a small peaked attic room in the center. **(Illustration 188.)** Another example, the *Kiddies Bungalow*, was constructed with six die-cut snap together sections. Copyrighted in 1922, it was published by the Douglas Manufacturing Company of Kansas City, Missouri.

The Dowst Manufacturing Company started making tiny cast white metal toys in 1878 and soon became a supplier of miniature prizes found in Cracker Jack boxes. In 1920 they began producing the Tootsietoy dolls' house furniture and it became a very popular play item for girls. In 1925 they developed a series of cardboard houses. Four architectural styles were offered, — a colonial house, a southern colonial house, a clapboard cottage and a Spanish style house, a clapboard cottage and a Spanish style house. All the exteriors had painted doors and windows, and the front windows are cut out and backed with isinglass sheets. Other exterior decoration included window boxes, shrubbery, and climbing roses and/or vines. Although the four houses vary slightly in size, all have a somewhat similar interior arrangement. All have two stories with five rooms plus a bathroom, and all have a stairway located either in a hallway or a room. Interior walls are not decorated, but the floors are decorated with printed rugs, while kitchen and bathroom floors are covered with printed patterns simulating linoleum. Few of these cardboard houses have survived the wear and tear of constant play, and fortunate is the person who has one in reasonably good condition.

Schoenhut, the well-known toy maker from

Illustrations 187: *Dolly's Breakfast* is a unique booklet of cut-outs featuring a child-size breakfast set. Cups and saucers, cereal bowls, coffee pot and more, are printed double to be folded at top center, and are equipped with a patented base. Published by the Reilly & Britton Company of Chicago, Illinois, in 1917. Booklet size is 9 x 12in (22.9 x 30.5cm).

Illustration 188: An original sales folder picturing *The Dick-Bilt House*, a folding cardboard house with color-printed interior and exterior. Patented, manufactured and offered for sale by Hobart DeLancey Rapson of Germantown, Pennsylvania, in the early 1920s. *Photo by Barbara Whitton Jendrick.*

Philadelphia, Pennsylvania, produced a knock-down dolls' house in 1933 and 1934. It was a two-story house with a peaked red roof with simulated tiles. The cream-colored front and sides are supported by grooved wooden corner posts. The facade has an opening front door and three die-cut white cardboard windows equipped with green shutters. The side windows are pasted on. The floors are heavy cardboard covered wth lithographed paper with a parquet design. The

house is 12 inches (30.5cm) high, 14¾ inches (37.6cm) wide and 7½ inches (19.1cm) deep when erected. Interior walls are a cream color without decoration. The back is open for play access.

During the 1950s when the Ginny doll was in vogue, a small cardboard Ginny house appeared along with a companion dog house. The die-cut corrugated bungalow featured slot and tab construction and was colonial in style. Basically

white with red trim, it had a blue shingle roof and was mounted on a green base. The house was landscaped with small evergreens and the white chimney was lightly covered with green vines. The one-room interior was undecorated. It was produced by the Container Corporation of America during the year 1957 only.

Chapter X.

THE THEATER AND THE TINSEL FIGURES

The toy theater provides various avenues of study, first as a toy, second as a study of the art of the theater, third as a reflection of the social and moral desires of its audiences, and finally as a record of the history of drama of the period.

As a toy, many a child of the late 18th and early 19th century spent hours of his or her leisure time captivated by the magic of the paper theater. The coloring of the characters and the scenery, pasting them onto cardboard, carefully cutting them out, then erecting the stage and the proscenium was a challenge. In some instances the lighting of the theater was provided by short candles or small oil lamps that stood in a row along the front edge of the stage, casting flickering lights on the small figures that were manipulated back and forth by the means of wire slides, or from wires overhead. Each country seemed to have its own method of producing the movement of the paper characters. The small booklet that was given with each play provided a printed dialogue, the scene setting for each act, and directions as to the movements of the various characters. Some of these booklets gave detailed methods for producing sound effects such as thunder, rain, marching men and cannon shots. After many rehearsals, reading the dialogue, and timing the movements of the characters, a child or sometimes a group of children were ready for the opening performance. Its success depended on how many people in the household could be convinced to attend, and then to present a smooth performance that would hold them in their seats. This was the most difficult problem a young producer faced, and unfortunately many an actual performance was never finished.

When one considers the paper theater as an art form, they should start with its birth in England, in 1811. It started in the form of a theatrical souvenir, an engraved sheet picturing costumed actors from a current play. While not originally published as cut-outs, the idea of cutting the figures out was soon conceived and a new paper toy product emerged. Publishers sent artists to the theaters to sketch the various actors and actresses in costume, to copy the actual scenery and the proscenium fronts. While the majority of those rendering the artwork were not well-known artists, they did authentically copy the stage fronts, the scenery, the characters, their costumes and dramatic poses. By the early 1820s complete toy theaters were available, all authentic copies of all phases of the original stage productions in miniature.

The "Tinseled Picture" was an interesting paper item in vogue in Great Britain during this same period and was closely related to the early growth of the paper theater. This practice, or craft developed from the theatrical portraits which also had originated in the early 1800s. These portrait sheets were prints of actors and actresses of the period, dressed as a particular character, and posed in a dramatic position. The sheets were labeled with the actor's name and the character he played. In the 1820s the idea of tinseling the theatrical portraits developed, and ten years later it became a popular pastime. Tinseling was a craft whereby the engraved portrait sheets were decorated by pasting various kinds of materials onto the costume surface. The face was left untouched, but the balance of the figure was decorated with metal foil, various fabrics, ribbons, leather, and feathers. As the interest in tinseling grew, the publishers began offering tinsel and other materials in ready cut shapes. Thus the later engraved sheets started to become somewhat similar, so that they would accept the already cut stick-on shapes that were available. They also tended to become over decorated. Many of the portraits would require as many as a 100 to a 125 paste-on pieces. The completed picture, in some cases a work of art, was usually framed and displayed for viewing. Many hours were put into these projects and, depending on the complexity of the decorations, quite a bit of money was expended for supplies. **(Illustration 189.)**

Turning back to our original line of thought that the toy theater provided various avenues of study, in this case it was the reflection of the social and moral desires of its audiences. The audience determined the type of play that was acceptable or unacceptable. In the 1700s, the English stage provided traditional verse drama which the limited wealthy audiences loved and accepted. By the end of that century this type of drama declined in popularity as a new kind of audience was developing. The period known as the Industrial Revolution was gaining momentum. New machines were producing products in great quantities — products that were formly handmade. People were moving from the rural areas to the cities; more people were working, and they had money to spend. These people looked for entertainment, and the stage presentations provided this for them. Existing theaters were enlarged, and new ones were built. The old drama, full of eloquent dialogue, was not to their liking. They demanded action, dancing, acrobatics, mystery, adventure, and historical battle episodes. Melodrama and pantomine took the place of the earlier traditional drama.

Early paper theater publishers were legion in England. William West was active from 1811 to

Illustration 189: A Tinseled Picture titled *Mr. King as Little John*, published by A. Park, 17 Leonard St., London, England. Dated November 22, 1811. Tinseling was a craft whereby the engraved sheet was decorated by pasting various kinds of materials on the costume surface. Materials such as metal foil, cloth, ribbons, fine leather and feathers were utilized. *Strong Museum Collection.*

1831, publishing about 140 plays. J.K. Green started working for West in 1811 and later went into business for himself in 1834. At that time he advertised himself as the "Original Inventor and Publisher of Juvenile Theatrical Prints, Established 1808." Green published many plays and was active until 1857. Hodgson & Company, who were in business from 1822 to 1830, published nearly 70 plays, most of which were slanted

towards children. **(Illustrations 190 & 191.)** Orlando Hodgson was active between 1832 and 1836 and published six new plays, Martin Skelt, in 1835, purchased the stock, copper plates and equipment of several other publishers and developed a very active business. Skelt used cheaper paper, published in volume, and developed an extremely fine method of distribution. **(Illustration 192 A - B.)** The Skelt family business

continued into the 1860s when it was taken over by W. Webb. **(Color Illustration 23.)** In 1860, J. Redington took over the earlier publisher J.K. Green's business and republished 19 plays. He, in turn, was succeeded by Benjamen Pollock, one of the last well-known English paper theater publishers.

Paper plays published after 1850 were, for the most part, similar in style to those produced in the first half of that century. While the English stage changed, the publishing of juvenile drama did not. Their printing practices remained old-fashioned, the engraving with copper plates continued, coloring was done by hand and later with stencils. Considering the methods used, the speed with which the engravings were colored with phenominal. It was not unusual for a publisher to offer a complete toy drama for sale four days after the opening night of an original play. By 1870, few toy theater publishers were active in England. The importation of the larger lithographed theaters from Germany furthered the decline. However, the paper drama sheets did leave a most complete pictorial record of the first half of the 19th century English stage, its actors, their costumes, and the scenery used.

It is recorded that the start of the toy theater in Germany and France originated in 1805, when sheets of characters in costumes were designed from plays of the period. However, in the 1803 G.H. Bestilmeier catalog we find the following paper theaters listed: No. 173 a Ombres Chinoise (Chinese Shadows) with various transparent presentations and 18 figures. **(Illustration 193.)** No. 58, a large theater with eight moving figures and many changes. No. 59, a large theater with all the changes and figures to be able to present the famous opera *The Magic Flute.* Unfortunately the publishers are unknown, the brief descriptions given above are as they appeared in the catalog. **(Illustration 194.)** As the years passed, the popularity and variety of the paper theaters increased. The German theaters and characters were of a larger size than those produced in England. **(Color Illustration 24.)** The plays were adapted from the dramas of the day, from operas, and from fairy tales. Originally written by famous

Illustration 190: An early Hodgson colored sheet of characters for the juvenile drama *The Maid and the Magpie*. Published by Hodgson & Company, 10 Newgate St., London, England, c.1825. *Strong Museum Collection.*

Illustration 191: Early hand colored juvenile drama sheet of characters for the play *Vision of the Sun*. Marked "Pub'd July 3, 1823 by Hodgson & Co. 40 Newgate St." London, England. *Strong Museum Collection.*

writers and composers, they were rewritten and adapted to the toy theater, J. Raab and C. Schramm of Nuremberg, Winckelmann & Sons and G. Kuhn both of Berlin, Joseph Scholz of Mainz, J.M. Hermann of Munich, and J.F. Schreiber of Esslingen were among the most prominent and prolific of the German paper theater publishers.

The box cover of the *Grand Theater* pictures an artistic representation of the famous Das Neue Theater located in Leipzig, Germany. A finely detailed photographed print of the theater itself reveals that it did not have the broad steps leading up to the columned entrance. Possibly the steps were added to the original building at a later date. **(Illustrations 195 & 196.)** The box cover carries the trade mark "AK," top center. Unfortunately I have not found a publisher with those initials. The box contains 44 beautifully colored characters ranging from beggars and housemaids to people of wealth, knights and royalty, a dog, and 24 accessories in the form of a variety of decorative props. Also included are two large back scenes, illustrated front and back, making four scenes, and an additional four matching side pieces illustrated front and back.

One of the most notable publishers of French toy theater sheets was Pellerin of Epinal who offered hundreds of sheets of theater material over its long production life. Theaters such as

145

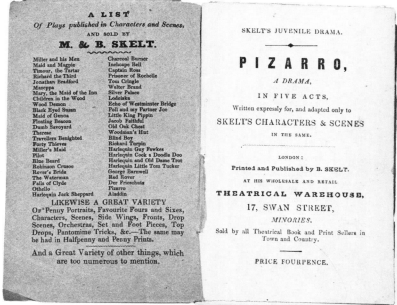

Illustration 192 A & B: A: Skelt's titled character sheet, one of eight, for the juvenile drama *Pizarro.* B: A list of the plays published by M & B Skelt, 17 Swan Street, Minories, London, England, c.1845. *Strong Museum Collection.*

Petit, Nouveau, Guignol, Francais, and *Grand Theater Nouveau,* were popular items. **(Illustration 197 A, B & C.)** The *Grand Theater Nouveau* was outstanding, being a large theater with a proscenium measuring 24¾ inches (63cm) high and 23 inches (58.4cm) wide. Its basic colors are orange-tan and tan with a lavender stage base and dome top. Decorative panels and wreath designs are alternately placed on the stage's front base. Statues on marble bases stand on either side of the stage, behind which double columns rise upwards and are surmounted by capitals holding a decorated frieze and a flat triangular pediment. The pediment is marked "Opera." Above this is a decorative grouping of musical instruments and sprays of leaves. At the central pinnacle are three cherubs, one with the mask of tragedy, one with a straight horn, and a third with a lyre. Deep red curtains with heavy gold braid are visable at the sides and the top of the proscenium opening. **(Illustration 198 A, B & C.)** Scores of senic backdrops depict town scenes, country landscapes, seascapes, and traveling fairs. Interior scenes of rooms are seen from the simple peasant home to the ornate splendor of a palace banquet hall. Also, costumed characters of all walks of life are included, all related to an assortment of plays. **(Color Illustrations 25 & 26.)**

In Denmark, one of the leading producers of paper theaters was a young Dane named Alfred Jacobsen, who started publishing theater sheets in the mid 1870s. A lithographer by trade, he combined his knowledge of printing with his interest in the Danish theater. Over the following 30-odd years he produced a large number of sheets that were equal in quality to those of any other juvenile theater publisher in the world. Jacobsen's early plays were based on old fairy tales, although a light political overtone sometimes filtered through them. Later the plays were divided into two trends — successful shows from the larger cities of Europe which he rewrote to suit the fancy of his Danish audiences, and plays based on legendary heroes and Danish patriotic incidents. While Jacobsen provided much of the artwork himself, he did use the talents of other artists to draw the striking prosceniums of the various Danish theaters, the character sheets, and the scenery used. All are positive records of the history of the Danish theater from 1875 to World War I.

The still standing, world renowned Tivoli Theater Copenhagen, Denmark was designed by Professor Vilhelm Dahlerup, and was erected in 1874. The Chinese theme in the design of the theater and the added feature of the novel peacock stage curtain is exceptional. When the curtain is lowered, the peacock folds it's tail and sinks below floor level to reveal the open stage, thus creating a lasting memory for anyone who has observed it. Generations of travelers from far points of the globe have been, and still are, enthralled by this fantasy. Alfred Jacobsen, the Danish lithographer, must have been enthralled and inspired with the new theater because he immediately produced a paper theater modeled after the prototype. The

model proved to be increasingly popular over the years, and appeared with slight variations until 1920 when it went out of print. This wonderful paper theater was republished in 1960, and it is this revived treasure that is pictured in **Color Illustration 27.** This boxed set includes the pictured stage, a light with battery, a secondary curtain, six background scenes, 16 die-cut characters or grouping of characters, six small metal stands, two metal stands mounted on stiff wires that are used to provide movement to the characters, and an eight-page pamphlet providing copy on the background of the original Tivoli Theater, the creation of the paper theater and three plays. The titles of the plays are *Pierrot's Calamities*, in three scenes; *Harlequin Mechanical Statue*, in four scenes; and *Pierrot Madly In Love*, in four scenes. All pieces are marked "Printed in Denmark, Vilhelm Prior." Prior was also a pioneer in the development of the Danish paper theater

sheets. This pantomime theater front measures 13¼ inches (33.7cm) high, 17½ inches (44.5cm) wide and 5¾ inches (14.7cm) deep.

In Japan, the paper theater was produced with the wood block printing style peculiar to that country. It originated as early as 1750 and enjoyed popularity until about 1920. Plays and scenes were, for the most part, taken from the famous Kabuki dramas.

Another form of the juvenile theater was the *Ombres Chinoise*, a title given to the European shadow theater of the 18th through the 20th centuries. Its history predates that period, having first appeared in China before the time of Christ. It became a popular art form with the Chinese between 1000 and 1300 A.D. By 1300 it began to appear in other parts of the Far East, principally in Java. Considerable skill was required to make the jointed theater figures as the materials originally used were animal hides processed into

Illustration 193: No. 173, an *Ombres Chinoise* (Chinese Shadows) theater, as pictured in the 1803 G. H. Bestilmeier catalog. Georg Hieronimus Bestilmeier of Nurenberg, Germany.

Illustration 194: No. 58, a large theatre with moving figures and many scenery changes, enabling it to present the famous Mozart opera, *The Magic Flute*. It was offered in the 1803 Bestilmeier catalog.

Illustration 195: Cover of a box containing the *Great Theatre for Children*. The illustration represents the famous Das Neue Theater located in Leipzig, Germany. The box set contains a theater, 44 characters, 24 props, scenery and side pieces. Box cover carries the trademark "AK." Germany, c.1880.

parchment, cut into shape, and decorated. Moving limbs were loosely secured by small pivots, and the manipulating rods were made of buffalo horn. The actual performance of a play required a highly trained and skilled puppeteer, one that could manipulate a large number of puppets to perform life-like movements which were cast as shadows on a screen from a light behind. These movements were made in time to accompanying music, which sometimes lasted for hours. The shadow theaters of China, Java, Thailand, and later Greece and Turkey, were mainly for adult audiences. They served many purposes other than entertainment, such as moral instruction, an offering to the gods, acts of purification, or the aversion of an impending calamity.

When the shadow theater was introduced in Europe it was aimed at entertaining adults, but later became a toy for children. **(Illustration 199.)** At this time the figures, some still jointed for movement, were cut out of black cardbaord. **(Illustration 200.)** Highly colored prosceniums framing a semi-transparent white screen were offered by a variety of publishers in Germany, France, England, and Denmark. **(Color Illustration 28.)** Some were sold in boxed sets containing a folded stage setting, a number of pre-cut silhouette figures, and a playbook giving the story line. The silhouettes were made up of people from all walks of life, animals, transportation vehicles, trees, and flowers. The *Ombres Chinoise* was also offered in a construction form. An example is a small book containing 144 pages, which is in the author's collection. It is an early paperback book titled *Theatre des Ombres Chinoises, Paris, Le Bailly Edit., 15 Rue de Tournon.* **(Illustration 201.)** A brief introduction deals with the development of the shadow theater in France, the construction of a homemade shadow theater, the cutting out of silhouette sheets (in this case sheets published by Pellerin & Cie), their means of movement and manipulation, and a listing of nine plays. The balance of the book is made up of nine complete plays, scene by scene. On the back cover of the book is a listing of 46 shadow theater titles published by Pellerin for use in the Ombres Chinoise Theater. **(Illustration 202.)**

In the United States, the paper theater never came close to the level of popularity it enjoyed in Europe. A booklet of a play in three acts titled *The Pirate of The Florida Keys*, brings to light one of the earliest publishers of American paper theaters. The *Seltz's American Boys Theater*, published by Scott & Company of New York City, lists seven plays, the majority of which seem to have a strong British influence. **(Illustration 203.)** Unfortunately I have not seen any of Scott & Company's plays or associated materials other than the play booklet mentioned above. A patent for a toy theater was issued to a J.W. Scott of New York City on December 11, 1877.

J.H. Singer of New York City patented what he called a "Toy Theatrical Stage" on May 15, 1883. The stage was a solid wood slab with parallel grooves running across stage from left to right. The balance of the theater, with the exception of the cloth drop curtain, was cardboard and colorful lithographed paper. The proscenium was placed up front, side scenes or wings placed at set grooves which were numbered or lettered for use, as found in the accompanying direction sheet.

Illustration 196: Photograph of the original *Das Neue Theater* in Leipzig, Germany, 1864-1867. Compare with picture on the box cover of **Illustration 195**, one with steps, one without.

Illustration 197 A - C: Three theater sheets published by Pellerin of Epinal, France, c.1890. **A:** *Theatre Guignol*, a traveling show on a Moyennes Constructions sheet measuring 11⅝ x 15¾in (29.5 x 40.1cm). **B:** *Theatre Des Marionnettes* on a Grandes Constructions sheet measuring 15¼ x 19⅜in (38.8 x 49.2cm). **C:** *Petit Theatre, Theatre Français*, on a Grandes Constructions sheet, same measurements as **B.**

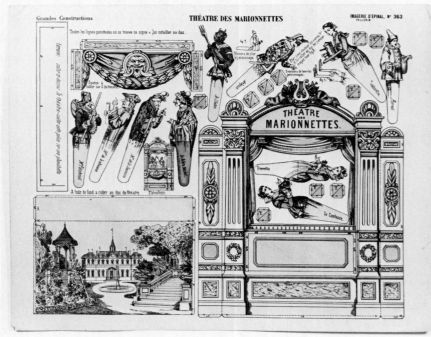

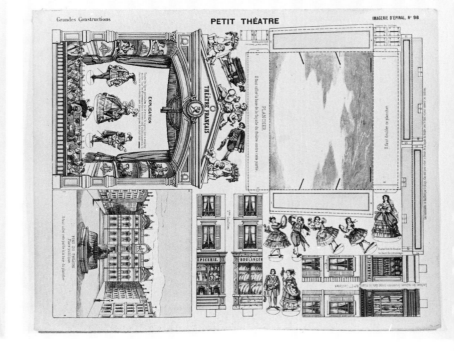

Illustration 198 A - C: Three theater sheets published by Pellerin of Epinal, France, c.1880. **A:** *Grand Theatre Nouveau*, a large theater printed in soft tan, orange tan, red and lavender. The proscenium measures 24¾in high and 23in wide (63.0 x 58.4cm). **B** & **C:** Two colorful sheets picturing draped front curtains to be used with the Grand Theatre. Sheet size 13 x 16¾in (33.0 x 42.6cm).

Illustration 199: A colorful example of a shadow theater, Ombres Chinoises, in the form of a vertical panorama. Moved by turning the small brass cranks on the upper and lower left side of the box-like proscenium. A continuous roll of unrelated scenes may be reviewed as one of the cranks is turned. Marked on the box cover, "Saussine, Edit. Paris" and "Lith. H. Jannin, Paris." c.1875. Overall size of toy 12⅞ x 16⅛ x 2in (32.7 x 40.9 x 5.1cm).

The background scenery fit into the rear groove. The cut-out characters and smaller props worked in intermediate grooves running through the center stage, and were manipulated on and off stage by a thin wire. Singer produced two sizes of theaters, the *Theater Royal* was 12 inches (30.5cm) wide and 8½ inches (21.6cm) deep, and the *Theater Imperial*, which was 15¼ inches (38.8cm) wide and 11¼ inches (28.6cm) deep. Plays such as *Red Riding Hood, Cinderella, Jack the Giant Killer,* and *Blue Beard* were offered in three scenes. *Beauty and The Beast, Sleeping Beauty, The Young Soldier, Pocahontas, Robinson Crusoe,* and *The Battle of Bunker Hill* were

issued in four scenes. **(Illustration 204.)** Singer's play *The Battle of Bunker Hill* consisted of four scenes. Scene I pictures a street in early Boston, Massachusetts (one side of a two sided background, picturing a cobblestone road with shops and dwellings on either side). Three colonists, Warren, Prescott, and Putnam, stand in the foreground discussing the hardships of living in Boston under the surveillance of the British troops, and how the colonial troops are mustering, gathering munitions and supplies in nearby Concord, Massachusetts. Scene II uses the same background, but a guardhouse and a squad of British soldiers are added to the stage. The

British generals, Gage, Clinton, and Howe stand in the foreground discussing their recent setback at Concord, and how the colonists fight unfairly, firing from behind walls and trees. Also, that Washington is on his way to lead the rebels and how they, the British, must plan the next move to defeat them. Scene III reverts back to Scene I. General Clinton and Doctor Warren discuss how the colonial troops are preparing for a showdown. Clinton feels the British are tired of fighting and will not show much effort. Doctor Warren disagrees, feeling the British will fight bitterly, although he feels they will ultimately be defeated. In Scene IV the background scene is reversed, showing the colonists in the background charging the British in the foreground, this is the Battle of Bunker Hill.

McLoughlin Brothers' *American Theater* appeared in their 1908 and 1919 catalogs. Set up, it measures 12 x 15 x 12½ inches (30.5 x 38.1 x 31.8cm). The proscenium is lithographed in color and contains a roll-up curtain. The stage floor is varnished wood with grooved cuts running cross stage, in the same manner as the stage used by Singer. Both the proscenium and the base are marked "Copyright 1901." Plays such as *Little Red Riding Hood, Puss In Boots, Sleeping Beauty,* and *Alice In Wonderland* were offered in 1911. **(Color Illustration 29.)**

Another paper theater from around 1900 was the *Fairy Theater* published by J. Ottmann Litho Company of New York City. The proscenium has white columns on each side with gold vinelike designs coiled around them. At the top of each column is a woman's head, one depicting comedy and the other tragedy. The curved top piece holds four cherubs surrounding a shield-shaped central ornament with the words "The Fairy Theater." Folding side pieces picture females in flowing robes playing with winged cherubs. The curtain is a warm red with tasseled gold braiding.

Playthings magazine from the mid 1920s advertised a theater called "Hollywood Dollies Theater." It was described as having a perfectly proportioned stage. It listed 150 movie stars of the period offered in paper doll form, each doll having four costumes designed exclusively for the films in which the star played. A sales pitch in the advertisement read, "130 million people attend the movies each week, these people are all possible customers." The theater, paper dolls, and costumes were published by Hollywood Dollies Inc., of 723 Seventh Avenue, New York City. The large uncut theater sheet, measuring 44 by 49½ inches (111.8 x 125.8cm), was lithographed by the Grinnell Lith. Company of New York City. It pictured a rather plain but colorful Greek-style proscenium with a fold back stage floor, a background scene of a high vaulted ceiling of a living room with a fireplace, a large window with luxurious blue draperies and a covered valance to match, plus a tall double door with diamond shape panes. Assembling instructions were printed on the sheet. The paper was of a heavy quality, yet the instructions state that it should be mounted on heavy cardboard. The proscenium, when erected, stands 22 inches (55.9cm) high and 32 inches (81.3cm) wide.

T. Mathews & Company of New York City and London, England, produced the *Empire Vaudeville Theater*. This was a die-cut model theater which could be erected instantly by pressing the various sections into position, such sections held firmly together by tabs and slots. Included were eight performers with jointed arms and legs, made to perform by inserting a hooked wire into a linen patch mounted on the back of each head, and manipulated from the back of the stage. An *Animated Circus* with four moving animal acts, and an *Animated Nursery* with six activated nursery rhyme figures, were also offered by the Mathews company. Both were offered with a snap together proscenium and stage, all die-cut and in embossed colors. **(Illustration 205 A & B.)**

The *Popeye Thimble Theater* with its cast of Popeye, his sweetheart Olive Oyl, the baby Sweetpea, Wimpy the hamburger lover, and the giant Toar, was an offspring of the comic strip *Thimble Theater*. Cartoonist Elzie Segar had created the strip ten years before Popeye was introduced in 1929. He immediately became the leading character and was accepted the world over as an underdog, a fighter, a do-gooder with a temper, and a sailor who convinced a lot of children to eat

Illustration 200: An uncut sheet of tradesmen, vendors and street people in the form of silhouette figures. Marked "Chinesche Schimmen, publisher Erve Wijsmuller." Germany. c.1870. Sheet size 13½ x 17in (34.3 x 43.2cm).

spinach. The *Popeye Thimble Theater* and its group of characters was published in the early 1930s. It is colorful, die-cut, and extremely difficult to find. It is a simple, plain theater with a lot of nostalgic appeal. **(Illustration 206.)**

Various magazines have contributed numerous cut-out theater construction projects, scenery, characters, props, and play scripts over the years. One prominant example is a series issued by *The Delineator* in 1918 and 1919, called *The Delineator Children's Theater*. Such titles as *Robinson Crusoe, Snow White, Cinderella, Jack and the Beanstalk, Launcelot and Elaine,* and *A Valentine Romance* appeared

monthly. Each play was presented on a full-color page drawn by Robert McQuinn. Each pictured a plain proscenium with appropriate background scenery at the top third of the page, four to nine characters in the center, and additional scenery, wings, and props in the lower third. Complete assembling directions and the text of the play was found on another page noted on the theater sheet. Also noted was: "Extra copies of this page, printed on heavy paper without lettering on the other side, may be obtained by sending five cents to the Picture Editor, care *The Delineator*, New York." **(Illustrations 207 A - D.)**

THÉATRE DES OMBRES CHINOISES

Paris, LE BAILLY Édit. 15 Rue de Tournon.

Illustration 201: The cover of a 144-page book which contains information about the shadow theaters. It includes the history, construction of a theater, the method of cutting the silhouettes, their means of movement and manipulation and nine complete shadow theater plays. Published by Le Bailly, Paris, France. c.1875. Book size is 6 x 3¾ x 1/2in (15.2 x 9.6 x 1.3cm).

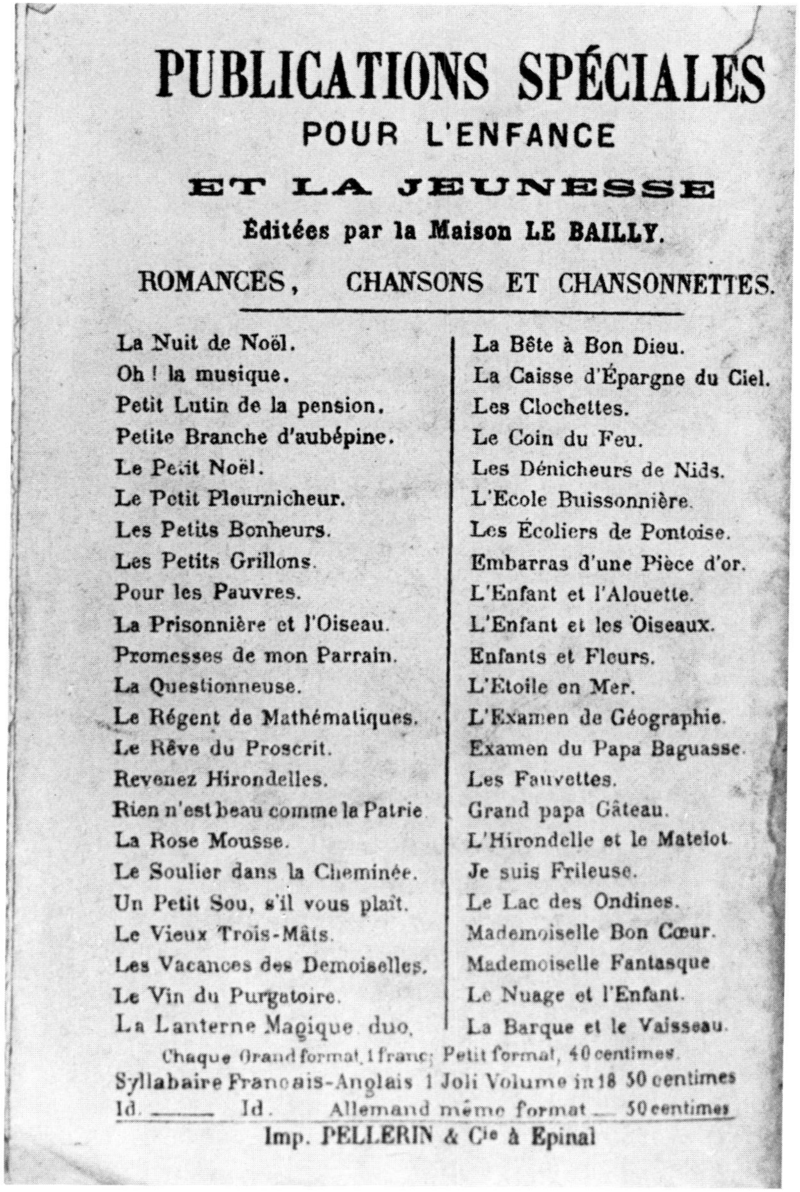

Illustration 202: The back cover of the book, *Theatre des Ombres Chinoises*, published by Le Bailly. It lists 46 shadow theater titles published by Pellerin for use in a shadow theater. c.1875.

SELTZ'S
American Boys' Theatre.

DIRECTIONS FOR PERFORMING.

I will commence at the beginning and tell you how to make your stage. This, of course, may be made very elaborately, and a boy of mechanical genius can easily improve on the following simple directions. All that is actually necessary is a flat board for the floor of the stage, with a post at each corner, and cross pieces at the top to hold them together. A ledge should be fastened to the front to hold the footlights and musicians, as shown in the cut. The sides of the floor and the top piece directly over should be cut with a saw, to the depth of an eighth of an inch, to hold the scenes and side wings. The proper proportion of each piece is given on the diagram. The appearance

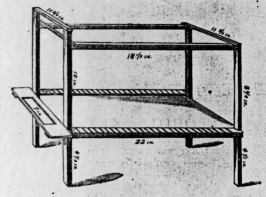

of the stage will be much improved if a proscenium is glued on the front. This can be bought at any bookstore for ten cents.

The sheets forming the play should all be carefully pasted on card board, the scenes on rather heavier card than the characters, which latter should be of good quality, as all the characters have to be neatly cut out leaving a piece of the blank paper under their feet about a quarter of an inch deep, and extending from toe to toe. The name of each character, with the number attached, should be pasted on its back. The performance of the play is much facilitated by keeping the characters used in the different acts together. The book of words will show you when and on which side the characters are to be put on and taken off the stage. The best plan is to have two boys to perform the play; one moving the characters on or off, and the other reciting the speeches.

SCOTT & CO.,
PUBLISHERS OF
Seltz's American Boys' Theatre,

146 FULTON STREET, NEW YORK CITY.

The following Plays, complete in 16 sheets of scenes, characters, wings and book.

PRICE, 25 CTS. PLAIN, 50 CTS. COLORED.

The Miller and his Men.
Sir Launcelot and Guinevere.
The Pirates of the Florida Keys.
Redheaded Jack, the Terror of London.
The Boy Sailor; or, The Pirate's Doom.
The Red Skeleton; or, The Dead Avenger.
The Fiend of the Rocky Mountains. (Pantomime.)

Scott & Co. have a large stock of

STAGES AND SETTINGS

All made expressly for the above.

Stages, 22x12x15 in ....price, $1 00
Oil Footlights.. " 50
Gas Footlights... " 1 00
Rubber Gas Tubes to connect with burners, per foot.................. " 15
Proscenium, colored... " 10
Slides, per doz.. " 35
Long Slides, per doz... " 45

Scott & Co. would caution the public against purchasing worthless imitations, as the plays of SELTZ's AMERICAN BOYS' THEATRE are the only miniature theatricals ever published, giving full directions for working, &c. Every piece of this admirable series is put together and tested by professionals before being issued to the public, insuring the correct working of every piece.

Published only by SCOTT & CO., 146 Fulton Street, New York, where everything connected with the plays can be had, wholesale and retail. The plays can also be had of all Booksellers and Newsdealers, in the U. S., and wholesale of THE AMERICAN NEWS CO. Be sure and ask for, and take none but SELTZ'S EDITION

Illustration 203: Two pages from an instruction folder regarding *Seltz's American Boys' Theatre*. Directions explain how to make the theater frame, how to cut out figures and scenery, and several play performing hints. Also listed are the plays available and a price list of accessories. c.1878.

Illustration 204: The proscenium of the *Theater Imperial* published by J. H. Singer of New York City. On stage is the final scene of the play, *The Battle of Bunker Hill*. c.1885. The theater is 12in high, 15¼in wide and 11¼in deep (30.5 x 38.8 x 28.6cm).

Illustration 205 A & B: Two examples of children's die-cut theaters produced by the T. Mathews & Company of New York City and London, England, c.1920. Erected instantly by pressing the various sections into position; the sections are held firmly together by tabs and slots. Both measure 9½in high and 12in wide (24.2 x 30.5cm).

Illustration 206: The *Thimble Theater Mystery Playhouse* appeared in the early 1920s. The composition characters include *Popeye*, his sweetie *Olive Oyl* and *Wimpy*. American. Manufacturer unknown.

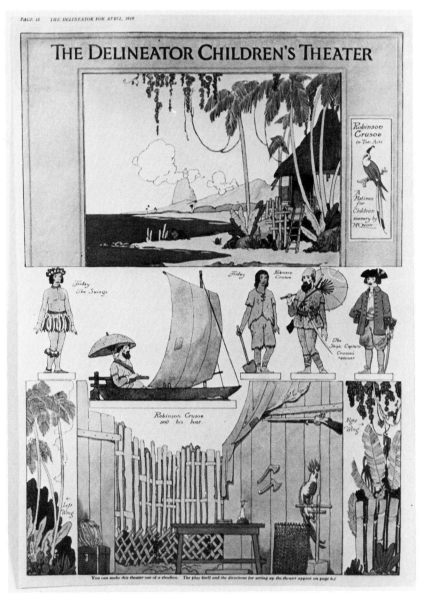

ABOVE AND FOLLOWING PAGE: Illustration 207 A - D: Four pages from *The Delineator* magazine. A portion of a series titled *The Delineator's Children's Theater*, which appeared in 1918 and 1919. The characters and scenery pictured are from the plays *Launcelot & Elaine*, *Robinson Crusoe*, *Snow White* and *Jack and the Beanstalk*.

160

Chapter XI.

THE CIRCUS, THE CLOWNS AND THE SIDE SHOWS

In every paper toy collection that is viewed, there appears to be a sampling of circus-related material. This is as it should be, whether you have a deep interest in the circus or not. Everyone is immediately fascinated when observing a skilled performer on a trapeze, an unusual clown act, an elephant performing a difficult routine, or a tiger leaping through a blazing hoop. People of all ages have enjoyed circus acts and parades throughout history.

One of the earliest examples of showmanship was recorded on a fresco excavated at Cnossus on the Island of Crete. It pictures three young people and a bull taking part in an ancient stunt, Bull Leaping. Performed in an arena, the leapers waited for the challenge of a wild bull. As the bull charged with head lowered, the nearest leaper would grasp the horns and would swing upward turning a somersault and be caught by a fellow performer behind the moving animal. These young acrobats would perform this act in a continuous sequence of dodging, leaping, and catching, a performance that required great courage, daring, and skill. Historians have dated this ancient fresco to 2,400 B.C.

Ptolemy II, ruler of Egypt, devoted much of his wealth in establishing a zoological collection. He gathered animals and reptiles from the far corners of the then known world. It became a custom to parade many of these exotic beasts with much pageantry before the people at important religious festivals. It is known that the Greeks and the Romans held the training of animals in high esteem. During these same periods, men and women trained themselves in acrobatics, juggling, rope walking and other feats of skill, to entertain in exchange for a few tossed coins. These few acts, plus numerous others, are the history of what we know as the circus today.

George Speaight, in the introduction to his book *A History of The Circus*, states that the circus is an international art, its development taking place in many countries over a long period of time. He states that while the circus as we know it today originated in England, it was later influenced by the circus in America, which was somewhat different from other circuses of the world. The circus of today was originated in 1773 by a Philip Astley, who is known as "the father of the circus." Astley brought together the various elements that make up a circus: feats of skill, animal training, and comedy acts, all performed in a ring. In 1780, he introduced a clown on horseback, and clowns have been a part of the circus ever since.

In America, during the early 18th century, show people of all kinds appeared: acrobats, strong men, horsemen, and animal trainers. The first lion appeared in 1716; performing monkeys in 1751; the first elephant in 1796. Some animals were trained, others were simply exhibited as curiosities. In 1793, John Bill Ricketts, an Englishman, established the first circus in America. The first American born circus owner was James W. Bancher, who appeared in 1824 with Bancher's New York Circus. By 1828 there were 17 circuses in America. As America's frontier moved westward, so did the traveling circus. As the growth of the circus in Britain, Europe, and America developed, it was natural that the circus theme should appear in toys in various parts of the world. It is in this category that paper toys are well represented.

Some nice examples of circus scenes are found in an action book published by Schaller & Kirn of Furth, Bavaria. Titled *To the Fair! To the Fair!*, it contains three perspective pictures, with moveable figures and verses for the amusement of good children. No. 1, folded, pictures the en-

Illustration 208: The entranceway to *Kreuzberg's Renowned Menagerie*, from the moveable book titled *To The Fair! To The Fair!*. Published by Schaller & Kirn of Furth, Bavaria, c.1875. Page size is 14¼ x 11½in (36.3 x 29.2cm).

Illustration 209: *In The Menagerie,* pictures one of the busy scenes inside *Kreuzberg's Renowned Menagerie.* A fold-out picture done in brilliant color is accompanied by verses in the foreground. c.1875. Fold-out page size 8¼in high, 11½in wide and 14¼in deep. (21.0 x 29.2 x 36.3cm).

walking upright on their hind legs. The background pictures a trainer with a hoop and three dogs, whom he is enticing to jump through the hoop. An assistant holds a stepladder with a poodle perched on top, and in the back top center is another dressed dog swinging on a trapeze. No. 3, in folded position, pictures the entranceway to *Kreuzberg's Renowned Menagerie.* **(Illustration 208.)** Opened it reveals a jungle-type enclosure containing several cages of wild animals. In the foreground is a cut-out giraffe, a large bird cage, a parrot, and three groups of interested spectators **(Illustration 209.)** All this is done in brilliant color, and each scene is accompanied by a companion verse printed in English in the foreground.

A second example is in the form of a fold-out panorama. Titled the *Great Menagerie,* it was published by J.S. Schrieber & Company for the English speaking market. It features six fold-out panels: *The Lion Tamer* **(Illustration 210)**, and *The Aquarium,* featuring a fold-out transparent pool containing a variety of sea life. The third panel, the *Snake Charmer,* pictures a cut-out family peering into a booth containing a woman performer with snakes coiled around each arm, her neck, and her waist. A colorfully dressed black witch doctor dances in the rear. Another panel features a fold-out cage and is titled *Tigers & Monkeys.* The next panel pictures a cut-out elephant who has just removed the hat from an enraged onlooker, who in turn is trying to beat the elephant with his closed umbrella. This amusing fold-out is titled *Jumbo.* **(Color Illustration 30.)** The last panel pictures two little girls looking into a fold-out cage of monkeys, titled *Our Ancestors.*

A single fold-out from France featuring a trainer, a monkey, and several dogs is titled *Le Cirque Corvi.* It is marked "A. Capendu, Editeur, Paris." It is one of a series mentioned elsewhere in this book. Opened, it reveals a brightly colored proscenium with a trainer in a clown costume, a dog firing a cannon, a monkey in a military uniform riding on the back of a dog, and a third dog pulling a miniature coach containing two costumed dogs. This small scene measures 7¾ inches (19.8cm) high, 10 inches (25.4cm) wide

trance of a typical European circus building. The open position reveals the interior arena by looking through a colorful proscenium. The act consists of male and female equestrians standing on the backs of a pair of galloping horses. Other performers include a ringmaster, a female trainer, and two clowns holding large paper-covered hoops. Two couples and three children are positioned in front, watching the performance. The audience is painted on the background. No. 2, folded, pictures a second entranceway to a hall of entertainment. Opened, it reveals a second proscenium with two rows of people in the foreground looking at a stage containing two performers with a group of dogs. Three of the cut-out dogs are dressed in fancy clothing and are

Illustration 211: A pull-up scene, four tiers deep, picturing a circus performance within a colorful proscenium. Titled *Le Cirque Corvi*, it is marked "A. Capendu, Editeur, Paris" (France). Opened it measures 8¾in high, 10½in wide and 12⅜in deep. (22.3 x 26.1 x 31.4cm).

and 5 inches (12.7cm) deep. **(Illustration 211.)**

Mention was made earlier of the beautiful cards offered as supplements in the magazine *Poupée Modèle* in the chapters on "Paper Dolls" and "Cardboard Dolls' Houses, Room Settings & Their Furnishings." In the late 1880s they offered a set of thirteen 11 by 7 inch (27.9 x 17.8cm) cards, colorfully illustrating a complete circus set up. It includes a circus ring, animals, performers of all kinds, clowns, a circus band, rows of seated

Illustration 210: *The Lion Tamer* is one of six fold-out panels of a panorama titled the *Great Menagerie*. Published by J.S. Schrieber of Esslingen, Germany, c.1885. Each panel measures 13 x 8¾in and opens out to 3½in (33.0 x 22.3 x 8.9cm).

audience, and aristocrats sitting in box seats. Also included is a triangular sheet of light tan colored paper which shows the floor plan with exact markings as to where the cut-out pieces should be placed. This floor plan measures 25 inches (63.5cm) wide and is 14½ inches (36.9cm) deep. The 8½ inch (21.6cm) diameter center ring is unmarked, leaving the young builder to place and replace the numerous performers and animals at his discretion. In all there are 35 performers consisting of clowns, bareback riders, balancing acts, jugglers, and animal trainers. There are also two elephants, two pigs, and 12 horses which supplement the various acts. Unfortunately it is impossible to picture all 13 cards, although they are worth the space. However we will illustrate three cards. **Illustration 212** shows the people at the entrance, with excitement on their faces, watching the dancing girls who are entertaining them while they wait for the circus performance to start. **Illustration 213** shows the

Illustration 212: The exterior to a circus, with people waiting for the next performance to start. The dancing girls and a huckster are trying to entice passerbys to purchase tickets. One of 13 cards published as card supplements to *Poupée Modèle*, c.1895. Card size is 11 x 6⅞in (27.9 x 17.4cm).

Illustration 213: A view of the circus show exit shows bandsmen seeking the attention of passing pedestrians, while the clowns try to convince people to buy tickets for the next performance. One of 13 cards making up a French circus published for *Poupée Modèle*, c.1895. Card size 11 x 6⅞in (27.9 x 17.4cm).

exit ramp, with three clowns making merry and trying to entice some of the onlookers to buy tickets for the next show. Three bandsmen and a climbing monkey lend their efforts to support the clowns. At the top of both of these cards you will notice some of the animals and performers who are part of the act. **Illustration 214** shows one of

two similar cards picturing a row of the various citizens of France, while above sit members of the upper class, all apparently enjoying the performance.

An early uncut sheet picturing several performers, animal acts, and numerous circus props is shown in **Illustration 215.** This hand colored

sheet displays the use of egg white for the purpose of highlighting some of the figures. While this is highly appealing to the eye, it sometimes presents a problem when photographing. Unfortunatley the publisher of this sheet is unknown.

The *International Circus*, created by Lothar

Illustration 214: Views of the spectators watching the various circus acts, the commoners on the benches below, the wealthy in box seats above. The third of 13 cards depicting a French circus. Published for *Poupée Modèle*, c.1895. Card size 11 x 6⅞in (27.9 x 17.4cm).

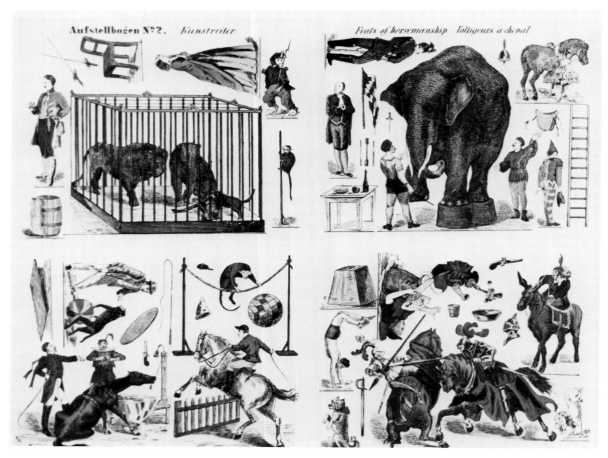

Illustration 215: A sheet picturing various circus acts and feats of horsemanship. Marked "Aufstellbogen No. 2," publisher unknown, c.1865. Sheet size 14 x 17⅝in (35.6 x 44.8cm).

Meggendorfer is possibly one of the finest examples of a paper toy with a circus theme. It was first published by J.F. Schreiber in 1887, and today is considered one of the top collectible action books. This panorama-type book opens to reveal six foldout scenes featuring various circus acts. Each act is accompanied by such captions as: "Mr. Funtolo performs on his horse as he leaps over a flaming gate"; "Clara Springel leaps and somersaults through a loop"; "Miss Ella rides her stately horse while the clowns have trouble riding their

donkey"; "The Sultan's Courier straddles his galloping horses"; "The clever acrobats of the Oriental Company perform amazing balancing tricks"; and "The Brabo family show their graceful skill riding bareback on two horses." This fabulous piece when opened out measures 13 inches (33cm) high, 52½ inches (132.1cm) wide and 4 inches (10.2cm) deep. **Color Illustration 31** pictures a reproduction of the original which was issued in 1982.

A fine example of a mechanical circus toy may

be found in Chapter XIII. (**Illustration 245.**) This pictures an uncut sheet of a Turner or a bar acrobat, with his traveling troup, performing for a group of children. This construction sheet, when cut and assembled, becomes a sand toy — one that is activated by falling sand. In this case it provides movement to the acrobat on the bar. This sheet was published by J.F. Schreiber of Esslingen, Germany, about 1910.

The French publisher Pellerin & Cie. issued an interesting bit of scenery for his *Grand Theater Nouveau* that portrayed a circus theme. The traveling circus, along with its associated forms of entertainment, is pictured with the town buildings in the background. The well-dressed townspeople and their children meander through the streets, some taking part in the festivities, some just looking. The ball tossing booth, the entrance to the circus arena, the round-a-bout, the climbing pole, and the booth of strange people and freaks, are all very typical of the traveling circuses that criss-crossed Europe. (**Color Illustration 32.**) A further Pellerin example is titled *Cirque Miniature*. This sheet makes up into a circular open-air structure with a shallow cone-shaped roof. The round floor, which rotates, holds four cut-out equestrians performing tricks on the outer perimeter. A ringmaster stands in the center with several performers doing balancing and juggling acts in a small circle around him. (**Illustration 216.**) Notice the detailed line drawing of the fully constructed toy, and the building directions printed in French in the upper right corner.

One of the earliest paper circus toys published in the United States was the *American National Circus* which appeared in 1858. The boxed set contains a wonderful elephant dressed in spectacular red, gold, and blue trappings, a horse with similar trappings, a bareback pony with a red, white, and blue bellyband, five equestrian figures, two changes of costume, and three decorative headpieces. This beautiful, highly colored set was designed and lithographed by J.G. Chandler of Roxbury, Massachusetts, and published by Brown, Taggard & Chase of Boston, Massachusetts. It is an accurate pictorial record of the

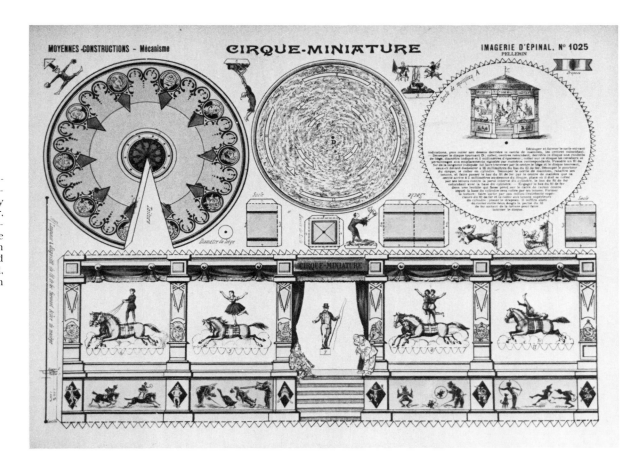

Illustration 216: The *Cirque-Miniature.* The sheet makes up into a round-a-bout. (See illustration of finished toy in upper right corner.) The round floor, which rotates, holds the four equestrians on the outer perimeter. The ringmaster stands in the center with the performers doing their acts around him. Published by Pellerin of Epinal, France, c.1890. Sheet size 11⅝ x 15¾in (29.5 x 40.1cm).

circus of the pre-1858 period when the equestrians were the featured performers. May it be noted here that the design and richness of color of this early lithographed set is one of only a few examples produced in the United States that can compare in quality with German sets of the same period. **(Color Illustration 33.)**

McLoughlin Brothers offered *The Lion's Den* from the Little Showman's Series in the early 1880s. It opens upward, forming a three-dimensional form for a cage in which a leaping lion

jumps through a hoop held by a lady trainer. **(Illustration 217.)** Three verses, titled *The Lion Queen*, are printed on the foreground base. This fold-out, in colors of yellow, tan, brown, red, pink, and light blue, measures 11¼ inches (28.6cm) high, 8 inches (20.3cm) wide and 11 inches (27.9cm) deep. In the same time period, McLoughlin published *The Monkey's Show.* A panorama type circus piece consisting of 12 panels illustrating humorous dressed animals imitating human circus performers. Its extended form is 8

inches (20.3cm) high and 12 feet (365.6cm) wide. **(Illustration 218.)**

The *Victoria Circus* was produced by J.H. Singer, and was patented on May 15, 1883. Its construction is very similar to the theaters produced by Singer in that it has a thick wooden base with a series of parallel cuts on it's surface. Thus the various colorful cut-out acts could be moved horizontally back and forth by means of pull wires or strings. The white cloth tent is held in position by three red poles in front, and a colorful cardboard background picturing a crowd enjoying the performance at the rear. **(Illustration 219.)** An accompanying bit of literature gives directions for setting up the tent, and further directions state: "Place the Parapet in the front groove, the Ringmaster in the center and arrange the figures and animals in the other grooves at will." The tent measures 12 inches (30.5cm) high,

12 inches (30.5cm) wide and 9 inches (22.9cm) deep.

A series of ten two-sided rocking cards featuring brightly colored, realistic circus acts are marked "Copyright 1913, by Syndicate Publishing Company, New York." Two excellent examples are pictured in **Illustration 220**. Others feature lady bareback riders presenting various trick perfor-

mances, tight rope performers, clowns, and various animal acts. The sizes vary slightly, but average 10 inches (25.4cm) high by 9½ inches (24.2cm) wide.

Uncle Bill's Big Circus was published by the M.R. Chesney Company of Kansas City, Missouri. Its most unusual feature is the folding and assembling of a most realistic circus tent, completely made of cardboard. When the animals are cutout, a strip along the back is left uncut and folded, leaving a standing two-sided animal.

Several magazines took advantage of the circus theme to develop children's interest in their publications. *A Cut-Out Circus for the Children* **(Illustration 221)** appeared in the July issue of the *Ladies Home Journal* in 1913. A fine example drawn by C. Durand Chapman, it was part of a series issued one per month. On examination of the illustration you will note that all the figures and props have a tab or two at their base. The caption, in fine print at the top center of the page, provides a reason for these tabs. It tells how to make a lazy-susan type cardboard ring that will support the tabbed figures: "To make the rings select a block of wood three inches square for the base. From stiff cardboard cut a circle 12 inches or more in diameter for a large ring, and one six or seven inches in diameter for a small ring. Cut small slits in both rings and put the two rings on top of wooden base with small ring on top and fasten through the center with a wire pin. Cut out the figures and stand them in the slits in the rings."

The second paragraph in fine print, bottom center, continues with these directions: "Cut small slits in all parts marked with dotted lines. The tabs on the feet of the figures and on the base of the objects will then fit in these slits, or the slits in the rings. If the objects are mounted on heavy paper they will stand better." It continues, suggesting where to place the performers on the ring, but finishes by stating that you can have great sport inventing new combinations yourself.

A large eight-page booklet titled *Circus Push-outs* was issued by the Platt & Munk Company of New York City. This type of die-cut push-out book was published by many other publishers, and

Illustration 217: Titled *The Lion's Den*, it is from the *Little Showman's Series*, published by McLoughlin Brothers of New York City in the early 1880s. It opens upward, forming a cage which contains a lion leaping through a hoop held by a lady trainer. Measures 11¼in high, 8in wide and 11in deep (28.6 x 20.3 x 27.9cm).

Illustration 218: The cover of a folding panorama titled *The Monkeys Show*. Consists of 12 panels illustrating dressed monkeys imitating human circus performers. Published by McLoughlin Brothers of New York City, c.1885. In its extended form it is 8in high and 12ft wide (20.3 x 3m 66cm).

covered many subjects. The center page spread of this circus book pictures a number of performers and trained animals mounted on half-round bases with fold-back tips which enable them to stand in an upright position. **(Illustration 222.)** In all there are 41 figures and animals, several props, such as tubs, balls, hoops, and flags, a ticket booth, and admission tickets.

The Walt Disney *Pinocchio Circus* uncut sheet measures 20 by 18 inches (50.8 x 45.7cm) and has a die-cut black top hat that a child might wear when playing the part of the ringmaster. The sheet is marked "1939 Walt Disney Productions." **(Illustration 223.)**

In 1945, The Citadel Press of New York City published a stiff page spiral-bound book titled *The Swinging Circus.* **(Illustration 224.)** This is a construction-type unique paper toy that is described in a quote from the directions: "With this book any child can put on an acrobatic show right in his own room. Take two chairs and put them a short distance from each other. Then take a piece of string and stretch it between the two chairs — thats your tight rope. Push the colored figures through the page — you will find that they have been cut for you. Then bend back the flaps which are marked 'fold back.' Hang the figures over the string, blow, and watch them swing." The

15 circus performers of *The Swinging Circus* were designed by Grace L. Schauffler. The figures vary slightly in size but average 8½ inches (21.6cm) high and 5½ inches (14cm) wide.

Throughout the book I have avoided the use of paper advertising material as I believe it is a field in itself. However, mention should be made of several large size push-out circuses issued by Lever Brothers of New York City, Post Cereals of Battle Creek, Michigan, and General Electric which produced a 60-piece *Big Top Circus* and a 65-piece *Wild West Rodeo*.

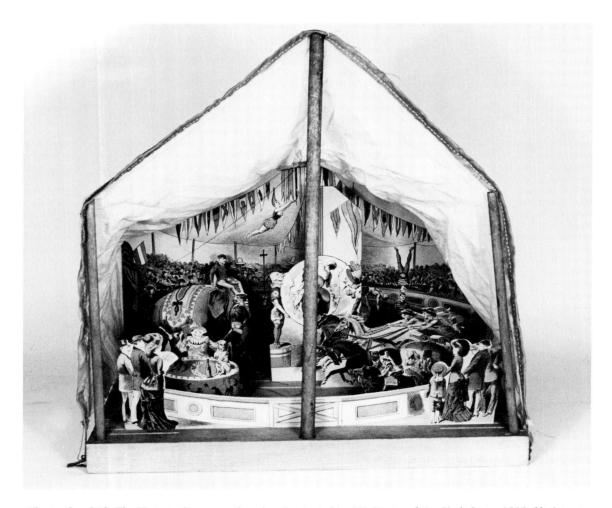

Illustration 219: The *Victoria Circus*, produced and patented by J.H. Singer of New York City, c.1883. Cloth tent, wood base, background, ring, flags, performers and animals are colorfully lithographed paper. The tent is 12in high, 12in wide and 9in deep (30.5 x 30.5 x 22.9cm).

Illustration 220: Two of a series of ten two-sided rocking cards that illustrate colorful circus sets. Marked "copyright 1913, by Syndicate Publishing Company, New York." Sizes vary slightly but average is 10in high x 9½in wide (25.4 x 24.2cm).

Illustration 221: *A Cut-Out Circus for the Children* appeared on a full page of the *Ladies Home Journal* magazine in July 1913. Drawn by C. Durand Chapman, it was one of a series that appeared monthly.

Illustration 222: A page from a booklet titled *Circus Pushouts*, published by the Platt & Munk Company, Inc., of New York City, c.1940. Eight large pages of colorful die-cut push-out performers, animals and props. Note half round bases with fold-back tips which enable figures to stand. Page size 12 x 10in (30.5 x 25.4cm).

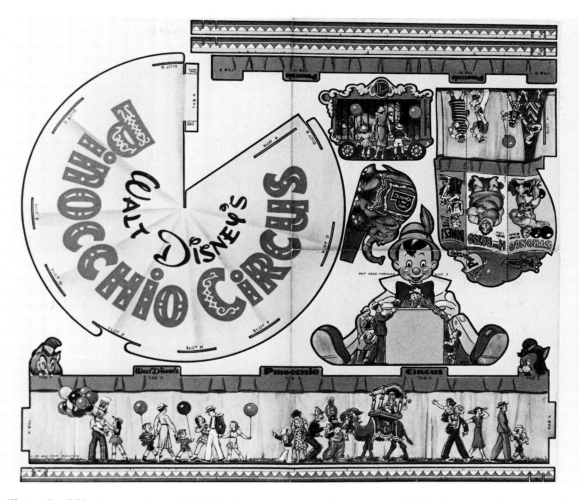

Illustration 223: An uncut sheet titled *Walt Disney's Pinocchio Circus.* Marked "1939 Walt Disney Productions." Accompanying the sheet is a die-cut black top hat that a child might wear playing the part of the ringmaster. Sheet size 18 x 20in (45.7 x 50.8cm).

Illustration 224: The cover of a construction book titled *The Swinging Circus*. The book contains 15 performers equipped with fold-back flaps so that they might be hung on a horizontal string. The figures are then blown on to make them spin or swing. Published by The Citadel Press of New York City, and copyrighted in 1945 by Grace L. Schauffler. The figures vary slightly in size but average 8½in high and 5½in wide (21.6 x 14.0cm).

Chapter XII.

CONSTRUCTION SETS, BUILDINGS & ZOOS

Early examples of construction sets are found in the 1800-1803 Bestelmeier catalog, along with a brief description. Some interesting sets are illustrated with the following copy: "No. 1031. The Great Church Festival; all is cut out of cardboard and beautifully painted, made to be assembled; there are also various boutiques with toys, many dancing peasants all in Nürnberg costumes, the musicians are on a stand; altogether 66 pieces in a beautiful box." A second example reads as follows: "No. 780. A Hunting Scene. It consists of the following pieces, which are cut out of cardboard and beautifully painted; two stags, one deer, five dogs, two hunters on horseback, 20 trees, shrubs and various other pieces, all packed in a beautiful box."

A slightly later example of a boxed set is titled *Zoological Garden* in five languages, and carries an identification mark "Verl Eigth, G.M." It is magnificent in detail and in depth of color. Consisting of 47 cut-out cards picturing people and animals of all kinds, a few are single units, many are in groups. Cut-outs ranging in size from a small porcupine measuring 1¼ inches (3.2cm) high by 3 inches (8.3cm) wide to a mid-size grouping of twelve exotic birds measuring 6¼ inches (15.9cm) high by 6¾ inches (17.2cm) wide, to a folding piece which represents the main entrance of the zoo and measures 9½ inches (24.2cm) high and 26 inches (66cm) wide. Each card is mounted on a wooden block, and each animal and bird is numbered. In all, some 99 species of animal and bird life are represented. All are hand colored and highlighted with egg white. **(Color Illustration 34.)**

A very complex model of the Cathedral at Köln (Cologne), Germany, could be constructed from a folder containing five folded sheets with 392

Illustraton 225: A drawing of the completed model of Der Dom zu Köln (Cathedral at Köln), Germany. This edifice could be constructed from the contents of a large folder containing five folded sheets on which are printed 392 parts, plus 30 figures. Unfortunately the publisher is unknown. c.1880. The finished model would measure 15in high, 14½in wide and 21½in deep (38.1 x 36.9 x 54.6cm).

uncut parts, plus 30 figures including church goers, an organ grinder, and two pedlars. Printed on large 28 by 17¾ inch (71.1 x 45.2cm) sheets, the colors run from cream through shades of brown, plus shades of blue to a blue green. The finished model would measure 14½ inches (36.9cm) wide, by 21½ inches (54.6cm) deep, and approximately 15 inches (38.1cm) high. **(Illustration 225.)** Instructions are printed in German on a fifth sheet, and assembling would require a lot of patience and previous model making experience. The finished project would be well worth the time and effort put into it. The attractive paper label on the heavy cardboard envelope is

Illustration 226: The face of the large folder containing the uncut parts to construct *Der Dom zu Köln*. Well marked in German, but not as to publisher. c.1880. Envelope size 14¾ x 18⅜in (37.6 x 46.6cm).

Illustration 227: A beautiful paper palace, put together many years ago, features heavy embossed decorations, a number of roof angles, fine cut-out detail in the paper curtains, and a fence that has weathered the years well. Of unknown origin, and possibly built before 1900, it measures 13½in high, 16½in wide and 10in deep (34.3 x 41.9 x 25.4cm). *Strong Museum Collection.*

printed in several shades of gray, black, two shades of red, and gilt. **(Illustration 226.)** It is strange that such a complex set of uncut sheets along with the original envelope is unmarked as to publisher.

Another unmarked cardboard edifice is pictured in **Illustration 227**, an early palace composed of various upright sections and a maze of roof angles and shapes. One of the outstanding features is the beautiful delicate embossing which is emphasized by the fact that it is an all-white building. There is no competition of color, the depth of the embossing casting a multitude of shadows that bring out its unusual beauty. The toothed quoins, the cut-out windows, the fine curtains, the details of the arched entrance, the statues at the head of each stairway, and the fragile fencing enclosing the front terrace, all enhance this unusual paper building. This remark-

able piece is 16½ inches (41.9cm) wide, 13½ inches (34.3cm) high and 10 inches (25.4cm) deep. There are a few minor breaks, bends, and surface blemishes here and there, but it is basically sound having spent a number of years in a glass enclosure. It could possibly date back to 1900.

Other equally interesting cardboard construction projects, with entirely different different subject matter, are presented here to show the variety of the German sheets. J.F. Schreiber published an exciting carousel triple sheet (see **Illustration 228**). Each sheet of stiff cardboard measures 17 inches (43.2cm) wide, and 14 inches (35.6cm) high. The broad grey cone top of the carousel measures 10¼ inches (26.1cm) in diameter and is decorated with red, green, and yellow striping. The circular central housing has simulated mirrored pillars enclosing rose-colored

panels decorated with vertical sprays of red roses. Above the panels are mirrored arches of a Gothic pattern, and strings of draped alternating red and white lights. An open section reveals a pipe organ with a brown wood casing, silver pipes, a drum with cymbals, and horns in gold, all framed within green draperies with a gold fringe. While the shallow cone roof, its outer edge, and the central housing are as colorful and decorative as those of the usual amusement park merry-go-round, the horses (or rather ponies), and the five seating compartments are plain by comparison. The ten ponies consist of a pair of whites, a pair of browns, two charcoal blacks and four dapple greys, each has a blue saddle blanket edged with red, and a simple brown saddle and harness. Included on the sheets are ten children in seated positions, six boys and four girls, dressed in clothing of the early 1920s. An added 6 by 10 inch

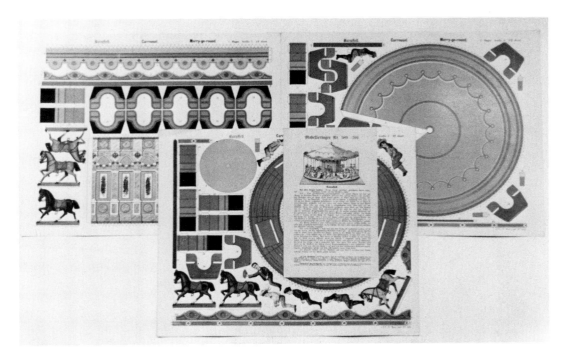

(15.2 x 25.4cm) sheet provides a black and white illustration of the completed merry-go-round and the construction directions in German.

A later Schreiber merry-go-round sheet titled *Micky Maus Karusell* features a number of Walt Disney's famous characters. **(Illustration 229.)** A riot of bright colors, this carousel has a highly decorative flat hexagon top which utilizes most of the colors of the rainbow. Made up as a child's toy, this uncut sheet would attract considerable attention in any fine collection or exhibit.

Joseph Scholz of Mainz, Germany, published a series of model architectural and technical sheets. Among those offered were both common and famous buildings found in Germany, and those of other countries as well. **Illustration 230** pictures a 17 by 13 inch (43.2 x 33cm) sheet consisting of three typical German dwellings. When cut out and assembled the houses average 5½ inches (14cm) in heigth, 2¼ inches (5.8cm) wide and 2¾ inches (7.1cm) deep, all rather small, but colorful and well detailed. A second sheet offers a grouping of three Venetian buildings along with an arched footbridge connecting two of the buildings. **(Illustration 231.)** The sheet size and the finished products are approximately the same size as the previously mentioned German buildings.

Crossing over the border from Germany to France we find an equal number of paper toys of the type covered in this chapter. An early boxed set titled *Le Grand Jardin Des Plantes* has a beautiful box cover marked, "H. Duru, editeur and Lith. Prodhomme, 89r du Temple." The box measuring 14¾ inches (37.6cm) wide, 11 inches (27.9cm) high and 2⅛ inches (5.4cm) deep, contains 50 rather crudely cut out figures set on wooden blocks. This set is quite similar to the previously mentioned German boxed set titled *Zoological Garden*, although most of the cut-out figures are of single animals, people, and ornamental trees, rather than groupings. Each animal is labeled with its French name. The artwork and hand coloring is superb. This magnificent set possibly dates in the mid 1800s, and although the cover is somewhat spotted, the cut-out figures are in remarkably good ocndition. **(Color Illustration 35.)**

ABOVE: Illustration 228: Three sheets of uncut parts are needed to construct this exciting carousel published by J.F. Schreiber of Esslingen, Germany, c.1920. Each sheet measures 14 x 17in (35.6 x 43.2cm). The added 6 x 10in sheet (15.2 x 25.4cm) pictures the completed carrousel and the building instructions in German.

LEFT: Illustration 229: The *Micky Maus Karussell* sheet provides the parts to construct a merry-go-round on which several of Walt Disney's characters ride. Published by J.F. Schreiber of Germany, circa 1954. The sheet measures 14¼ x 16¾in (36.2 x 42.5cm).

177

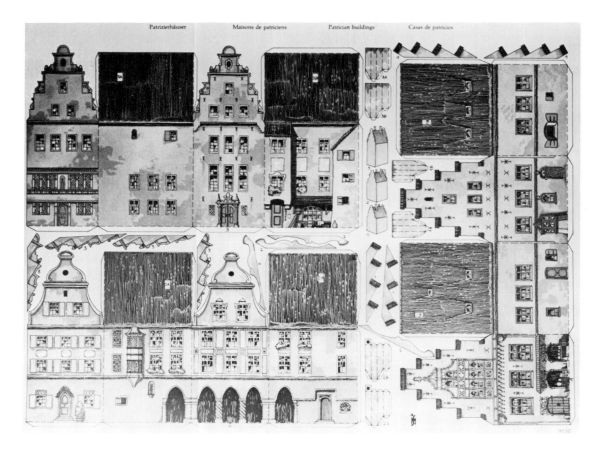

Patrizierhäuser   Maisons de patriciens   Patrician buildings   Casas de patricios

The great French publisher Pellerin offered a wide and diversified selection of paper sheets pertaining to buildings, gardens, zoos, and the like. Pellerin did not confine his colorful sheets to French subjects, but illustrated subjects of mystery and enchantment from distant parts of the globe. French children cut, assembled, studied, and learned of the various designs of living quarters and other types of buildings in far-off lands. A colorful Arabian tent, a Sheik, his many wives, his camels and followers, are pictured on a small sheet titled *Tente Arabe* which measures 11¾ by 9 inches (29.9 x 22.9cm). **(Illustration 232.)** A second example, titled *Citadelle Chinoise au Tonkin*, is on a larger sheet labeled *Moyennes Constructions*, which measures 15¾ inches

(40.1cm) wide and 11¾ inches (29.9cm) high. **(Illustration 233.)** Here are the makings of a model of a Chinese fortress with a high outside wall topped with numerous cannons. To a French child the fortification and the cannons are not new, but the strange building in the center prompted questions. The inquisitive child would ask about the building and the people who might inhabit it, hence the learning process continued. Some other fascinating and intriguing titles found in the *Moyennes Construction* series are *Palais de la Reine a Madagascar*, *Fontaine Musulmane pres Constantinople*, *Pagode De Bhatgaon* and *Kiosque Chinois*, names and places of mystery in far-away places. **(Illustration 234 A & B.)**

Some interesting examples of British paper construction toys are found in a series titled *The Childrens Models*. **(Illustration 236.)** Each unit consists of six rather large square sheets measuring 14¾ by 14 inches (37.6 x 35.6cm), all enclosed in a large envelope with one of the scenes colorfully printed on its face. Published by A. & E. Dickens of London, England, and printed in Holland, there are three titles in the series. They are classics of children's literature: *Robinson Crusoe*, *Cinderella* and *Little Red Riding Hood*. The top two-fifths of each card consists of a background scene, the lower three-fifths consists of the characters and props involved in each particular scene.

The six scenes found in *Robinson Crusoe* are

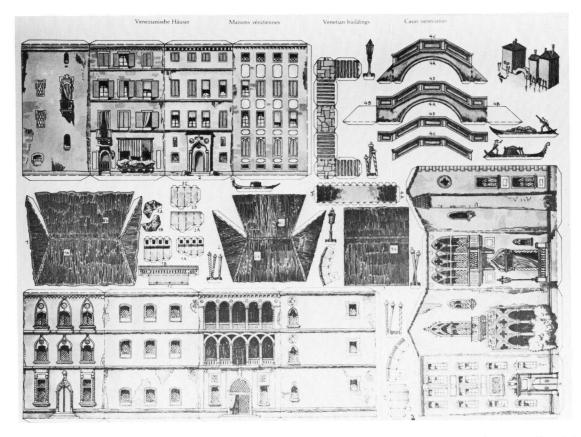

Illustration 231: Titled *Venetian Buildings* in German, French, English and Spanish, this sheet pictures three dwellings of the type found in Venice, Italy, along with a canal bridge. Published by Joseph Scholz of Mainz, Germany, c.1910. Sheet size 13 x 17in (33.0 x 43.2cm).

as follows: *R. Crusoe goes to Sea, R. Crusoe as a Shipwrecked Man, The Household of R. Crusoe, R. Crusoe meets Friday,* **(Illustration 235)**, *R. Crusoe Teaching Friday,* and lastly *R. Crusoe Saved from the Island.* The six scenes of Cinderella **(Illustration 236)** picture her in the *Kitchen, With the Fairy, At the Ball, Losing her Slipper, Trying on the Slipper,* and finally *Her Betrothal to the Prince.* A small two-sided printed sheet included with each set lists the three titles and the six scenes pertaining to each set. The reverse side gives directions which suggest the use of cardboard backing and a diagram for construcing the supports for the backgrounds, and also the stands for the various figures and props. Unfortunately there is no date marked on

either of these sets, but an educated guess would place them in the 1920s period.

In England, during the period of World War II, cardboard modelers were offered packets of tiny highly detailed construction cards, each measuring 3½ by 5 inches (8.9 x 12.7cm). Known as "Micromodels," these little construction packets contained the makings of many of Britains famous old buildings, fascinating railroad locomotives, and well-known historical ships. An Englishman, Geoffrey Heighway, began publishing these super, small scale sets around 1940. They were quickly accepted by the modeling experts and the novice modelers as they were inexpensive and offered a challenge, because of their tiny size. Their immediate success might be

attributed to timing — being at the right place at the right time. Both civilian hobbyists and the British soldiers in the trenches, found that the concentration required to build one of these tiny models temporarily blocked out the war environment, and moved the mind into a period of peacefulness and history. A Micromodel packet, a razor, a tube of glue, tweezers, a six-inch ruler, and toothpicks were all the tools needed, and they could be carried anywhere in a small box. Each Micromodel packet carried the slogan "Your workshop all in a cigar box." These tiny construction packets were so enthusiastically received, that the company, Micromodels Ltd., continued production until 1960, when Heighway passed away. Occasionally one will find a packet offered today.

They are highly desirable and collectible.

In the United States we find a rare example of a cut-out and assemble toy building that was printed in the Christmas issue of the *New York Herald* newspaper, in 1895. Rare because of its condition, age, and completeness, it was printed in a yellow-tan and black on a full page of cheap newsprint, and it has survived. It consists of seven drawings of units that, when cut out and assembled, would represent a model of the Herald Building, where the newspaper was printed and published. **(Illustration 237.)** The instructions printed in the upper left corner reads as follows: "Paste on heavy cardboard and cut on black lines, then paste together as directed on blank edges. The elevation on the left is the Broadway side; the elevation on the right is the Sixth Avenue side; the centre piece is the roof; the elevation at the top is the front of the building, on Thirty-fifth street;

the elevation at the bottom of the page is the rear of the building, on Thirty-sixth street; the skylight and chimney are to be pasted on the roof where indicated." The caption read: "A Christmas Toy For The Heralds Little Readers."

The 1896-97 Milton Bradley catalog offers a house full of rooms, in which each room is separated on a single sheet. Titled *A Home for Paper Dolls*, it was offered in three sizes: Home No. 1, contains six rooms in a portfolio. Home No. 2, contains ten rooms in a box. Home No. 3, contains fourteen rooms and two lawns packed in an elegant box. The object of the project was to appropriately furnish each room by cutting out pictures of people and furniture from catalogs, magazines and fashion books, then pasting them on the sheets until each room was completely furnished and occupied. While the objects were usually pasted in securely, alternate methods

were used, such as leaving an opening on the top of the crib or bed where a baby or a child could be half inserted into a position where he or she appeared to be asleep. This depended on the ability and ingenuity of the paster. A complete instruction circular and a story titled *Emma's Christmas Present* accompanied each set.

The 1911 McLoughlin catalog advertised "The New Pretty Village" in three sizes. The large set has 17 buildings that fold into a box that measures 14 by 20 inches (35.6 x 50.8cm). The medium set consists of eight buildings in a box measuring 11 by 15 inches (27.9 x 38.1cm). The small set is made up of four buildings in a box 12 by 8 inches (30.5 x 20.3cm). These sets were sold with a colored ground plan showing roads, paths, grass areas, and blank spaces designating where the assembled buildings should be placed. **(Illustration 238.)** In the catalog page it quotes from a

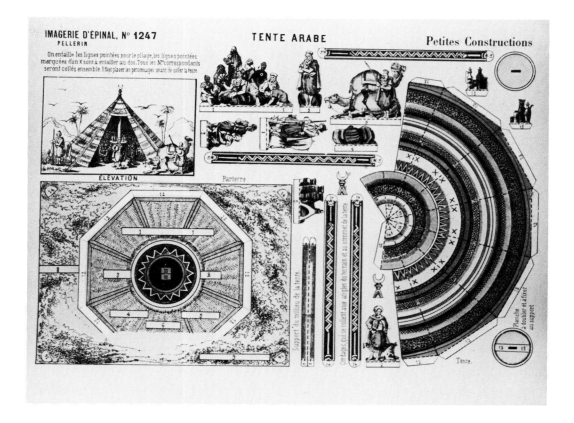

Illustration 232: *Tente Arabe* is a *Petites Construction* sheet published by Pellerin of Epinal, France, c.1900. A colorful Arabian tent, a sheik, his wives, his camels and followers, are pictured on the smallest of Pellerin's sheets. Size 9 x 11¾in (22.9 x 29.9cm).

letter written by Ethel Lloyd Patterson to Santa Claus, which was published in the *New York World* on December 21, 1910. The quote, in part, reads: "Say Santa Claus, if you want to give us something cheap, just to fill in, we like that paper village pretty well. There are 17 little houses, a church, a school and everything, and they are all packed flat in the box and you take them out and fit them together." These little cardboard houses were often set up as decoration under the Christmas tree before and after the 1911 date. McLoughlin Brothers added a statement of their own on the same catalog page: "Of course, everybody knows what our Pretty Village is. We have been selling it for 25 years." Subtracting the 25 years from 1911 would give a date of 1886 for the first Pretty Village. Yet the Village is not mentioned in the 1886 McLoughlin catalog. **(Illustration 239.)**

McLoughlin's competitor, Milton Bradley, offered three Toy Villages in his 1909 catalog. Bradley's Toy Village consisted of a number of folding houses made of cardboard and hinged with strong cambric. The two-piece houses, roofs and folded walls, were simple to erect, firm when set up, and easy to take down, fold, and store in their box. Each set was supplied with a lithographed sheet of people and objects to be cut out, and small tinplate stands which held the figures in an upright position. Also included was a ground plan showing streets, paths, lawns, flower beds, and blank spaces on which to place the houses. The three sets offered were No. 4422, the "big town" of the series. It contained 17 buildings among which were a hotel, a boat house, a florist's shop, a fire department, church, village store and post office, a blacksmith's shop, a tent, Uncle Tom's cabin, and the balance in dwellings. The large lithographed ground sheet measured 23 by 47½ inches (58.4 x 120.7cm). No. 4421, Bradley's Toy Village, represented a smaller town consisting of eight buildings, the uncut sheet of people, trees and objects, tin stands and a ground sheet measuring 23¼ by 23 inches (61.7 x 61cm) No. 4420, the smallest set, contained four buildings, a sheet of figures and objects, the tin stands, and the ground plan measuring 11¼ by 23¼ inches (28.6 x 59.1cm). The 1913 catalog carried the same three villages plus a smaller scale edition of the small set mentioned above. These four sets of Toy Villages appeared in the later 1914, 1917 and 1918-19 catalogs.

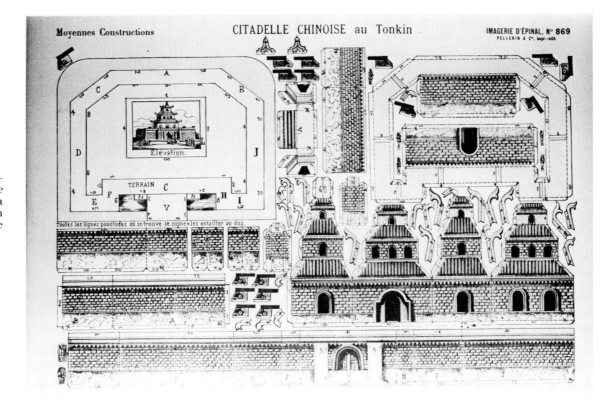

Illustration 233: This *Moyennes Constructions* sheet, *Citadelle Chinoise au Tonkin*, provides the makings of a Chinese fortress. Published by Pellerin of Epinal, France, c.1900. Sheet size 11¾ x 15¾in (29.9 x 40.1cm).

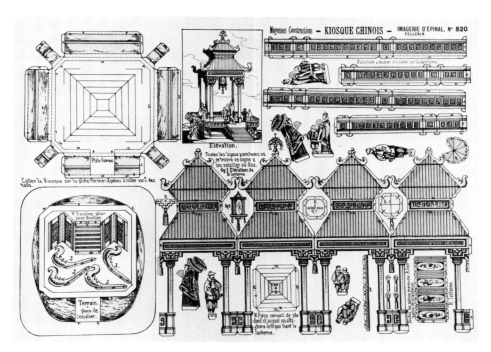

Illustration 234 A & B: The uncut sheet and the finished model. **A.** A *Moyennes Constructions* sheet, *Kiosque Chinois*, published by Pellerin of Epinal, France, c.1900. **B.** The finished model stands 6⅞in high on a 4¼ x 5in base (17.4 x 10.9 x 12.7cm). *Photo by Barbara Whitton Jendrick.*

Illustration 235: *Robinson Crusoe Meets Friday*, one of six cut-out scenes from a series of three children's stories titled *The Childrens' Models*, c.1925. Published by A. & E. Dickens of London, England. Sheet size 14 x 14¾in (35.6 x 37.6cm).

Illustration 236: The cover folder of *The Childrens' Models of Cinderella* which contains six large cards of characters and scenes to be cut out and erected. c.1925. Published by A. & E. Dickens of London, England. Folder size 14⅛ x 14⅞in (35.9 x 37.8cm).

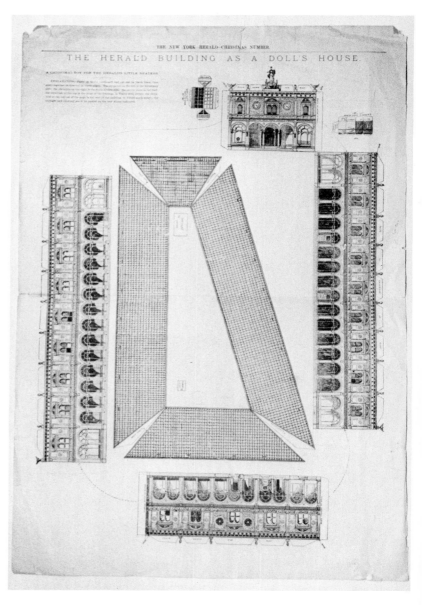

Illustration 237: *The Herald Building as a Doll's House* appeared as a cut-out construction sheet, full-page, in *The New York Herald-Christmas Number* newspaper, in 1895. When cut out and assembled, the model represents the Herald Building on Broadway in New York City. Newspaper sheet size 22⅞ x 15⅞in (58.1 x 40.3cm).

PRETTY TOY VILLAGES

The Pretty Villages are so made that the buildings can be taken apart and put away in a very small space. The roofs, chimneys, and all extra parts are removable, and each part is numbered so that mistakes are impossible in placing the pieces. All printed in full colors. The popularity of this toy has led us to make it in several sizes at different prices.

No. 545.—NEW PRETTY VILLAGE	No. 546.—NEW PRETTY VILLAGE	No. 547.—NEW PRETTY VILLAGE

No. 545.

Size of box, 12 x 8½ inches

Each set contains 4 folding buildings. Also trees, flowers, people, etc.

Put up in dozens

No. 546.

Size of box, 11½ x 15½ inches

Each set contains 8 folding buildings. Also extra figures of people, trees, etc.

Put up in ½ dozens

No. 547.

Size of box, 15 x 20½ inches

This set contains 16 folding buildings; houses, stores, churches, etc. Also an extra number of trees, flowers, people, gates, seats, etc.

Put up singly

Illustration 238: *The New Pretty Village* was offered in three sizes in the 1911 McLoughlin Brothers' catalog. These colorfully lithographed buildings came folded flat, were easy to erect and to break down and store. See box sizes on catalog page.

Illustration 239: A close-up of some of the buildings included in the larger set of The New Pretty Village. They were supplemented by a horse and wagon as pictured, by figures of people, trees and various other props. The die-cut buildings measured from 4 to 9in (10.2 to 22.9cm) in height.

Chapter XIII.

MOVEMENT BY SAND OR HOT AIR

It is recorded that the Greeks used both sand or hot air to produce movement in some of their figures. In Europe during the middle ages, religious figures were gravity activated by the use of falling sand. Karl Grober in his book, *Children's Toys of Bygone Days*, mentions an early cut-out hot air toy. Quote: "An Ulm engraving of the year 1470 displays a horse and two apes joined together in the middle by a bar and fastened to the back of the horse by a pin. When placed above a stove, the heat made the apes swing to and fro."

In the early 19th century, glass faced boxes appeared containing jointed figures in the front half and a sealed compartment in the rear. The rear compartment contained a funnel at the upper half with a form of paddle wheel below it. A horizontal shaft ran from the center of the wheel through the upright central partition into the back of the jointed figure in the front section. The rear sealed compartment also contained a measured amount of clean fine sand. To activate the figure, the box was held upright in both hands, slowly turned twice counter clockwise bringing the sand to the top of the box where it fell into the funnel and slowly dropped onto the paddle wheel. As the wheel turned, the connecting shaft provided movement to the figure, movement that lasted for two or three minutes. **(Illustration 240.)** While the majority of these sand toys contained a single jointed figure, others were more complex, some with additional movements, still others containing two or three figures. The boxes with additional movements or more than one figure required additional levers and buffers in the rear enclosure to provide movement to the figures.

Some of these toys were encased in paper

Illustration 240: An early sand toy picturing a violinist. When activated, the right arm moves up and down drawing the bow across the strings, the musician's right foot taps and the cat's tail moves from side to side. This toy is unmarked. Possibly German, c.1890. Size 9 x 5½ x 2in (22.9 x 14.0 x 5.1cm).

Illustration 241: A *Moyennes Constructions* sheet titled Le Savetier (the cobbler or the shoemaker). A small sketch, top center, shows the front elevation of a shop with children watching the cobbler at work. A small drawing in the upper right pictures the sand wheel that, when activated by falling sand, moves the cobbler's right arm up and down in a hammering motion. Published by Pellerin of Epinal, France, c.1890. Sheet size 11⅝ x 15¾in (29.5 x 40.1cm).

covered wooden boxes, although the majority of the later type were completely made of paper and cardboard, plus the glass face. Because of their paper construction, many of these sand toys have not survived the passing of time, and few are found in working condition. Wear along the outer edges of the sealed rear compartment allowed the sand to escape. The proper repair of these toys requires patience, dexterity, and a supply of matching old papers to make it appear as it did originally. These sand toys were produced in Germany and France, with a few being produced in the United States from the 1870s on. The previously mentioned 1800-1803 Bestelmeier catalog pictures and lists several hand painted cardboard mechanical toys with moving figures and/or parts that are activated by falling sand.

Another type of sand toy appeared just before the beginning of the 20th century in the form of paper construction sheets, similar to those mentioned in Chapter XI. Construction sheets to be cutout and assembled, had moving parts so constructed that they could be activated by either falling sand or the heat rising from a candle or a stove. These sheets, published in both France and Germany, were popular with the older children of the time and are eagerly hunted by present-day collectors.

The French publisher Pellerin offered scores of construction sheets which provided this mechanical action. For example, **Illustration 241** pictures a *Moyennes Constructions* (middle size sheet) titled *Le Savetier* which, when assembled, is a small three-dimensional cobbler's shop. Five children stand outside watching the figure inside the shop repair a shoe. The cobbler hammers away at the shoe he holds in his lap. The simple, but life-like movement of his right arm is provided by the falling sand turning the paddle wheel. The small line drawing located in the upper right corner of the sheet illustrates the construction of the mechanism. A further example, **Illustration 242**, pictures a stream, with a woman on her knees washing clothes. In the background is a village setting, two small footbridges, several buildings, and a water wheel. When assembled the water wheel turns and the woman's right arm moves up and down beating the wet clothing.

Notice the two small line drawings in the upper right-hand corner of the sheet, picturing the front and back elevations of the mechanism. See how the sand hopper is built into the upper right corner, how it feeds onto the wheel, which turns and provides movement to the water wheel and the woman's arm.

The two larger Pellerin sheets, *Grandes Constructions*, offer action figures framed within a formal proscenium. The first, **Illustration 243**, titled *Le Bucheron*, pictures a man chopping wood. The action provided in the finished construction is the up and down chopping action of the axe and the two arms. Notice the large drawing of the rear of the finished mechanism in the lower left corner of the sheet. This enables you to clearly see the construction of the cardboard mechanism. A second example, **Illustration 244**, pictures a Prussian soldier and a Zouave fighting. When assembled, both will have arm movement. Here again is a clear-cut illustration of the construction mechanism. Reviewing all four examples, the cardboard mechanisms are the same in principle, yet each is slightly different in design as it must fit into an area where it can easily provide movement.

Some examples of the highly colored German paper mechanical toys follows: A sand toy sheet published by Schrieber pictures the various parts to construct a small traveling circus act. **Illustration 245** pictures an upright striped tent with three bandsmen playing in the upper half; the lower portion houses the sand powered mechanism. Notice the drawing of the front and side views of the mechanism. The star performer, an acrobat turning on a bar, is located in front of the tent. A drummer and two assistants watch his every move, while a young lady collects donations from a young audience. **Illustration 246** shows a line drawing of the completed toy along with assembling instructions in German.

Paper toys in the form of cut-out figures mounted on an upright wire shaft which was topped by a series of horizontal vanes, is a form of hot air toy. The vanes turn, due to heat rising from a stove, a candle, or other heat producing medium. This type of hot air toy existed in

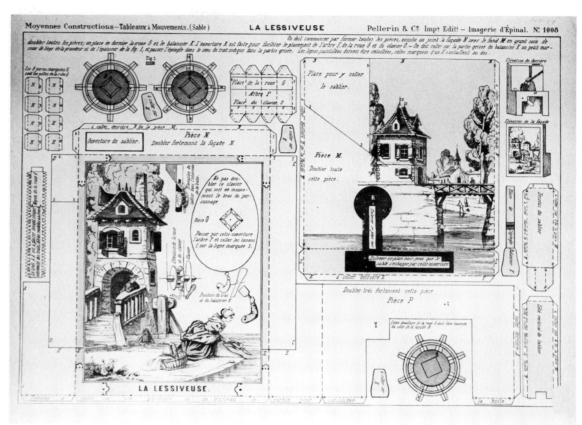

Illustration 242: *La Lessiveuse* (the washerwoman) pictures a woman on her knees at the side of a stream, paddling her wet clothes. A *Moyennes Constructions* sheet of the parts to make a mechanical toy motivated by falling sand. The movement is in the woman's right arm. Published by Pellerin of Epinal, France, c.1900. Sheet size 11⅝ x 15¾in (29.5 x 40.1cm).

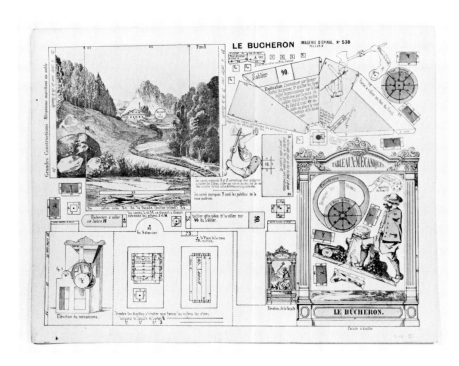

Illustration 243: A *Grandes Constructions* sheet, titled *Le Bucheron* (the woodchopper). The finished toy is activated by falling sand poured into a hopper and passing through to a mill wheel which turns. A connecting lever is attached to the woodchopper's shoulder and it supplies movement to the two arms. Published by Pellerin of Epinal, France, c.1900. Sheet size is 15⅜ x 19⅜in (39.0 x 49.2cm).

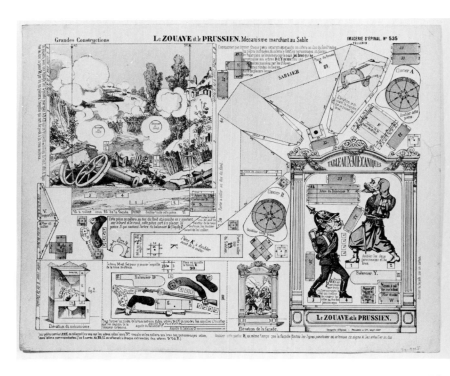

Illustration 244: A *Grandes Constructions* sheet titled *Le Zouave et le Prussien*. The arms of both soldiers have movement motivated by the sand mechanism pictured in the lower left corner of the sheet. Crossed rifles move up and down. Published by Pellerin of Epinal, France. c.1910. Sheet size 15⅜ x 19⅜in (39.0 x 49.2cm).

Europe far back in time. They were manufactured in the United States from 1860 on. Edward Ives, one of Americas leading toy makers in the 19th century, made hot air toys when he started in business in Plymouth, Connecticut. **(Illustration 247.)** William C. Goodwin of Hamden, Connecticut, received a series of three design patents on December 27, 1870. They pictured "Two Children on a See Saw," "A Cupid Hammering Out A Dart" **Illustration 248**, and "A Woman Washing Clothes."

In the late 1890s, McLoughlin Brothers produced an outstanding hot air toy which was considerably different from others that appeared before and after this time. Called a "Gyrating Shadow Lantern," it was constructed on a square flat wooden base with an upright center pole with a nail on top; hung on the nail is a 16-blade horizontal fan. Hanging from the fan are three lengths of very fine chain which holds a thin tin circular rim equipped with clips. An assortment of black silhouette cardboard figures and animals may be clipped onto the hanging rim. This toy structure is enclosed on all four sides by a white translucent material. Holes in the square base provide support for two or four candles which, when lit, give off rising heat which turns the horizontal fan above, thereby turning the silhouette figures. An added feature is that the flickering light from the candles casts shadows of the moving figures onto the four-sided translucent enclosure, creating an erie effect. This toy measures 13½ inches (34.3cm) high and is 11 inches (27.9cm) square. **(Illustration 249.)**

At the beginning of the 20th century, the two well-known German publishers Schrieber and Scholtz were still publishing colorful and interesting sheets. A Schrieber sheet provided the makings and backdrop for a hot air toy. **(Illustra-**

Illustration 245: A sheet depicting a traveling circus act in the form of a sand toy. The two diagrams in the center of the sheet show how it looks and works. Published by J.F. Schreiber of Esslingen, Germany, c.1910. Sheet size 14¼ x 17in (36.3 x 43.2cm).

Illustration 246: A closeup of the *Turner* sand toy and building instructions printed in German. This small sheet, 8 x 6in (20.3 x 15.2cm), accompanied the traveling circus act sheet shown in **Illustration 245.**

tion 250.) The backdrop measuring 8¼ inches (21cm) wide and 7¼ inches (18.5cm) high, shows a mountain with a range of snow covered peaks in the background. At the foot of the mountain is a small village on the edge of a lake, and in the foreground is a small boat with two fishermen. When the three-sided background is cutout, folded, and set up, check the illustration of the back view, showing vertical post and wire "T" shaft that turns overhead horizontal vanes and the two small paper zeppelins. It also requires that two candles be placed alongside the upright shaft and under the horizontal vanes. When the

candles are lit, the rising currents of heat turn the vanes, thereby moving the two zeppelins around the outside perimeter. Another well-known publisher of this type of mechanical sheet was the previously mentioned Joseph Scholtz of Mainz, Germany. **Illustration 251** pictures an uncut sheet of parts to construct a hot air toy of a man attempting to shear a goat. As you can see from the drawing of the back view of the finished toy, both of the mans arms move as well as the head and shoulders of the goat. Again you will see the necessity of using a stiff wire, a candle, and the use of a block of wood as a base for stability.

Another example by Scholtz, **Illustration 252**, is very similar to the one mentioned earlier that was published by Pellerin. **(Illustration 244.)** Scholtz pictures two German soldiers drilling in bayonet combat. Both figures are jointed at the shoulders and elbows, which provides action to the guns bearing bayonets when the toy is activated by heat. The line drawing, top center, illustrates a rear view of the finished toy.

Illustration 247: Two pages of American hot air toys from an Ives, Blakeslee & Williams Company catalog of 1893. Ives was making hot air toys when he started in business in Plymouth, Connecticut, in 1860.

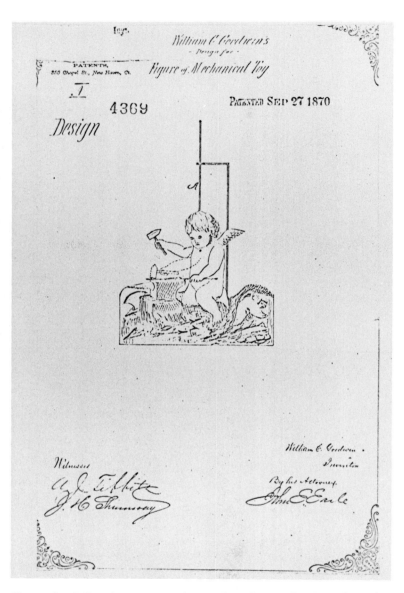

Illustration 248: A design patent drawing by William C. Goodwin of Hamden, Connecticut, for a hot air toy dated 1870. These paper toys were mounted on an upright wire shaft which was topped by a series of horizontal vanes. When the toy was placed over a source of heat the vanes turned, providing movement to the paper figure.

Illustration 249: A hot air toy powered by the heat of two candles, enclosed within a shadow box. It appeared in the late 1890s. The silhouette figures on the turning ring cast erie shadows on the semi-transparent sides of the toy called a *Gyrating Shadow Lantern*, it was manufactured by McLoughlin Brothers of New York City. The toy measures 13½in high and 11in square (34.3 x 27.9 x 27.9cm).

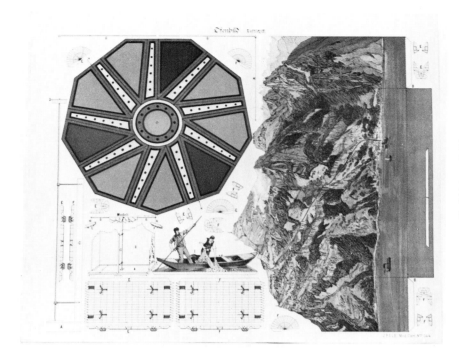

Illustration 250: An unusual hot air toy may be constructed from this sheet published by J.F. Schreiber of Esslingen, Germany, c.1910. It makes up into a picturesque mountain scene with the fishing boat on the lake in the foreground and the two zeppelins rotating above when the vanes are activated by the heat producing candle. Sheet size 14⅛ x 17in (35.9 x 43.2cm).

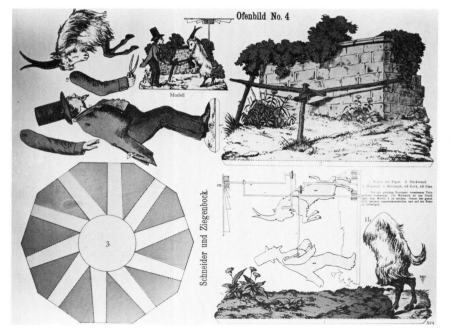

Illustration 251: *Ofenbild No. 4 Schneider und Ziegenbock* (Stove Picture No. 4 Tailor and He-Goat), published by Joseph Scholz of Mainz, Germany, c.1900. The constructed model would present a humorous confrontation between the tailor wanting to shear the goat, and the goat objecting. Rising heat would provide movement to the man's arms, and the head and shoulders of the goat. Sheet size 13 x 16¾in (33.0 x 42.6cm).

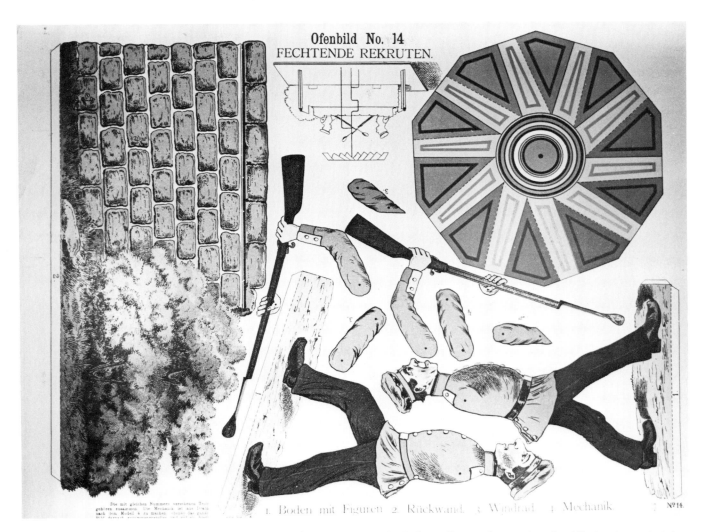

Illustration 252: *Ofenbild No. 14, Fechtende Rekruten* (Oven Picture No. 14 Fighting Recruits) presents a sheet that makes up into two soldiers at bayonet practice. Both figures are jointed at the shoulders and elbows, which provides action to the guns when the finished toy is heat activated. Published by Joseph Scholz of Mainz, Germany, c.1915. Sheet size 13 x 16¾in (33.0 x 42.6cm).

Chapter XIV.

OPTICAL TOYS

Of all the wonderful toys produced during the 19th century, few are as fascinating as the group identified as optical toys, sometimes called philosophical toys by the Victorians. While this group covers a large number of kinetic toys made of various materials, we will concern ourselves with those made of paper and cardboard, possibly supported by a minor piece of wood, glass, or a mirror. The principle of operation of these toys is the phenomenon known as persistence of vision, meaning when an object is suddenly removed from the field of vision, the impression of its image is momentarily retained by the retina of the eye. It was the development of these simple toys, each improving on its predecessor, that finally gave us the crank operated moving picture projector in 1895 — and look where we've gone from there!

One of the early optical toys is *Les Metamorphoses*, which was first marketed in 1850 by Jullien in Paris, France. The toy made use of anamorphic drawings — distorted drawings usually in the form of a flat-type curve. This art principle has existed since the 16th century and has offered a challenge to scores of known artists of bygone years. The anamorphoscope, or cylindrical mirror which is used to reconstitute distortion, appeared in 1850. McLoughlin Brothers offered their version of the anamorphoscope in the 1880s. Packed in a wooden box with a sliding cover, it is titled *The Magic Mirror, or Wonderful Transformation*. The box contains a 4 inch (10.2cm) round top mirrored glass cylinder 1⅛ inches (3.2cm) in diameter and 24 distorted drawings on cards measuring 6¼ by 7¾ inches (15.9 x 19.8cm). Each card offers a highly colorful distorted character or animal and a small circle designating exactly where the mirrored cylinder

Illustration 253: A boxed set of *Thaumatrope* discs made in France. The round box cover is marked "L. E. T. Trompe-L'Oeil, Les Plaisirs de Jocko, Amusement de Societe." Each side of the disc pictures a different image, but when spun the two sides merge forming a complete picture. Example: a bird on one side, a cage on the other, when spun the bird appears to be in the cage. c.1835. Disc size 2⅝in (6.7cm) diameter.

should be placed. Illustrations include a man carrying his overly fat stomach on a wheelbarrow, a cobbler at his workbench, a squirrel eating a berry, Puss in Boots, a ballerina, an elephant and several military figures of different shapes. **(Color Illustration 36.)**

The *Thaumatrope* was introduced in 1825 by Doctor John Ayrton Paris. It was published and offered to the market in April of 1825 by William Phillips in London, England. The first issue appeared in a small round flat box titled *Thaumatropical Amusement*. It contained a number of stiff paper discs with short strings attached on either side so that the discs could be twirled between the forefingers and thumbs. Each side of the disc pictured a different image but, when spun, the two sides merged together forming a complete picture. Examples might be a bird on one side and a cage on the other. When the disc was spun, the bird was inside the cage. A man on one side and a horse on the other side, when the disc was spun, the man was riding a horse. **(Illustration 253.)**

The *Phenakistiscope* was introduced in the early 1830s by two men working independently and unaware that the other was working on the same project. S. Stampfer of Vienna, Austria, developed what he called the *Stroboscope*, while the Belgian scientist Joseph A.F. Plateau built a similar device which he called the *Phenakisto-scope*. The toy is constructed as follows: The outer edge of a large cardboard disc is deeply notched or slotted at equal distances, below which is a progression of slightly varying hand colored drawings that simulate movement of a figure or figures in related positions. The disc is fastened in the center to a wooden spindle. When the *Phenakistoscope* is held up to a mirror and spun, the viewer, peering through the revolving slots, observes the image in the mirror performing a continuous series of movements. **(Illustration 254.)** The designs, layout, and ideas, hand executed on the cardboard discs are intriguing, each being different and usually very amusing. **(Color Illustration 37.)**

The *Phenakistoscope* proved to be a somewhat tiring device to operate since it required continual turning by hand, and had the further disadvantage that only one person could watch the moving pictures. These two disadvantages were subsequently overcome by the development of an optical device known as the *Zoetrope*. The *Zoetrope* is made up of a wide cardboard cylinder in the shape of an old-fashioned hat box, which revolves

Illustration 254: The *Phenakistiscope* was one of the early forms of moving pictures, introduced in the 1830s. When held up before a mirror and spun, the viewer peers through the revolving slots on the outer edge of the disc observing, in this case, a couple waltzing gracefully, turning to and fro. The figure in the inner circle beats a steady tatoo on his double drums. Disc published by Ackermann & Company, London, England. c.1845. Disc size 9½in (24.2cm) in diameter.

on a central verticle axis stand. The upper half of the cylinder is pierced at regular intervals with verticle slits. Inside the cylinder, one would place a long strip of figures, drawn in a manner similar to those mentioned in the description of the *Phenakistoscope*, but in a straight line rather than circular. The number of figures or pairs of figures would equal the number of peephole slits on the top edge of the cylinder. This arrangement was an improvement on the *Phenakistoscope* because several spectators could arrange themselves around the turning cylinder and view the action through the slots. The variety of designs of figures and animals that were produced for the Zoetrope strips are a fascinating study in themselves. Some display the movements of dancers, jugglers, circus performers, boxers, all usually with a comic theme. Others might be a bit horrifying, such as a lion swallowing a man, or a man eating a mouse.

The first *Zoetrope* was designed by W.H. Horner of Bristol, England, in 1833, and he called it the *Daedelum*, the wheel of life. The idea did not become popular until 1860 when it was patented by a Frenchman, Desvignes. On April 23, 1867, it was patented in the United States by William E. Lincoln of Providence, Rhode Island. The patent copy reads: "This invention consists of a toy arranged so that a number of figures are seen moving in imitation of life, or in other and complicated movements, and is constructed so that any number of plates can be adjusted to it, putting no limit to the variety of the subjects that can be shown. This invention is based upon the optical fact that an image once seen is retained for a moment of time upon the retina of the eye after the image is withdrawn." He then goes on with a detailed description of the toy. Lincoln assigned the patent rights of his *Zoetrope* to Milton Bradley & Company of Springfield, Massachusetts. **(Color Illustration 38.)**

While more than one person could observe the action of the *Zoetrope*, it still retained the disadvantage that slits were employed as a means of presenting the phases of movement to the eye. Because the slits were separated from each other by a fairly large space, the amount of light reaching the observer was limited. The idea of eliminating the verticle slits on the cylinder and substituting a series of mirrors in the interior center did away with these disadvantages. The arrangement of the mirrors reflected each single stage on the figured strip. This idea was patented by Emile Reynaurd in 1877, and was called a *Praxinoscope*. **(Color Illustration 38.)**

The *Polyorama Panopique* is made up of a paper-covered box with an expandable front bellows containing a small round glass peephole. One of several framed slides may be inserted in a slot at the rear of the toy. The slides picture famous buildings or historic sights. Each paper slide is perforated in particular areas to permit the entry of light. The top of the box is equipped with a hinged door which, when opened to light, offers the viewer a daylight scene. When this door is closed and a second door at the rear of the box is opened, the light shines through the perforations and offers the same scene at night. **(Illustration 255.)**

Illustration 255: The *Polyorama Panoptique* offers day or night scenes of the same pictured image. The paper slide at the rear of the toy is perforated in particular areas to permit the entry of light. When the slide is pushed in and the hinged door at the top is opened, as pictured, the viewer observes a daylight scene. When the top door is closed and a door in the rear is opened, the viewer sees the same view at night. The lamp post and windows light up and there are stars in the sky. Marked "POLYORAMA PANOPTIQUE//BREVET D INVENTION S Gte du Gouv." French, c.1880. Size 9 x 10⅜in (22.9 x 26.3cm).

A very interesting paper toy that was popular in the 1800s is called *Jacobs Ladder* here in the United States. So illusionary is its action, it may be rightly classified as an optical toy. It consisted of a series of flat cardboard oblong sections illustrated on both sides, and connected together by two strips of cloth tapes. Sometimes it was equipped with a finely turned wooden handle fixed to the top section, and sometimes it was made without a handle. Occasionally it is found with just five sections, but usually with many more. To function, the toy must be picked up by the handle and held in a horizontal position with the sections hanging in a vertical position. By twisting the handle a half turn, the second section is lifted to the same level as the first section, at which point the upper side of the second section falls into an inverted position, and appears to pass downward on the other sections, first upon one side of the ladder and then upon the other, until it reaches the bottom. This effect is only an illusion, as the second section in reality only falls back to its original position. In that movement it becomes reversed. What was formerly the lower end becomes the upper end, the front having exchanged places with the back. This change of position of the second section brings it parallel with the third section which is then released, and the third section drops over the fourth when the next section is released, and so on throughout the remaining sections. **(Color Illustration 39.)**

A diagram for making a *Jacob's Ladder* toy appeared in the November 1868 issue of *Poupée Modèle*. **(Illustration 256.)** The drawing on the left illustrates where the connecting tapes were located. The drawing on the right pictures the front and back views and their relationship to each other.

A simple paper optical toy that should be mentioned here is the Flicker of Flip Book. This popular novelty was prominent in the United States between 1900 and 1935, although it has appeared occasionally since then. It consists of a series of animated drawings on some 30 to 50 pages, bound at one end so that they could be flicked with the thumb at any speed desired.

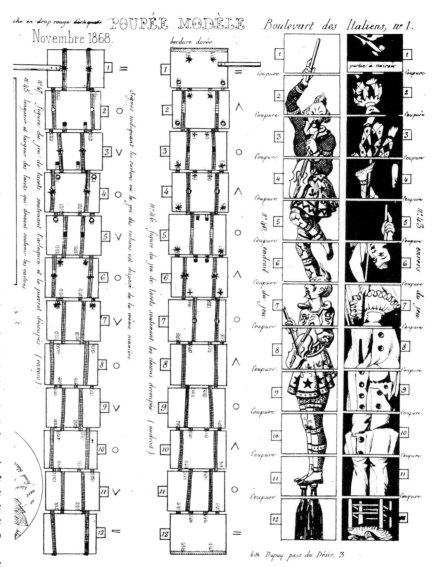

Illustration 256: These two diagrams, along with directions for making a *Jacob's Ladder* toy, appeared as a *Poupée Modèle* supplement in 1868. The two drawings on the left picture the arrangement of the tapes. Those on the right picture the front and back views of the subject matter and their relationship to each other.

These little Flip Books, usually 1½ by 2½ inches (3.8 x 6.4cm), offer hand held moving pictures of characters such as Charlie Chaplin, circus acts, or the flight of an airplane. A further variation of the Flip Book is the Multi-Flip Book published in Europe and titled *Donald & Pluto*. **(Illustration 257.)** This 9 by 4¼ inch (22.9 x 10.9cm) book contains a grouping of five Flip Books, each page printed on both sides, thereby providing ten episodes of lively entertainment showing the escapades of Donald the plumber and his pet, Pluto.

Illustration 257: Examples of Flicker or Flip Books. The small books on the right are reproductions, but are similar in size and action to those commonly found from 1900 to 1935. Published by Merrimack Publishing Company of New York City, they measure 1¾ x 2¾in (4.5 x 7.1cm). The larger variation is a Multi-Flip Book, five two-sided flip books in one. Printed in France, copyright Walt Disney Mickey Mouse Ltd. 1939. It measures 9 x 4¼in (22.9 x 10.9cm).

Chapter XV.

TRANSPORTATION VEHICLES & TOYS THAT FLY

The development of the live steam engine was possibly the most important development in the early years of the Industrial Revolution. The power of steam was known by scholars before the time of Christ. Hero of Alexandria, a Greek scientist of the 1st century A.D., wrote of this power and constructed several experimental models relating to it. However, the use of steam was not put to a practical use until after 1698, when Thomas Savery developed a crude steam engine. Thomas Newcomen and James Watt, among others, contributed many added and improved features that later provided a smooth running engine. In 1769, a Frenchman Nicolas Cugnot developed a steam carriage. In 1804 a Welshman, Richard Trevithick, built an engine that ran on rails. In both instances the horse was replaced by a man-made engine, and both were the start of a mode of various forms of transporation which would have a profound effect on the way man would live in the future. The development of man-made transportation vehicles, from early steam to the present atomic powered space ships, has taken place in a relatively short span of time.

Publishers of paper toys have kept pace with the development of the various forms of transportation. Youth has always been infatuated with speed and eagerly awaited the offerings of paper construction toys that made up into boats, trains, automobiles, and aircraft.

In France, the firm of Pellerin offered construction sheets covering all forms of transportation of the period. Some of the boats and ships offered existed before the age of steam, one example being Noah's Ark **(Illustration 258)**, and highly ornamental barge propelled by a galley of oarsmen. **(Illustration 259.)** Other ship construction sheets include a sheet of a full-rigged sailing ship

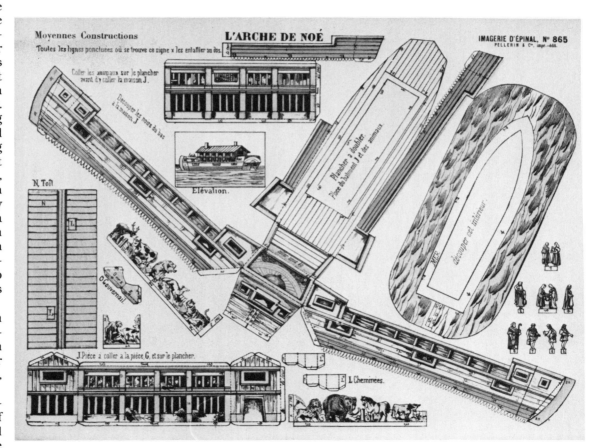

Illustration 258: *L'Arche De Noe* (Noah's Ark) a *Moyennes Constructions* sheet published by Pellerin of Epinal, France, c.1895. Sheet size 11¾ x 15½in (29.9 x 39.4cm).

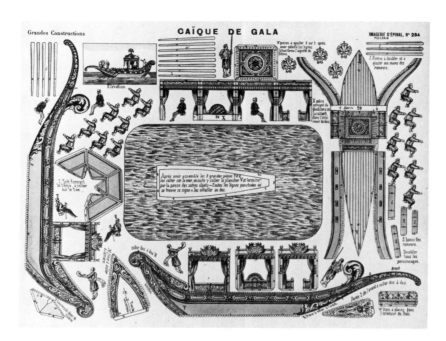

Illustration 259: An elaborate barge propelled by many oarsmen. *Caique De Gala* is the title of this *Grandes Constructions* sheet published by Pellerin of Epinal, France, c.1895. Sheet size 15⅜ x 19¼in (39.0 x 49.0cm).

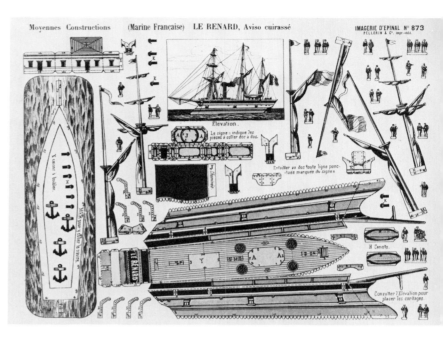

Illustration 260: *Le Renard, Aviso-cuirasse* is a model of a ship of the conversion period from sail to steam. A *Moyennes Constructions* sheet published by Pellerin of Epinal, France, c.1890. Sheet size 11¾ x 15½in (29.9 x 39.4cm).

of the conversion period, when it was also equipped with a steam engine. **(Illustration 260.)** The last seagoing sheet is an unusual example titled *Canot Automobile*, a pleasure craft. **(Illustration 261.)**

Pellerin also issued construction sheets featuring early trains. A large *Grandes Construction* sheet titled *Chemin De Fer* pictures the numerous parts to cut out and assemble for an early European train. **(Illustration 262.)** They also published three construction sheets which built an American 4-6-0 steam locomotive, a tender and a baggage and parlor car. **(Illustration 263 A - C.)** Another example titled *Gare Americaine A Maryland*, pictures a European type train with a 2-2-2 locomotive, a four-wheel tender and three six-wheel passenger cars. Included on the sheet are the parts to construct an elaborate station topped with American flags. **(Illustration 264 A & B.)**

The sales of early 20th century European automobiles were based on the speed and endurance which they performed. Long distance auto races were popular in France and Germany, and this is the theme found in Pellerin's *Automobile de Course*. Pictured are the parts for a sporty race car, c.1910, with driver and mechanic dressed in foul weather gear. **(Illustration 265.)** A second road vehicle titled *Autobus*, pictures the construction parts for a typical bus found in France in the early 1920s. This complex bus model, all of eight inches (20.3cm) long when completed, required the expertise of a child 12 or more years of age with previous paper construction experience to assemble. **(Illustration 266.)**

Micromodel of England, mentioned previously, issued many tiny transportation construction kits for modelers between 1940 and 1960. Ships such as the *Santa Maria*, the *Mayflower*, the *Mauretania* and the *Queen Mary* were popular.

Locomotives and tank engines modeled after the *Rocket, Puffing Billy* and various other British examples were offered to the delight of railroad enthusiasts.

Man has always been interested in flight. Watching a bird flying upward and then soaring through the air becomes more fascinating the longer one observes it. Possibly the earliest form of a man-made flying object would be a kite. Kites made of wood and cloth have existed in China for 2,000 years or more. They were flown for pleasure, for religious purposes, as a fighting kite with cutting strings, and as a surveying and measuring device. They were also used as an instrument of war, to record the weather, for observation purposes and, later, as a most important scientific contribution for the study of flight in the development of the airplane. Kites began with a variety of small shapes and developed into a large man lifting kite. From that point they progressed to a glider form. These gliders eventually were constructed to carry a man, and later became engine powered developing into the airplane. The Frenchmen Santos-Dumont, Gabriel Voisin, Louis Beriot, the German Otto Litienthal, and the Wright Brothers in the United States were all pioneers in the development of powered flight. It was the primitive flying machines invented by these men that Pellerin pictured on some of this construction sheets. **(Illustrations 267 & 268.)**

When the German Count Ferdinand Zeppelin invented the rigid airship named after him, great things were expected of this invention, which was principally a new form of group air travel. An early design of the dirigible was found on the Pellerin construction sheet *Le Zeppelin, Ballon Dirigeable Militaire Alemand.* It was a delicate project to construct, but when completed it evolved into a most satisfying model. **(Illustration 269 & 270.)**

Several high quality construction booklets containing the parts to build models of the world's leading planes have come out of the Slovakian area of Europe. **Illustration 271** pictures the cover of a Czechoslovakian publication which contains the colorful parts and detailed assembling instructions, in four languages, to build the four planes illustrated on the cover. Pictured are a French *Spad* of 1918, the Ryan *Spirit of St. Louis* of 1927, the Avia *BH 9* built in Czechoslovakia in 1923, and an Italian *Macchi Castoldi* of 1931.

As one would expect, the prolific publisher of German paper toys J.F. Schrieber produced a number of transportation sheets over the years. Some of these, illustrating early American forms of transportation, have been published in recent years. A stiff four-page folder featuring the various parts to construct an early American 4-4-0 wood burning steam locomotive is pictured in **Illustration 272.** Another picturing a Mississippi sidewheeler steamboat with a lot of fine detail is shown on a large four-page folder. **(Illustration 273.)**

In 1929, Samuel Gabriel Sons & Company of New York City published a series of five construction books called *The Put-Together Series.* One of these, titled *Build It With Scissors,* offers six cut-

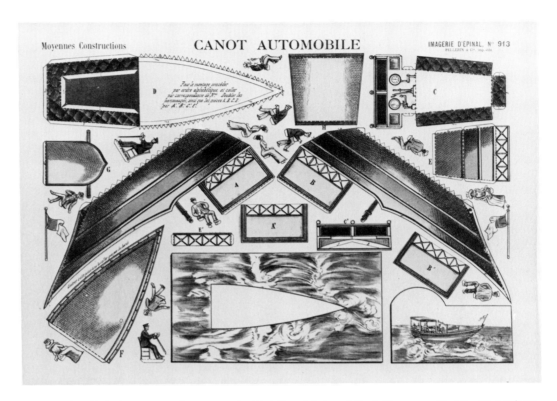

Illustration 261: A sea-going pleasure craft titled *Canot Automobile.* A *Moyennes Constructions* sheet published by Pellerin of Epinal, France, c.1910. Sheet size 11¾ x 15½in (29.9 x 39.4cm).

out and fill-in pages consisting of an electric locomotive, a tug boat in a floating drydock, a huge 4-6-4 steam locomotive and tender, an automobile of the late 1920s standing in front of a gas station, and two monoplanes of the same period. **(Illustration 274.)** The directions printed on the back of the title page explains the book and its purpose with this statement: "The six fill-in pages of this book represent the background of modern mechanical achievements. Opposite each background picture there is a color page, gummed and ready to paste. These gummed sheets are to be cut out carefully, each part by itself, and fitted together to give a complete picture if the pieces are pasted accurately into the outline on the opposite page. The numbers on the background

next to the pieces on the gummed sheets are guides to piecing the pictures together. Not until the entire cut-out portion of the picture has been laid in position, is it advisable to paste the various pieces in place, as occasionally one of the gummed parts overlaps another. When finished, the color pictures will have a realistic and plastic effect and will illustrate the story, at the same time giving the child a definite knowledge of the names of the principal parts of electric and steam locomotives, drydocks, automobiles and airplanes."

A large and extremely well done book titled *Ships Aloft, A Construction Book For Future Flyers* was published by Harper & Brothers of New York City and London, England, in 1936. The extremely informative copy was written by Harold

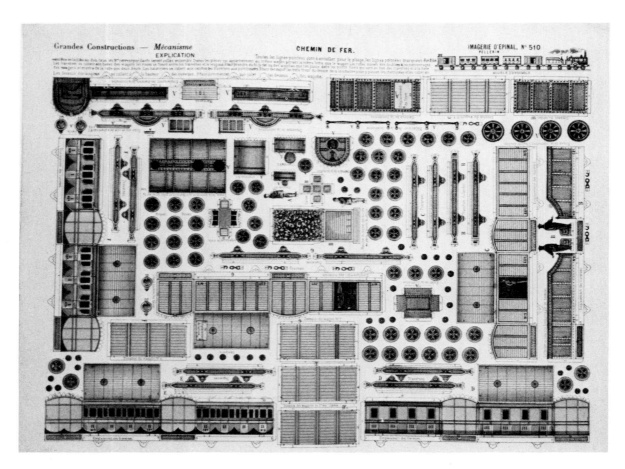

Illustration 262: *Chemin De Fer,* a sheet of parts to assemble an early steam locomotive, a tender and five carriages. A *Grandes Constructions* sheet published by Pellerin of Epinal, France, c.1890. Sheet size 15¼ x 19⅜in (38.8 x 49.2cm).

Platt, and the realistically colorful illustrations and their various colorful parts to be cut-out and applied are the work of a fine artist, Clayton Knight. The pictured models include a Douglas Airliner, the Martin China Clipper, the Boeing Bomber, and a fighter plane from an aircraft carrier. **(Illustration 275 A & B.)**

In 1942, the Crestcraft Company of Chicago, Illinois, issued a series of flying glider-type models of famous planes. Included in the assortment was Lockheed *Lightning,* a Bell *Airacobra,* a Brewster *Buffalo,* a B-17 *Flying Fortress,* a Douglas *Dive Bomber,* and a Curtis *Warhawk.* The following year, Whitman Publishing Company issued a booklet containing five plane models, printed and die-cut, ready to assemble. The models included a North American B-25, a Boeing B-17 E *Flying Fortress,* a Consolidated B-24 *Liberator,* a Douglas A-20A *Light Bomber,* and a Short *Sterling Bomber* (British). **(Illustration 276.)**

While thousands of paper construction planes have appeared since man's first flight, a new form has evolved in the past 25 to 30 years and become rather popular — paper airplanes that fly or glide in graceful flight. Articles and books on the subject have been published which are possibly a bit too scientific for youngsters, but readily accepted by devotees world-wide. In 1966-67, the *Scientific American* magazine sponsored a paper glider competition that drew 12,000 entries. This event triggered a renewed interest in paper gliders. In the past few years colorful booklets of stiff paper cut-outs or punch-outs of space planes

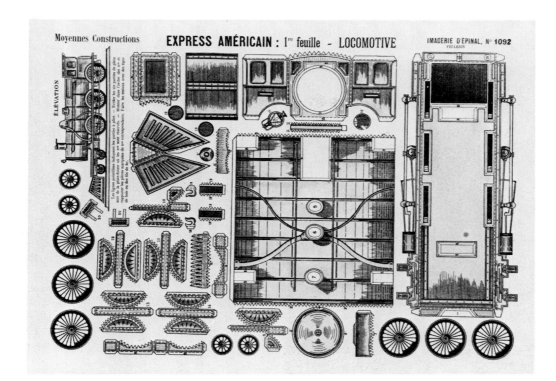

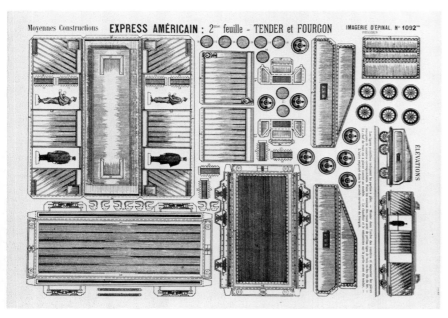

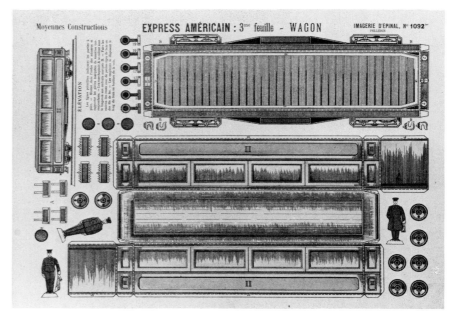

Illustration 263 A - C: Three *Moyennes Constructions* sheets titled *Express Americain.* **A.** Locomotive. **B.** Coal tender and baggage carriage. **C.** Passenger carriage. Published by Pellerin of Epinal, France, c.1895. Sheet size 11¾ x 15½in (29.9 x 39.4cm).

RIGHT: Illustration 264: A *Grandes Constructions* sheet titled *Gare Americaine (sic) A Maryland*. An American railway station in Maryland, topped with a pair of American flags. An early steam locomotive, tender and three passenger coaches of European outline stand in front of the station. Published by Pellerin of Epinal, France, c.1890. Sheet size 15¼ x 19⅜in (38.8 x 49.2cm).

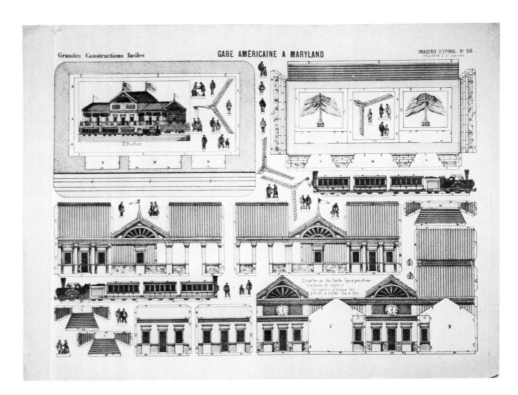

BELOW: Illustration 265: *Automobile de Course* is a *Moyennes Constructions* sheet with the parts to make an early racing car, along with the figures of the driver and a mechanic. Long distance races in Europe were the backbone of their automobile industry. Published by Pellerin of Epinal France, c.1910. Sheet size 11¾ x 15½in (29.9 x 39.4cm).

BELOW: Illustraton 266: *Autobus* is an example of a typical French bus of the 1920s. This *Moyennes Constructions* sheet has all the parts to make this model. Published by Pellerin of Epinal, France. Sheet size 11¾ x 15½in (29.9 x 39.4cm).

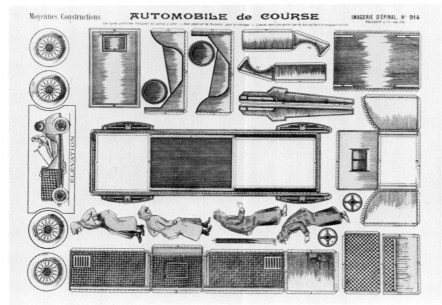

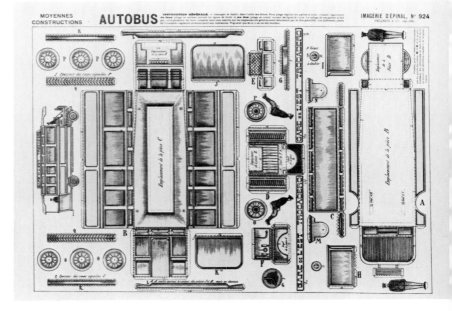

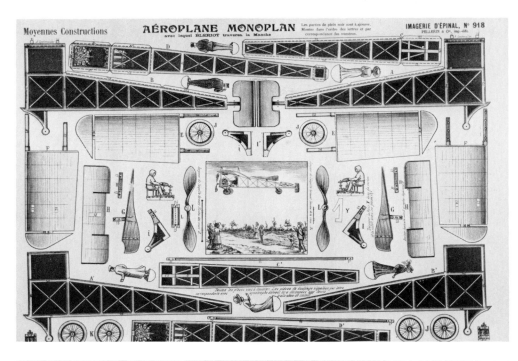

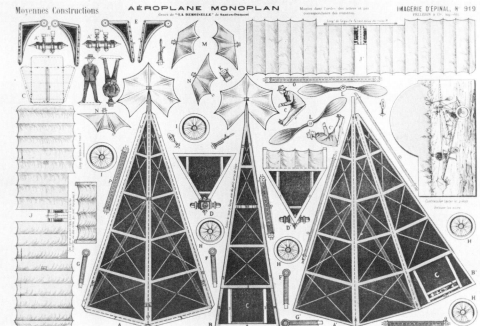

have proven to be highly popular with young boys.

While we have covered the major paper toys, there are other types that are both important and interesting. The following selections are picked at random in an effort to show the wide variety and scope of such toys.

In the 1803 Bestelmeier catalog the following items were listed: "No. 964, A Mongolfish Balloon, made of two or three sheets of fine colored paper, on the bottom is a gondola made of sheet metal with a bottom of braided wire. If you want to make the balloon rise, one person has to hold it up while another puts burning pressed paper into the gondola. The balloon will unfold and rise. A single sheet of paper will drive the balloon up higher than a church steeple, from there it will slowly drift down without damage. Such an amusement can be repeated may be 50 times." **Illustration 277.** The same catalog offers "Parachutes, made of paper, with which a small dog or cat can be let down. Children will have lots of fun with that." In the United States a patent was issued for a paper balloon in the shape of an elephant which, when filled with hot air, would float. It was issued to Edward F. Linton of East New York, New York, on August 8, 1882. Among other things, think of the thousands of pinwheels that have been played with by children of the past and the present.

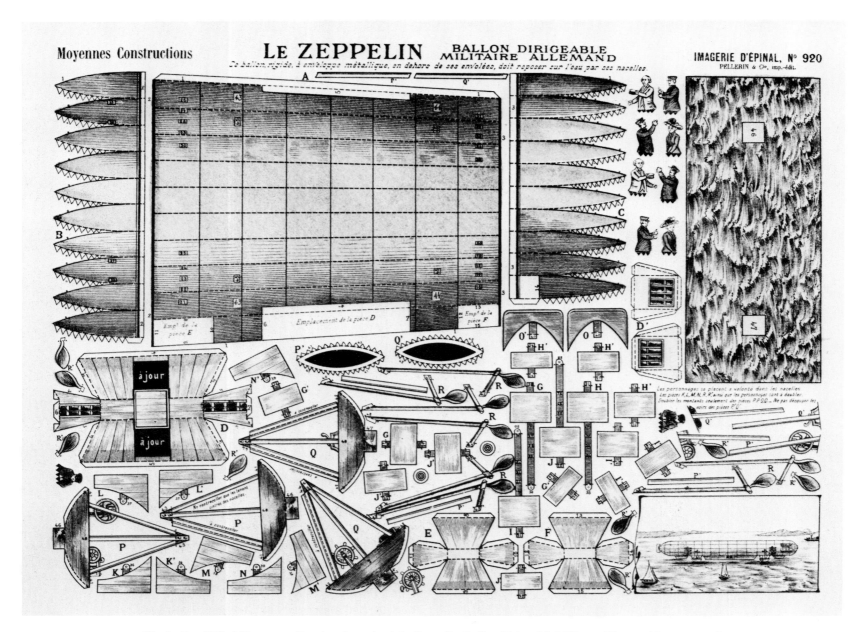

Illustration 269: A *Moyennes Constructions* sheet, *Le Zeppelin, Ballon Dirigeable Militaire Allemand*. It consists of parts to construct a German military zeppelin. Published by Pellerin of Epinal, France, c.1900. Sheet size 11¾ x 15½in (29.9 x 39.4cm). *Strong Museum Collection. Photo by Tom Weber and Mike Radke.*

Illustration 270: The finished paper model of Pellerin's *Le Zeppelin, Ballon Dirigeable* pictured in **Illustration 269**. This early airship was apparently made to land on water. Notice the propellers protruding from the sides of the airship above each gondola. *Photo by Barbara Whitton Jendrick.*

Illustration 271: The cover of a stiff page booklet containing cut-out parts to construct four outstanding planes of the world from 1918-1933. Included are the 1918 French Spad, the Ryan Spirit of Saint Louis of 1927, the Avia BH9 or 1923, and the Italian Macchi Castoldi seaplane of 1931. This booklet was published in Czechoslovakia, c.1950. Booklet size 9½ x 14in (24.2 x 35.6cm).

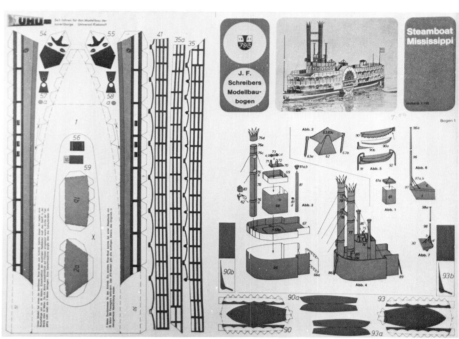

Illustration 272: A four-page folder featuring parts to build a paper model of an early American 4-4-0 steam locomotive. Published by J.F. Schreiber of Germany, c.1950. Folder size 12¾ x 8½in (32.5 x 21.6cm).

Illustration 273: A large five-page folder containing parts to build a paper model of the *Steamboat Mississippi*. Published by J.F. Schreiber of Germany. c.1950. Folder page size 12½ x 17⅛in (31.8 x 43.5cm).

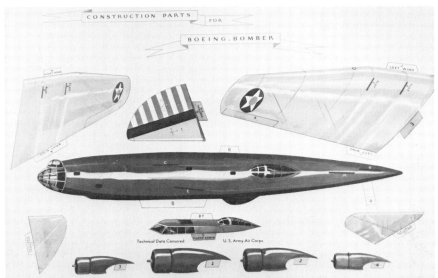

Illustration 274: This *Build it with Scissors, A Modern Put-Together Book* offered six building projects. One of the projects, the locomotive pictured above, was made up of 18 colored, pre-glued sections on two pages. These were to be cut out, the pre-glued backs moistened and applied one by one on a two-page spread until the locomotive was completed. Published by Samuel Gabriel Sons & Company of New York City, in 1929. Cover measures 10¼ x 12in (26.1 x 30.5cm).

Illustration 275 A & B: *Ships Aloft, A Construction Book For Future Flyers* is similar to the one mentioned in **Illustration 274. A** pictures a page of parts to be cut out and applied to the body pictured in **B**. Published by Harper & Brothers of New York City & London, England, in 1936. Cover size 11½ x 20in (29.2 x 50.8cm). *Collection Seymour Merral.*

Illustration 276: *Bombers*, the cover of a stiff page booklet containing the die-cut parts to assemble five plane models. Published by the Whitman Publishing Company in 1943. Cover size 11¾ x 9in (29.9 x 22.9cm).

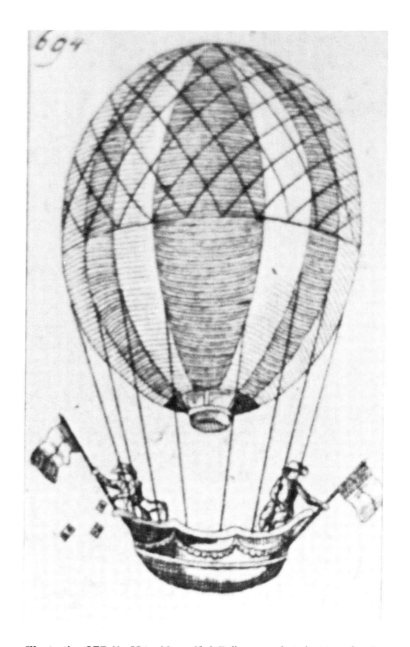

Illustration 277: No. 694, a Mongolfish Balloon, was listed, pictured and described in an 1803 Bestelmeier catalog. The balloon was constructed from sections of colored paper, the gondola of braided wire. Burning compressed paper in the gondola would cause the balloon to rise.

Chapter XVI.

BEAUTIFUL OR UNUSUAL ODDITIES

A group of paper educational objects which possibly could have been included in an earlier chapter, is pictured in **Color Illustration 40**. The world globe is shown hanging horizontally from the two poles, within its own cylindrical container. This early globe traces Captain Cook's three trips to explore and map islands and coastlines, mainly in the Pacific and Antarctic Oceans. The initial trip was made on the *Endeavor*, which left Plymouth, England, on August 25, 1768, in search of a supposed continent located in the South Pacific. Cook sailed and charted the vast ocean area between Tahiti, Australia, and New Zealand, but never found the supposed continent. He returned to England July 12, 1771. A second expedition of two ships, the *Resolution* and the *Adventure*, left England July 13, 1772. They returned home in 1775 after making many new discoveries in the South Pacific. A final trip was made on the *Resolution*, which left England July 12, 1776. Sailing to the same general area he discovered the Hawaiian group. Later, he sailed northward along the west coast of North America, up around the Aleutian Islands and into the Bering Strait, where he was stopped by an ice pack. Cook turned and headed back to Hawaii and warmer weather. It was there, in 1779, that he was killed by natives during an argument. James Cook (1728-1779) is remembered as one of the leading nautical explorers of the 18th century.

The two small square boxes contain variations of the game *The Earth and its Inhabitants*. The box on the right, nearest to the above mentioned globe, is possibly the earliest of the two examples. It carries a slightly different label, *The World with its Inhabitants*. Both have a small world globe and a folded panorama-like strip, with each panel

Illustration 278: An early game called *Myriorama* or *Endless Changes of Landscape*. The nine cards offer an almost limitless number of combinations as the lines at either side of any one card match the lines on the sides of all the other cards. The publisher and country of origin is unknown. The illustrations were the work of F. Giveinwald, c.1835. Each card is 7½in high x 2¾in wide (19.1 x 7.1cm).

picturing a native of each of the many countries of the world.

The early English game *Geographical Recreation or A Voyage Round the Habitable Globe* was published by John Wallis of London, England, in 1809.

An unusual early game called a *Myriorama*, or *Endless Changes of Landscape*, consists of nine cards which are engraved and hand colored, each picturing a section of a landscape. This form of puzzle appeared around 1825. **Illustration 278**

pictures a landscape consisting of a strip of land spotted with trees and shrubs, a goat, two sheep, and three people looking over a lake to the opposite shoreline which contains a church and a few buildings with sloping fields and mountains in the distant background. Although each card is marked with a Roman numeral, they may be arranged in any side-by-side order and produce a perfectly blended landscape scene. It allows an almost limitless number of combinations, as the lines at either side of any one card match the lines

on the sides of all the other cards. The line of the shoreline in the photograph, the distant shoreline, and the line of the horizon, all meet exactly on either side of all cards. Each card measures 7½ inches (19.1cm) high by 2¾ inches (7.1cm) wide. The original slip box measures 7⅝ by 3½ inches (19.4 x 8.9cm). The illustrations were done by F. Giveinwald, but the publisher is unknown.

There were several forms of *Metamorphoses* or *Changeable Portraits* available before and after the 1850s. These were a simple form of puzzle that offered high amusement rather than a degree of difficulty. While it can be found in several forms, it is basically a series of sliced cards. Each card has a beautifully colored figure of a person or animal. Each card may have a horizontal cut across the center with diagonal cuts from corner to corner in each half, or various other combinations of cuts. While the figures and costumes are all different, the widths of the illustrations along the sliced lines are equal, and therefore interchangeable. Hence all sections may be moved to form many humorous combinations.

A large French set titled *Jeu de Quiproquos* contains nine cut cards, each picturing a figure such as a fisherwoman, a house maid, a mother, a soldier, a doctor, a young lady, a fisherman, a gardener, and an old maid. Each card is cut into six pieces — three horizontal cuts on the upper half, with two diagonal cuts on the lower corners. The majority of the personalities pictured express a bit of French humor, as does the box cover seen in **Illustration 279**. This set was published by H. Rousseau of Paris, France, and lithographed by H. Jannin of the same city.

An early German *Metamorphoses* boxed set is titled *Rider Changements, Prince Albert, husband of the Queen, Victoria of England.* The box cover carries the title in five languages, and pictures a dashing young Prince Albert in military dress astride a bay horse. The 8 by 6½ inch (20.3 x 16.5cm) cards are divided by two angle cuts. There are six cards in the set. They picture the same Prince Albert that appeared on the box cover, Napoleon on a white charger, a Turkish Warrior on a brown horse, an Arab on a black steed, a Spanish Cabellaro on a brown horse, and

Illustration 279: An elaborate boxed set of *Metamorphoses* or *Changeable Portraits* titled *Jeu De Quiproquos.* As you can see, the top two-thirds of each card has three horizontal cuts, while the bottom third has two 45° angle cuts at each corner. All parts are interchangeable and offer many humorous combinations. Published by H. Rousseau of Paris, France, c.1865. Box size 12¼ x 15½in (31.2 x 39.4cm).

a Clown in military costume riding a large white goat. The liberal use of egg white to accent the richly colored illustrations is obvious. (**Illustration 280.**)

There are three small examples of German sets of *Metamorphoses* cards pictured in **Illustration 281**. The largest set pictured measures 5½ by 4 inches (14 x 10.2cm). The set on the left titled *New Metamorphoses for Young Ladies* is made up of eight cards, each with two equal horizontal cuts. The center set is titled *The Sister, in a beautiful variety of costumes* and contains six hand painted cards, each with two horizontal cuts. The last set is labeled the *New Metamorphoses, A collection of 5832 comical figures formed by joining, the annexed 54 engraved and coloured parts*. This set contains 18 cards, each with two horizontal cuts. All types of characters and animals, both wild and domesticated, are pictured.

A further example is an early, c.1840 boxed *Metamorphoses* set titled *The Collection of Likenesses or Portraits*. The contents consist of 14 cards, each portraying either human portraits or the head of an animal, some of which are rather grotesque. Each card measures 5⅜ by 3¾ inches (13.6 x 9.6cm) and is cut horizontally and vertically in eight equal sections. The 112 sections offer the opportunity to create hundreds of very unusual and humorous portraits. (**Color Illustration 41.**)

A very rare early American example of *Metamorphoses* was published by V.S.W. Parkhurst of 47 Westminster Street, Providence, Rhode Island. The box and its contents are pictured in their entirety in **Illustration 282**. The box measures 5 by 2¾ by 1/4 inches (12.7 x 7.1 x 0.65cm); all illustrations are carefully hand painted.

Turning from our *Metamorphoses* oddities to a lovely French boxed set we find we have a paper toy with a theatrical theme. The decorative box contains a four-panel folding background screen picturing a country landscape, cut-out figures of a young boy and girl standing on flat round wooden bases, and a group of nine overlay costumes. Included is a small green covered book which introduces a French family, Monsieur and

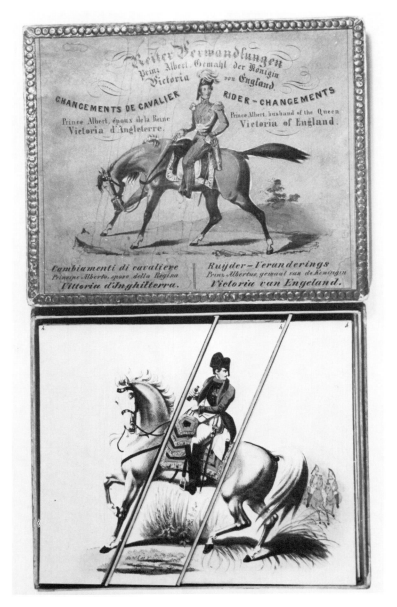

Illustration 280: An early *Metamorphoses* boxed set titled *Rider Changements Prince Albert, husband of Queen Victoria of England*. A set of six 6½ x 8in cards (16.5 x 20.3cm) are divided by two angle cuts. Pictured is the box cover and one of the cards picturing Napoleon. Publisher unknown. Possibly German. c.1850.

Illustration 281: Three examples of the simplest form of *Metamorphoses*. All cards with two horizontal cuts and engraved figures beautifully hand colored. Titled in three to four languages, unfortunately not marked as to publisher. Germany, c.1845. Center box cover measures 5¾ x 4in (14.7 x 10.2cm).

Illustration 282: A rare American example of *Metamorphoses* published by V. S. W Parkhurst of Providence, Rhode Island, c.1865. The hand colored cards are divided into three equal sections by horizontal cuts, offering hundreds of humorous combinations. The box measures 5in tall, 2¾in wide and 1/4in deep (12.7 x 7.1 x 0.65cm).

Madame de Mericourt, their daughter Amelie, and son Charles. The parents extremely satisfied with the zeal and application that their children give to their studies, decide to develop and write three or four simple plays that the children might act out during their coming school vacation. Monsieur de Mericourt writes four short plays, each having three to four acts, and each requiring just two characters. The four plays with complete dialogues are printed in the book. Madame de Mericourt designs and sews the various costumes necessary for the children to wear in the four plays. These costumes are represented in the paper costumes in the photograph. **(Color Illustration 42.)** The boy and girl figures stand 3½ inches (8.9cm) tall. The set was printed by G.

Doyen of Paris, France, in 1826.

A magnificent boxed set titled *Grand Theater of Metamorphoses* with a sub-title *In serious and grotesque representations* has a lavishly illustrated cover with the title given in four languages — German, French, English, and Spanish. **(Illustration 283.)** The contents of the box are equally beautiful. A second box forms a stage with an elaborate cut-out proscenium decorated with illustrations expressing a youthful theme. The background of the stage, which represents a distant landscape, has a long horizontal cut about an eighth of an inch (0.31cm) wide and is located about four inches (10.2cm) above the stage floor. Included in the set are seven pairs of related figures. Each cut-out figure has a flat hoop skirt-like black base. On each base is the colorful lower half of a costume. A tiny wooden pin joins this lower base to the double cut-out upper body, arms, and head. A small wooden turning knob behind the joining pin is made to slide along the horizontal cut on the back screen of the stage. It also enables the operator to slide a character on stage and, by a simple twist of the rear knob, change the character of one figure to another. For example: from beauty to the beast, a knight to a hound, or a pretty girl in a long pink dress to a scolding older woman. (**Color Illustration 43.**)

Another form of paper toy that falls into the category of beautiful and unusual oddities is the overlay cards. Here a series of like size cards, each usually decorated with a highly colored costume and a cut-out vertical oval above the neckline of the costume, may be placed on a base card that carrys a head and face. (Mention was made of overlay books in an earlier chapter.) **Illustration 284** pictures an early hand painted set of five cards and the original folder titled *Marchandes*. The bust of the young woman framed within the flower decorated oval is the base card. The four overlay cards picture her as different characters, the last one in a very uncomplimentary position. These cards measure 3¼ by 2¼ inches (8.3 x 5.8cm). **Illustration 285** displays the separated slipcase titled *Oriental Costumes* with a dressed figure on the back. The base card in this set pictures a head, while the remaining overlay cards depict various costumes. These richly colored cards measure 4¼ by 3 inches (10.9 x 7.6cm). Both of these examples date in the mid 1800s. Collectors will occasionally find a set of hand painted overlay cards cut out of isinglass and usually picturing natives and costumes of India. While they are not paper, they should be considered a welcome addition to any paper collection as an interesting overlay made of another material.

Our next oddity is both beautiful and humorous, and consists of two boxed sets which are related to one another — *The Comic Boy* and *The Comic Girl* both having a similar sub-title, *Amusement with a Swinging Pendulum Figure in*

Illustration 283: The box cover of the *Grand Theatre of Metamorphoses, In serious and grotesque representations.* (See **Color Illustration 43.**) This attractive cover commands as much attention as the theater itself. Published by G.W. Faber, Germany, c.1855. Cover measures 11¼ x 14¾in (28.6 x 37.6cm).

Many Forms. As you can see in **Color Illustration 44** each set has an assortment of five heads and a number of hats. All of these are adapted to slide on the upper bodies, which are supported on a wooden hanging assembly which holds a rocking and weighted upright shaft. The upper half of this shaft has a slot that accepts the forked slot on the neck of the heads. When a head is set in position and given a slight push, the head will slowly rock back and forth on the well balanced pendulum. The figures on the stands, without the hats, are 6¾ inches (17.2cm) high. The highly colored clothing and hair areas are varnished,

while faces, hands, and white areas are free of varnish. As you can see, the box covers are titled in German, French, and English. The boxes are marked "G.W. Faber" in script on the lower right corner. These toys appeared around 1850.

An interesting example of an uncut printers sheet picturing a complete paper doll set and the cover label is our next oddity. Color is applied by hand, some of it possibly by stenciling. Notice the color is applied with no attempt to keep it within the lines of the drawings. Any over painting would be eliminated later when the figures and dresses were cut out. Speed of coloring must have

Illustration 284: A small set of *Overlay Cards* consisting of the base card, the girl in the oval, four overlay cards with faces cut out and a slip case. Marked *Marchandes* and *De 5 Zinnen*. c.1850. Cards measure 3¼ x 2¼in (8.3 x 5.8cm).

Illustration 285: A set of 12 *Overlay Cards* with the base card picturing a male head and a front and back view of the slip case. Titled *Oriental Costumes*, it is not marked as to publisher or country of origin. c.1850. Card size 4¼ x 3in (10.9 x 7.6cm).

been a necessity to keep up with the presses. Notice, however, that the cover label is done with care; there is no overlapping of color. **(Color Illustration 45.)** This beautiful set has two identical child dolls, ten costumes, and nine headpieces, all having fronts and backs. What the method of securing the costume onto the figure was, poses a question. Could it have been applied straps at the shoulders, joining the dress front to the back and then slipping it over the doll's head? This sheet measures 20 inches (50.8cm) high and 26 inches (66cm) wide. Titled *Les Toilettes Du Bébé*, it is signed "B. Colldert, Saussine, edt. Paris."

The *Bal d'Enfants, travesti* is a beautiful oddity in several ways. The feeling of youthfulness in the decorations of the box cover, the unusual shape of the box and cover, the beauty of the contents, and the action provided to some of the tiny dolls when the scene is erected, is fascinating. The box cover is centered with a colorful illustra-

tion of a boy and girl dancing in the foreground, while other children and adult chaperons are dancing or conversing in the rear. This lovely illustraton is framed with an elaborate line-drawn design of cupids playing musical instruments, intermingled with scroll-like sprays of flowers and leaves. A pea-green embossed tape is applied to the edges of the eight-sided cover. The contents of this lovely box are set up as pictured in **Color Illustration 46**. The four small jointed dolls that are hung shoulder-high on a thread strung across the front of the elaborately furnished room, are provided with a dancing movement when the thread is lightly pulled from the outside wall. The thread is held taut by a small lead weight at each end. The jointed dancing figures are 2½ inches (6.4cm) tall. The beautiful room setting is 7 inches (17.8cm) high and 10¼ inches (26.1cm) wide. Seventeen tiny cut-outs of people and furniture, mounted on small half-

round wooden stands, complete this exquisite paper toy. The box cover is marked "de Lemercier Benard et Cie."

A second unusual dancing toy is a wonderful dancing doll with moveable legs and moveable flirting eyes. A paper doll, yes, but placed in this chapter because of her movements. The box cover is titled in English, German and French. Called *The Dancing Doll for Girls*, it has the subtitle, *A fine puppet with moveable eyes and limbs, and six different charming dresses, dances at the measure of a pendulum.* **(Illustration 286.)** The doll has an oversized head, possibly to accommodate the movement of the flirty eyes. The moving legs are formed as a three-piece unit with a small wire twist at the crotch and one at each of the knee joints to allow for movement. A broad cardboard loop at the rear of the shoulders of the doll would accept and hold the hanging weight of a pendulum, the swinging of which would move

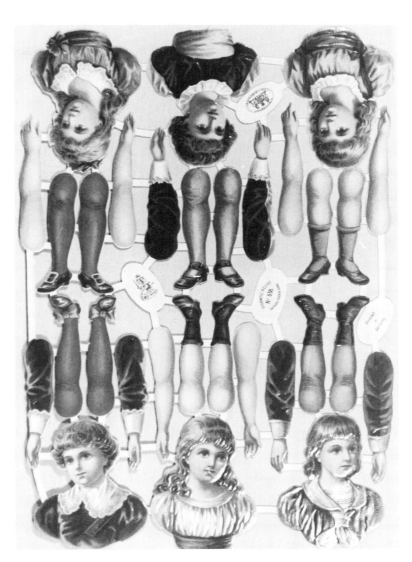

Illustration 286: Titled *The Dancing Doll for Girls. A fine puppet with moveable eyes and limbs, and six different charming dresses, dances at the measure of a pendulum.* A loop at the rear of the head may be hung on the pendulum of a wall clock. Such movement causes the doll's eyes and legs to move from side to side. This German set has no markings as to publisher. c.1870. Doll stands 8¼in (21.6cm) high.

Illustration 287: This sheet of embossed scrap clearly illustrates the thin white tabs that held the various related parts together. This example was published by Raphael Tuck of Great Britain and printed in Germany, c.1895. Size 8 x 4¾in (20.3 x 12.2cm). *Photo by Barbara Whitton Jendrick.*

Illustration 288: A small box of 24 hand colored cards titled *Feronica's hierogryphical riddles*. Included is a four-page folder titled: *A new, easy and agreeable method of sharpening young people's wit.* Publisher unknown. Marked "Made in Germany." c.1860. Cards measure 3⅝ x 2¼in (9.2 x 5.8cm).

the eyes and the legs to the left and back to the right, and so on. Unfortunately one dress and one headpiece appear to be missing, but all other parts are intact and show good color with slight wear. Here again, the use of egg white for highlighting the hand colored costumes is evident. This German-made set c.1870, has no publisher or printer identification marks.

The collecting of paper scraps and the pasting of them into books was a popular pastime during the 19th century. At the beginning of the 18th century, it was a practice of young women to cut out small prints, verses, love notes, and other momentos, and paste them in a blank book. In

many cases some early printed scraps were used to decorate the English theatrical portraits mentioned in an earlier chapter. In Europe, bakers and candymakers decorated their products with colorful scraps and appropriate verses. By 1825, a means of engraved steel embossing evolved and cutting dies soon followed — hence more and better scrap became available at lower prices. Children became involved and found it a fascinating pastime, and the demand for scraps soon doubled. These lovely glossy embossed chromolithographed sheets with figures and objects of all kinds in slight relief, were mainly a product of Germany. The demand became so great, world-

wide, that the German publishers established branches in countries with whom they traded.

The last quarter of the 19th century seemed to be the Golden Age of the production of scraps as both the quantity and quality reached a high level. The variety of the subject matter offered seemed unlimited. **Color Illustration 47** pictures a complete set of scraps titled *The Kings and Queens of England, The Entire Series of 37 Rulers from William the Conqueror to Queen Victoria*. It is extremely rare to have the 13 delicate units intact and showing good color. The original envelope, frayed and worn at the outer edges, is split; the printing however is clear and readable. **Illustration 287** pictures a sheet of scrap dolls showing how the pieces of scrap were held together by thin white tabs. Both examples pictured were products of Raphael Tuck of England.

The elegantly dressed figure pictured in **Color Illustration 48** is a jointed tab and slot figure. Made up of 23 hand colored pieces, he is 15 inches (38.1cm) tall when assembled. This mystic is a practitioner of sorcery; in his left hand he holds a staff that enables him to use his supernatural powers as he wishes and, from the expression on his face, he believes it.

Feronica's Hierogryphical Riddles is a boxed card game that possibly should have found a place in Chapter II. This small paper-covered wooden box contains 24 numbered hand colored cards in well preserved condition, and a four-page folder titled *A new, easy and agreeable method of sharpening young people's wit*. The contents of the folder are worth repeating here: "We shall forbear giving any directions for solving the hieroglyphic enigmatical language in which we offer the present number of proverbs, convinced, that nothing will tend more to the improvement of the juvenile mind, than a habit of guessing and solving the meaning of things, in whatever shape or form they may present themselves. We know moreover by experience, that patience and perseverance will overcome the greatest difficulties, and as both may therefore be numbered among the principal virtues that adorn mankind, we flatter ourselves, that our attempt of inculcating and promoting these virtues, in a manner both diverting and instructive, will meet with the approbation and support of parents and guardians. And should the difficulty of solving our riddles, in some instances, be increased by orthographical inaccuracies, we hope to be forgiven considering in how few instances the idiom of the English language admits of images, instead of words and letters; however not to deprive the lazy mind of the satisfaction of finding out the meaning of our riddles, we shall subjoin the solution for their perusal. At the same time we beg leave to offer our riddles as materials for playing forfeits. On being distributed indiscriminately among those who intend to join the game she or he who cannot, after the expiration of some minutes, read the contents of the card received, will be obliged to pay a forfeit. With the redeeming of these forfeits we shall not interfere, and all that remains to be said on our part, is, that we wish our young friends a good deal of patience and perseverance, but still more pleasure." Also included on the two-page folder are the solutions to the 24 riddles. The box cover is marked with the title and the words "Made in Germany," c.1860. **(Illustration 288.)**

This next example must be considered an oddity — a sheet portraying three male figures with separated heads. The feature is that the heads are drawn without a top or bottom. Each head has two faces, one entirely different from the other. One must turn the page upside down to observe the second face. For your convenience two identical sheets have been photographed, so that turning is not necessary. **(Illustration 289.)**

An early grouping of beautiful oddities are pictured in **Color Illustration 49**. Although four colorful riders and their assorted steeds are pictured, there are extra riders. The surprising feature of the set is that each rider is detachable and reversable as is the steed, and that the opposite side is entirely different. For example, reading from left to right, the boy in the military uniform on the dark brown horse becomes a cat holding a cage containing a mouse, and the steed becomes a white Billy Goat. The boy with the flowing plummed hat riding the white horse is

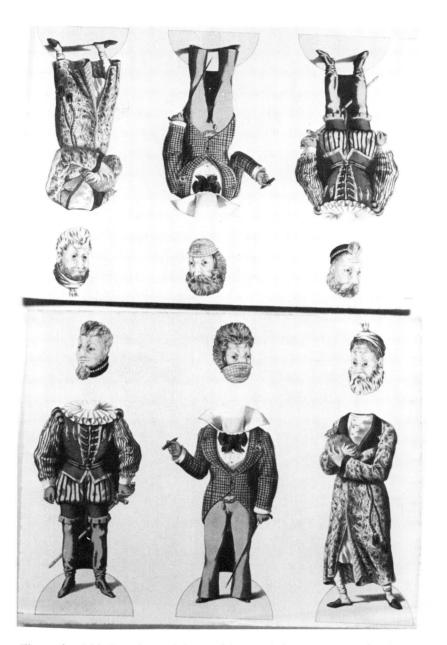

Illustration 289: Two identical sheets of three male figures with two-faced heads that have to be turned upside down to see the second face. Publisher unknown. French. Sheet size 14⅜ x 17¼in (36.5 x 43.9cm). *Photo by Barbara Whitton Jendrick.*

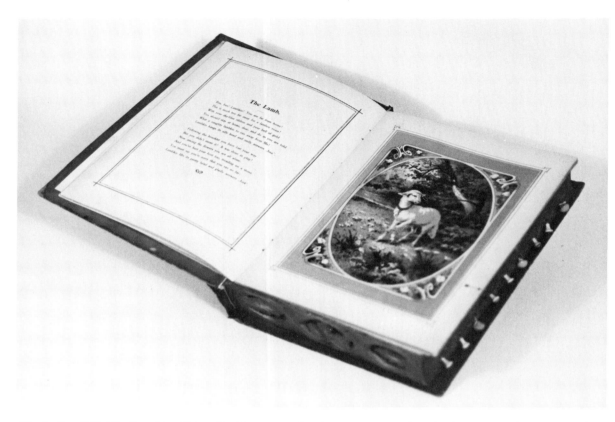

Illustration 290: *The Speaking Picture Book* has nine color plates picturing either a bird or an animal accompanied by verses on the opposite page. Each plate is marked with an arrow on the right margin, indicating which pull knob will make that animal speak. Patented by Theodor Brand of Sonneberg, Germany, in 1878. The book measures 12½ x 9½ x 2¼in (31.8 x 24.2 x 5.8cm).

turned to become a colorful Arab wearing a turban, and riding a large black bear. The monkey in military dress riding the rooster reverses to become a boy riding a zebra. And lastly, the boy riding the dog becomes a black prince riding a white dove. The two extra figures portray a farm boy playing a horn who, when reversed, becomes a well dressed city boy, and a handsome young man who becomes a tailor with an overly large nose. All are highly colored, and all clothing surfaces are varnished. The original box is missing, and possibly two more steeds. These were made in Germany, c.1875, but there is no identification as to publisher.

Another oddity is *The Speaking Picture Book*, a creation of Theodor Brand of Sonneberg, Germany. This is a novel toy book with lovely color plates picturing various domestic animals and birds which, at the pull of a cord, speak to the young reader. There are nine full-page color plates, each accompanied by verses on the opposite page. Pictured are a rooster, a donkey, a lamb, a bird feeding it's young, a cow, a cuckoo, a goat, and a mama and papa. Each plate has an arrow marked on the right margin of the page pointing to the pull knob that makes the animal in the picture speak. The grouping of nine squeak boxes, each with a different appropriate tone, are built into a box in the back three-quarters of the large 12½ by 9½ by 2¼ inch (31.8 x 24.2 x 5.8cm) book. Information on the title page of this novel book informs us of its high level of acceptance by children and parents alike. *The Speaking Picture Book* pictured in **Illustration 290** was exclusively printed for "F.A.O. Schwarz of 303-305 Fifth Avenue, New York City," and it was the 18th edition. It is also noted: "This work can be had at all Booksellers and Toy Shops in English, German, French and Spanish Editions." Brand was issued a United States patent for his book on December 30, 1879.

An unusual oddity is the boxed paper toy titled *La Dame De Paris*, which contains a cut-out stiff cardbaord doll similar to the one printed on the box cover. **(Color Illustration 50.)** She holds up her skirt revealing a horizontal kidney shape opening at the thigh level. Included in the box is a pair of knee high white cotton stockings with black satin shoes attached. The stocking tops are delicately decorated with pink ribbon. As you may surmise, two fingers are to be inserted in the kidney shape opening from the back, and the pair of stockings and shoes are placed on the fingers. Then the moving fingers become kicking legs. The costume of the figure is varnished, the face, hands and white petticoat are not. The figure measures 7½ inches (19.1cm) high. The figure on the box cover is varnished in a similar manner and is framed within a gilt embossed border with a pea-green edging. The publisher is unknown, but the set was certainly made for the French market, c.1890.

Raphael Tuck & Sons, Ltd. of England were prolific producers of a huge variety of paper toys. **Color Illustration 51** pictures four different highly colored embossed toys. Each of these toys is part of an individual set. The Scotch Lassie at the rear of the photograph is from a boxed set called *Father Tuck's Marionettes*. This set, c.1920, consists of ten figures, and all have action. The pull of a cord lifts the arms up, with each hand

Illustration 291: *Rocking Horses* is the title of a boxed set of six rocking toys. Colorfully dressed figures or animals riding on self-standing rocking horses or their partners. Marked "Artistic Toy Novelty Series No. 120," it was published by Raphael Tuck & Sons, London, England, c.1920. Average heighth of toys is 5¼in (13.4cm).

holding a small doll-like figure. Each figure has a descriptive verse by Clifton Bingham on its back side. The figures in this set include the pictured Scotch Lassie, Santa Claus, Jolly Jack, Puss in Boots, Friendly Bears, The Golliwogs, Happy Jappy, Dinah, Red Riding Hood and The Little Kittens. The figures measure between 10 and 11 inches (25.4 and 27.9cm) in height.

The boy riding the horse on the left, is a part of the *Artistic Toy Novelty Series No. 122* (c.1910)

titled *Young Riders*. This boxed set consists of six boy and girl riders with patented double legs which straddle the backs of the six horses. The two inside legs of each horse are hinged enabling the horse to stand. The horse and rider stand 8½ inches (21.6cm) high.

The groom walking the horse carrying the little girl in the sailor outfit is from the *Artistic Toy Novelty Series No. 121* (c.1910) called *Healthy Pastimes*. This set is composed of four

self-standing pairs of figures each having a horse, in one case two horses. These figures stand 8 inches (20.3cm) high.

The rocking toy in the foreground is a selected piece from *Father Tuck's Toy Rockers, Series No. 52*. This set contains ten pieces consisting of the sailor boy, an elephant, a little girl, a cat, a girl with flowers, a dog in a clown costume, a clown, a black child, and an Oriental child.

Raphael Tuck & Sons published several other

Illustration 292: *Driving to Pasture* contains six stand-up figures of children tending groups of domesticated animals and fowl. Marked "Artistic Toy Novelty Series No. 123," it was published by Raphael Tuck & Sons, London, England, c.1920. Average heighth of figures 4½in (11.5cm).

boxed sets and envelopes or Rocking Toys, the subject matter of which was children or wild and domestic animals. **(Illustration 291.)** One extremely fine set *Artistic Toy Novelty Series No. 120* is titled *Rocking Horses*. Five of the cut-out toys feature rocking horses which carry a varied group of equestrians, such as Mother Goose and Punch, a monkey, a cat, a dog, and a black boy. The sixth figure is a Clown riding on the back of a second Clown who grasps the rockers with his hands and feet. These rocking horses have hinged legs and double rockers that may be spread enabling the rocking horse to stand, or with a

slight push rock. The toys stand 5¼ inches (13.4cm) tall and possibly date in the mid 1920s.

Some other novelty toys published by the Tuck firm included *The Artistic Toy Novelty Series No. 123*. It is titled *Driving to Pasture*, and consisted of six shepherd lads and lasses driving sheep, poultry, and other farm animals. **(Illustration 292.)** A further oddity shows a boxed set titled *The Flying Wonder*, which contains six embossed standing figures, each holding a springy wire in his or her hand, giving movement to the figure. **(Illustration 293.)** A unique boxed set which uses mirrors in a novel way is titled *See*

Yourself. It contains three groupings of two people using mirrors in a comic and humorous manner. The *Three Merry Mirror Groups* are pictured along with the box cover in **Illustration 294.**

A final example of Raphael Tuck & Sons' exciting work is pictured in **Illustration 295.** This is a game of chance in the form of a round-a-bout. This spinning game called *The Merry Go-Round* is a fragile bit of cut-out work and one wonders, after many spins, how the hanging riders have survived. The game dates c.1925.

Illustration 293: *The Flying Wonder* set consists of six figures holding a short length of springy wire with a toy or bird at the far end. A simple novelty toy with action, published by Raphael Tuck & Sons, London, England, c.1910. Average heighth of figures without wire 5in (12.7cm).

Illustration 294: *See Yourself,* "Artistic Toy Novelty Series No. 130," consists of three merry mirror groups. Published by Raphael Tuck & Sons, London, England, c.1910. Average heighth 7½in (19.1cm).

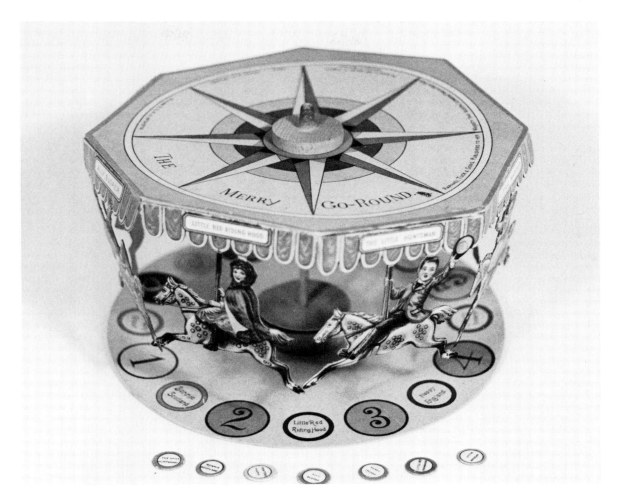

Illustration 295: *The Merry Go-Round* is the title given this spinning game of chance. Highly colorful with delicately cut-out horses and riders, it is surprising that it is still intact. Published by Raphael Tuck & Sons of London, England, c.1925. It is 6¼in (15.9cm) high and has a diameter of 9in (22.9cm).

Chapter XVII.

PAPER TOYS FOR TODAY'S COLLECTOR

Having read the book to this point and studied the photographs of the hundreds of interesting paper toys, the reader should have more than a passing interest in the subject. To some who are already collectors of paper ephemera, may your knowledge be broadened on the subject of paper toys and may your desires increase, for there are still beautiful items to be found.

To those of you who feel that collecting paper toys might be interesting and pleasant fun, it is. In all the various fields of present day collecting there are probably none that offer more in quantity and quality at an affordable price. Understandably there are hundreds of paper toys that have age and great condition, and that will command high prices, but they do not appear on the market frequently. There are also hundreds of different paper toys, be they 35 years old or less, plus scores of original creations and well done reproductions of earlier items, that have been published in the past five to ten years.

Card games, board games, and puzzles are still being published by the old leaders of the industry, Parker Brothers and Selchow & Righter. Once a new game or puzzle is discontinued, it becomes collectible. Old games, particularly card games, show up at antique shows and flea markets. Do not buy an old card game or puzzle if it is not complete, unless it dates before 1875.

Peep shows and panoramas are rather hard to find, particularly here in the United States. An example of an original well done peep show titled *The Enchanted Forest*, by Trina Schart Hyman, was published by G.P. Putnams Sons in 1984, and it is well worth space in any paper toy collection. It features a vista lined on both sides with old gnarled trees in which a number of elves, gremlins and forest animals are half hidden, all

peering out at the golden haired princess who appears to be lost in the wilderness. However, a prince on a white horse is rapidly approaching her, his castle looms in the distant background. If you are fortunate enough to be able to visit Europe, your chances of finding this type of toy are greater. A few well printed reproductions of ealry panorama-type books, such as *The Doll's House* and *The City Park*, both originally by Lothar Meggendorfer, are available at this writing. Three nice original fold-out panoramas were produced by Intervisual Communications of California in the past few years. Titles include *My House*, *Smiley's Super Service Station*, and *Uncle Tony's Farm*; all show great detail and imagination.

Toy books with movement offer many kinds of opportunities to the novice collector. Examples, sometimes in worn condition, can be found at antique shows and flea markets. Remember that good condition in paper toys is of prime importance. If it does not work mechanically, but all the parts are there and the price is fair, consider it. Ask yourself, "Do I have the time and ability to repair it correctly?" If exposed parts are missing do not buy it, another better example will turn up in the future.

Good reproductions of early moveable books have appeared on the market each year for the past five years. They are well done and can be handled without fear of damage. Keep it in your collection until you find an original at a fair price. Examples such as *Surprise! Surprise!*, originally by Lothar Meggendorfer, *The Children's Theater*, originally published by J.F. Schreiber in 1878, and *The Great Menagerie*, also originally published by Schreiber in 1884, are all available in book stores at the present time.

There are scores of new moveable books that have appeared on the market, particularly in the past five years. The quality of color, and the design of some of them is equal to the older examples. The mechanical action in some cases exceeds the best of the early examples. Classics such as *Cinderella*, *Robin Hood*, *Gulliver In Lilliput*, *Aladdin & The Wonderful Lamp*, *Alice in Wonderland*, *Pinocchio*, *Raggedy Ann*, and *The Wizard of Oz*, are found in modern moveable books with pop-up and pull-tab features. Moveable books based on comic strip characters with the same type of action, plus an occasional rotating disc, seem to be popular. Characters such as *Popeye*, a modern *Buck Rogers*, *Nancy & Sluggo*, the *Flintstones* series, the *Yogi Bear* series, *Snoopy's Secret Life* and the *Muppet Show* series, are all appealing. Action books featuring *Superman*, *Wonder Woman*, *Spiderman* and *The Incredible Hulk*, are available. Spage Age moveables include *Astronauts On the Moon*, *Space Mission*, *The Space Shuttle*, *Star Wars*, the *Star Trek* series, *The Black Hole* and the *Return of the Jedi*. Recent issues such as *Leonardo Da Vinci*, *Sailing Ships* and *The Human Body*, are outstanding examples of moveable books and are very educational. These, and many more good action books, are available to today's collector and they increase in value as the years go by.

Paper soldiers and their weapons will be with us for generations to come. They seem to appear in cycles and, since World War II, have slumped in popularity to a low level. Die-cut soldiers of the McLoughlin 1910-1925 period appear occasionally at antique shows. World War I and II figures frequently appear, seldom in complete boxed sets, but as individual pieces or in booklet form.

Europe is the place to find a variety of paper soldiers, not that they are plentiful, but publishers in several countries still occasionally produce them. In Britain, numerous sheets of knights of old and their weapons are readily available.

If your interest is in paper dolls and their attractive paper outfits, your choice and chance of obtaining them is probably greater than all the other paper toy collectibles together. Old, original paper dolls, usually cut out, can readily be found at auctions or flea markets at reasonable prices. Magazine sheets from 1910 through 1940 issues are available, although they are not as plentiful as they were five years ago. Pre-World War I boxed sets are rare, occasionally turning up at an auction and commanding a high price. Good reproduction paper dolls from various periods are readily available.

Many talented people have created fabulous original paper dolls, all of which are highly collectible. Tom Tierney, probably the most prolific, has produced examples from many periods. From *Great Empresses & Queens*, to an *American Family of The Colonial Era*, to *Pavlova & Nijinsky* and on to several of the glamorous movie stars, to recent issues of the *Nancy Reagan Fashion Paper Doll* and a *Ronald Reagan Paper Doll*. Pat Stall, Susan Sirkis, Peggy Jo Rosamond, Kathy Albert, Susan Johnston and others have created many wonderful and collectible paper dolls.

Books on the subject of the paper dolls are available and are a "must" for identification and the correct groupings within a set. *Those Fascinating Paper Dolls* is considered the "Bible" of paper doll books. A reproduction originally written by Marion Howard, it covers the earliest of paper dolls to those of the early 20th century. *Antique Advertising Paper Dolls*, authored by Barbara W. Jendrick, is a source of information and pictures of advertising dolls. *The Paper Doll*, by Barbara Chaney Ferguson, covers the birth and growth of paper dolls from the late 1700s to the present. Also included are tips on preservation, storage, and sources for paper dolls. These books and all the above booklets, plus a number of others, are available from Hobby House Press, Inc., of Cumberland, Maryland.

A variety of paper theater building booklets have appeared on the United States market during the past ten years. Some were for a children's audience, others for teen-agers, and some for adults. In 1978, Charles Scribner's Sons of New York City published *The Time & Space Theater*, designed and illustrated by Deborah R. Horner. It consisted of a cut-out and put-together highly colored stage along with line drawings of scenery, props, and marionette characters to color. Detailed drawings of stage construction were included. There are nine large pages of characters, some representing figures and animals from old fairy tales, and a second group representing space creatures. There is no printed story. The two groups meet in space, and the children maneuvering the puppets make up their own imaginative dialogue.

A second construction theater set is composed of a series of sheets which are colorfully printed with 32 dancers, numerous props, a puppet theater, and a carousel. The brightly colored large folder that boxes the sheets is the basic stage itself, after going through a refolding process. When assembled, this unit becomes a pictorial representation of the 1911 Paris Ballet Russes production of *Petrouchka*, in which the great Nijinsky danced the leading role. This beautiful production was designed by Jane F. Kendall, with an historical text by Leonard S. Marcus. It was published by David R. Godine of Boston, Massachusetts, in 1983.

A third example is in the form of a large 144-page paperback book titled *Make your own World of the Theater*. Written and designed by Rosemary Lowndes and Claude Kailer, it was published by Little, Brown, in 1982. Page after page features fine accurate, softly colored drawings of the stage sections — proscenium, scenery, characters and props, with detailed step-by-step assembling instructions and numerous drawings of the various stages of construction. When assembled, you have a 10¾ by 9 inch (27.4 x 22.9cm) three-dimensional theater which is modeled after the Royal Opera House in London, England. It is complete with fantastic interior and exterior detail and an orchestra. Also included are the parts to make up two productions: *The Sleeping Beauty*, a ballet in a prologue and four acts, five sets, dancers, and stage directions, and *La Boheme*, and opera in four acts with three sets, singers, and stage directions.

Publishers in Great Britain have offered many great toy theaters over the years, and are continuing the tradition today. Four or five reproductions *Pollock's Toy Theaters*, plays such as *Sleeping Beauty*, *St. George & The Dragon*, *Cinderella*, and *Ali Baba & The 40 Thieves*, are available. Visitors to Stratford-on-Avon, England, may purchase a booklet with parts to model Shakespear's Globe Theater. Models of Shakespear's birthplace and Anne Hathaway's cottage are also available.

Turning from theaters to other types of buildings, from houses to larger imposing edifices, we have quite a selection to choose from. In 1980, Dover Publications of New York City offered a well produced reproduction of McLoughlin Brothers' 1897 version of *The Pretty village*. The 24 pages in full color pictured 18 structures to be cut out, assembled, and glued. From an 1897 village we turn to a land of fantasy, the *Emerald City of Oz*. Art and design were by Dick Martin, and published by Dover. It is a cut-out assemble booklet containing 16 colorful pages with the makings for 14 structures and 15 two-sided paper dolls representing Dorothy, Toto, the Scarecrow, the Tin Woodsman, the Cowardly Lion, and the Wizard. Turning to another land of make believe we find *A Smurf Village*, a 32 page punch-out booklet by Peyo, designed by James Razzi, and published by Random House of New York City, in 1982. Some construction sets might be classified as edifices. A series called *The World at Your Feet*, by Allan Rose, offers many examples. Rose, a graphic designer in New York City, has offered a challenge in each of his beautiful paper construction projects. Some of the projects are: the U.S. Capitol and the Washington Monument, the Sears Tower, the Chrysler Building, the Booklyn

Bridge, the Tower Bridge & Tower of London, and the Eiffel Tower. All are spectacular, requiring patience, dexterity, and time to build. Captions on the covers read: "So Easy Even an Adult Can do it," and "Hours of Fun for the Ambitious Builder." They are produced by Perigee books, published by the Putnam Publishing Group.

German paper model kits are still published by J.F. Schrieber and are available in many of the better hobby shops. Available at the present time are nine of the great European castles, from the small Castle Hornfeld to the magnificent Castle Hohenzollern. Other new Schrieber cut-out packets, ranging from paper dolls to Punch & Judy shows, are available.

Edmund Gillon Jr. has designed three interesting groups of cardboard buildings in H.O. scale in 9¼ by 12¼ inch (23.6 x 31.2cm) booklets. An *Early New England Village*, *A Western Frontier Town*, and a group of four *Victorian Houses* are extremely well done and simple to erect. A.G. Smith has designed a replica of a *Main Street* in H.O. scale. The booklet, similar in size to those mentioned above, consists of 48 pages of parts and instructions. These four booklets are available from Hobby House Press, Inc., of Cumberland, Maryland.

Paper optical toys are rather hard to come by, possibly because collector interest in them is far greater than the supply. Few reproductions of paper optical toys have appeared on the market. Dover Publications published a copy of McLoughlins' *Anamorphic* set, 1885, consisting of 24 colorful cards picturing strange curved, elongated illustrations and a sheet of shiny silver mylar to be affixed to a short cardboard cylinder. This replaces the original mirrored glass cylinder. These distorted illustrations look normal when observed in the mirror-like cylinder. The Troubador Press of California has produced at least ten model books in the past few years. Three of them, *3-Dimensional Optical Illusions*, *Paper Movie Machines*, and *Photo & Scene Machines*, deal in the construction of paper optical toys. The *Photo & Scene Machines* booklet contains ten optical projects: Anamorphic Pictures, a Camera Obscura, a Photographic View Camera, a Magic Lantern, a Zoetrope, a Diorama Theater, a Kaleidoscope, a Bisceneorama, and a Stereoscope. This booklet contains full-size decorative black-and-white patterns, step-by-step drawings of different stages of construction, clear and simple directions, and bits of historical background about the objects and the men who invented them.

In 1979, a Borzoi Book, published by Alfred A. Knopf Inc., of New York City, appeared on the market. Titled *The Book of Moving Pictures*, it contained 12 stiff card pages illustrating the colorful discs of a Phenakistoscope. The punch-out discs, full-size, are highly original renditions of the early discs. They were created by a woman artist, Demi.

Bellerophon Books of California has published several construction books covering various forms of transportation. *Great Trains, to cut out and put together* was offered in 1979. It offers historical background of early and late steam locomotives, as well as construction parts to build four locomotives. The models include the Stourbridge Lion of 1829, the Brother Jonathan of 1832, an American 4-4-0 of the 1837-1885 period, and a 4-6-0 Ten Wheeler that was active from 1890 to the demise of the steam locomotive. This booklet is not in color but directions and drawings are well done.

Another well designed line of paper construction toys called the *Model Historic Aircraft Series* is the creation of Peter A. Zorn Jr., and Eugene and Asterie Provenzo. One example, the *Spirit of St. Louis, Ryan N.Y.P.*, provides the parts for Lindbergh's famous plane and, additionally, the parts to construct a small Model T Ford truck. Alan Rose, a master designer and modeler mentioned earlier, has designed several large, well detailed transportation models. Models of the famous *Titanic*, the supposedly unsinkable ship that sank after hitting an iceberg on her maiden voyage, and the modern *Saturn V Rocket*, are fantastic. Both booklets contain step-by-step assembling instructions along with an introduction containing the history and unique features of the prototype of each model.

A British company, Time Travellers, has produced a wonderful card model kit of an authentic replica of a 1910 London bus. Each pre-cut part is printed in full color and, when assembled, produces a realistic 14 inch (35.6cm) long model —even the wheels revolve. Designed as a double-deck bus, the top is open to the elements, as is the driver's seat, although it does have a bit of a roof overhead. Much attention is given to accurate detail of parts under the chassi, to the curving rear steps up to the second level, and to the construction of the seats on that level. The body is red with cream trim, and is well marked with various route destinations. The exterior sides of the upper seating level are covered with advertisements of products from the 1910 era.

A great number of space toys have appeared on the market that have been popularized by the trip to the moon and the movie versions of space adventures. Scores of colorful space ships and equipment have appeared in punch-out and assemble booklets. Random House of New York City has released several over the years. *Star Trek Action Toy Book* in 1976, *Star Wars* in 1978, *Super Heroes* in 1981, and *Return of the Jedi* in 1983, are four of several outstanding examples released by them. Wayne McLoughlin created and designed a fantastic *Space Shuttle*, a complete kit in a book. Included is background information on American space trips and a chronological listing of all known space trips in the world, from 1926 to March 30, 1982. This booklet was published in 1982 by Little, Brown & Company of Boston, Massachusetts, and Toronto, Canada.

While some of the above booklets had occasional flying or gliding planes within their contents, there are other booklets that contains only gliders that are hand propelled. Michael Grater's book *Cut & Fold Paper Spaceships That Fly* has 16 full-color models that glide. Published by Dover Publications Inc., it is dated 1980. Another paperback book of 120 pages is titled *Paper Flight*. Written by Jack Botermans, it offers complete instructions for making 48 folding models that fly. Some are very simple in design, others very complex with a varied range in between. The publisher is Holt, Rinehart & Winston of New York City, and it appeared on the market in 1983.

The last example is a booklet titled *U.F.O. Punch Outs* with a sub-title *They really fly! No scissors, No paste, Seven flying U.F.O.s, U.F.O. Launcher, Shuttlecraft & Space Station*. Published by Random House in 1979, the toys have good color, are well designed, and show fine detail.

The majority of the above construction booklets are attractively colored, well designed, and printed on a fine grade of heavy cardstock. They are a credit to the publishers, prices are reasonable and, if you wish to construct any of the models, the finished object is very durable.

The Metropolitan Museum of Art issues a catalog of mail order items under the title *Presents for Children*, usually before the start of the Christmas season. In the past few years they have offered several nice paper toys in the form of games, pop-ups, cut-out booklets, and masks. It is one source where the collector may find beautiful or unusual paper oddities that are pleasing to the eye. The following examples are some of the oddities that are offered. Players participate in a family board game called *By Jove*; they escape from the labyrinth and voyage with a character named Jason in quest of the Golden Fleece. Players vie to collect the necessary coins and awards to win, and may be influenced by the whims of unpredictable gods or the decrees of the oracles.

A book of *Medieval War Games*, by Nicholas Slope, tells the story of the age of knighthood and the world they lived in. It includes a fascinating boardgame that recreates a medieval tournament and a full color, three-dimensional pop-up diorama representing the setting and staging of a jousting tournament.

Another board game, *Made For Trade*, pictures an early American seaport town. With this board and accompanying deck of cards, four different games may be played. The simplest gives a wonderful glimpse of early town life. The more advanced games involve the intricacies of American trade, including options to purchase, taxa-

tion, and such set-backs as Indian attacks.

The Nutcracker is a ballet cut-out booklet by Jane Kendall. It contains a colorful fold-out theater with three scene changes, 24 costumed characters, and several props, one of which is a magical Christmas tree that grows. Included is the story and history of the ballet and instructions on how to assemble it. As an added feature, a Tchaikovsky's *Nutcracker Suite* cassette may be ordered with the book.

A fold-out, pop-up castle called *Pendragon Castle*, is a four-section panorama, complete with knights and damsels performing the activities of the day during medieval times. The castle was first built, according to legend, by King Arthur's father, Uther Pendragon.

The Nativity is a fold-out, pop-up, creche scene that opens out to a 24 inch (61cm) width. The four scenes are filled with religious figures based on the beautiful 18th century Neapolitan creche figures from the Metropolitan Museum of Art's famous Christmas tree.

Sturdy cardboard masks in full color, featuring principal characters from the *Wizard of Oz* may be found in booklet form. Cut out and assemble Dorothy, Toto, the Wicked Witch, and five other characters from Frank Baum's classic.

Possibly the most unusual oddity is a 40-page construction booklet titled *Make Your Own Working Paper Clock*. Copyrighted by James Smith Rudolph, and published by Harper & Row, Publishers Inc., of New York City, it appeared in 1983. It consists of 160 uncolored sections to be cut out; all you need is scissors and glue. It is operated by weights, can be rewound and regulated to keep perfect time, and it works.

As you can see there are many new paper toys available, many reproductions, and a limited number of the older examples. This offers several roads to a pleasurable and inexpensive pastime. You may become a collector of all types of paper toys, or decide to collect and enjoy just one type. It may be theaters or possibly soldiers, depending on your interests. You may wish to collect construction booklets because you enjoy building things. In this case purchase two of the same booklets

instead of one, using one to cut out and assemble, enjoying the challenge of constructing and the satisfaction of completing the project. Keep the second booklet intact as it will increase in value as time passes.

You may have a different need for the use of a paper toy. As a parent playing with a youngster, the child will receive much in the way of educational benefits plus companionship working on such a project. Teachers may use the booklets such as *Leonardo Da Vinci*, *The Human Body*, and *Inside the Personal Computer*, all will interest students in their respective specialized classes. Youngsters of all ages, if temporarily bed ridden, would be grateful to receive a paper construction toy. Building this toy will put him in a good frame of mind, and time will pass more quickly. Older people who are retired and have need for activities to keep them busy can become paper toy builders.

Paper construction projects are unlimited in scope if you create your own. They are for everyone, young and old alike. For those with little imagination write to the U.S. Patent Office in Washington D.C. and obtain one of the patented paper toys listed in the next chapter. Make a copy of the patented toy. The patent copy tells you how to construct the toy, and the drawing itself will assist you. Paint and decorate your copy to your own satisfaction. Display your toy along side a copy of the patent drawing. You will derive a lot of pleasure from this and, perhaps, your friends will suggest that you do others and many even try one themselves.

An alternative project would be to go back through this book, look at the photos and pick a toy that appeals to you, and that you feel is within your capability to build. Don't sell yourself short, try it, you may have hidden talent that needs experimentation and some development. If you are not very artistic, use colored paper to build. If you have a bit of artistic talent, paint and decorate it. You may even go a step further and customize it, or recreate it for a different time period. A simple example might be turning a Pantin Jester into a space person. Another example could be using an old building sheet as a pattern and, from it, design and build an important house or building in your home town. Build a peep show featuring something outstanding in your city or state, a building, a statue in a park, an historical or current event. Build your own theater, write a short simple play based on an event in your town, design the characters involved. Children can build a theater out of a shoe box. Cut an opening in the front, set two dowel reels in the back, and run the daily comic strips through it. Decorating the box theater and coloring the comic strips is additional fun. Express your capabilities in a paper toy. The first one may turn out to be only fair, but a second try might be great.

Chapter XVIII.

PAPER CONSERVATION HINTS & PAPER TOY PATENTS

Early paper contained a high rag content and it was this ingredient that gave it greater lasting qualities. Many years passed before paper production reached to a point where the demand for it was at a peak and the supply of rags lessened to such a degree that it was necessary to replace the rags with another substance — wood pulp. While wood pulp made a good paper, the paper lost its lasting quality because of the acid content of the wood. Acidity in paper is one of the principle reasons for its deterioration.

pH is a measure of the acidity or alkalinity of a solution. Numerically pH 7.0 is neutral, numbers above this neutral point become increasingly alkaline; below it, increasingly acid. Land is made up of scattered areas of acid or alkaline soil of varying degrees. This acid or alkaline content, along with other traces of mineral elements, are drawn from the earth in the form of nourishment and moisture by the roots of trees. These elements are deposited throughout the tree.

Unfortunately, most wood seems to retain these traces of acidity. Modern acid paper does not have a long life expectancy unless it is treated with an alkaline substance to neutralize it. This has presented many problems in its application. As pH 7.0 is neutral, the ideal safe pH level for paper would range between 6.5 and 8.5. To produce paper that has a neutral pH is expensive, impractical for use in paper toys and numerous other paper products. With this brief explanation of the problem of acidity in paper, let us turn to some common sense rules that we, as paper collectors, can follow. Hoping to keep our collection in a stable condition we must remember that sunlight and dampness are the two major contributors to the breakdown of paper. Remember, also, that the ideal humidity should be 55% in Summer and 45% in the Winter.

1. Intense sunlight or daylight thru windows must be avoided.
2. In display cabinets, protect objects against ultra-violet radiation from the light of florescent tubes. Cover tubes with U.V. absorbing plastic sleeves.
3. Objects placed in dark dry storage will have nearly double the life of an object exposed to light.
4. Heat can bring about extreme dryness which causes paper to become brittle, causing fibers within the paper to break down when handled.
5. Dampness causes paper to swell, and with continued dampness mold will flourish.
6. Keep objects free from soot and dust; protect them from furnace or oil burner soot.
7. Avoid thumb prints and finger marks, they contribute to the breakdown of paper and to the deterioration of colors and designs on the object.
8. Paper toys with serious tears or soiling should be put in the hands of a conservator. Check examples of his past work — there are all kinds of conservators.

The following is a list of patented paper toys, their numbers, the inventor, and the date the patent was issued. They date from 1867 to March of 1927. Board and card games and puzzles are not included. There were patents issued on a fantastic number of games and puzzles, unfortunately only about half of them were ever manufactured. It is for that reason they are not listed.

PATENT #	OBJECT	NAME & ADDRESS	DATE
72,855	Bird Kite	Edward I. Hughes Pittsburgh, PA	Dec. 31, 1867
79,782	Toy House	Emily Russel Plymouth, MA	July 7, 1868
100,466	Wind Wheel	Edward Taylor Hartford, CT	Mar. 1, 1870
Des. 4,368	Wind Toy	Wm. C. Goodwin Hamden, CT	Sept. 27, 1870
Des. 4,369	Wind Toy	Wm. C. Goodwin Hamden, CT	Sept. 27, 1870
Des. 4,370	Wind Toy	Wm. C. Goodwin Hamden, CT	Sept. 27, 1870
160,994	Paper Toy	W.H. Backus Boston, MA	Mar. 23, 1875
163,866	Paper Doll	W.H. Hart, Jr. Philadelphia, PA	June 1, 1875
169,020	Hot Air Toy	J.P. Michaels New York, NY	Oct. 19, 1875
184,384	Changing Picture	J. Kayser New York, NY	Nov. 14, 1876
198,050	Theater	J.W. Scott New York, NY	Dec. 11, 1877
223,108	Speaking Book	Theodor Brand Sonneberg, Germany	Dec. 30, 1879
239,281	Card Game	Walter Stranders New York, NY	Mar. 22, 1881
242,709	Dissected Picture	Walter Standers New York, NY	July 7, 1881
244,745	Dissected Picture	C.P. Goldey New York, NY	July 26, 1881
246,863	Game Cards	Milton Bradley Springfield, MA	Sept. 13, 1881
247,302	Toy Box	Thomas Candy Cincinnati, OH	Sept. 20, 1881
247,336	Panoramic Toy	W.F. George New York, NY	Sept. 20, 1881
258,651	Dissected Picture	G.H. Ireland Springfield, MA	May 30, 1882
261,775	Toy Box	H. & F. Smith Cincinnati, OH	July 25, 1882
262,441	Paper Balloon	Ed. F. Linton East New York, NY	Aug. 8, 1882
269,764	Panorama Box	F.M. Whitelaw Hartwell, OH	Dec. 26, 1882
270,511	Educational Disc	P.G. Thomson Cincinnati, OH	Jan. 9, 1883
276,586	Santa Mask	Ezra Holden Chicago, IL	May 1, 1883
277,798	Toy Theater	J.H. Singer New York, NY	May 15, 1883
279,976	Sectional Picture	Albert Operti New York, NY	June 26, 1883
294,868	Toy Doll	H.A. Goffe New York, NY	Mar. 11, 1884
299,015	Action Toy	Wm. B. Sales Oshkosh, WI	May 20, 1884
318,823	Slice Puzzle	Walter Stranders New York, NY	May 26, 1885
334,622	Theater	J.W. Sherman San Francisco, CA	Jan. 19, 1886
347,682	Folding House	J.P. Buckingham Brooklyn, NY	Aug. 17, 1886
371,900	Panoramic Device	J.S. Pihlstrom Chicago, IL	Oct. 18, 1887
390,966	Toy Picture	Cyrus Heller Williamsport, PA	Oct. 9, 1888
397,302	Cut Toy Figure	John McLoughlin New York, NY	Feb. 5, 1889
421,815	Stage Scenery	J.F. Byrnes Norwich, CT	Feb. 18, 1890
422,521	Sectional Picture	Wolff Hagelberg Berlin, Germany	Mar. 4, 1890
513,688	Doll House	E. McC. Smith Baltimore, MD	Jan. 30, 1894
515,090	Paper Doll	Madge McDonald Washington, DC	Feb. 20, 1894
521,253	Toy Holder	F.D. Arthur Scarborough, NY	June 12, 1894
524,855	Folding R.R.	Felix C. Krantz Dresden, Germany	Aug. 21, 1894
526, 901	Paper Doll	C.N. Hoyt Brooklyn, NY	Oct. 2, 1894
530,142	Panorama Toy	Joseph Walker Birmingham, England	Dec. 4, 1894
535,621	Paper Doll	Wm. T. Jefferson New York, NY	Mar. 12, 1895
535,779	Doll House	Vincent W. Wilson Pawtucket, RI	Mar. 12, 1895

PATENT #	OBJECT	NAME & ADDRESS	DATE
537,734	Piano	B.A. Trufant New Orleans, LA	Apr. 16, 1895
537,735	Baby Carriage	B.A. Trufant New Orleans, LA	Apr. 16, 1895
537,791	Paper Doll	B.A. Trufant New Orleans, LA	Apr. 16, 1895
543,767	Paper Doll	E.T. Gibson Minneapolis, MN	July 30, 1895
547,223	Paper Doll	Robt. McCalmont Franklin, PA	Oct. 1, 1895
553,893	Paper Doll	E.C. Betzig New York, NY	Feb. 4, 1896
554,410	Paper Doll	H.P. Bailey East Orange, NJ	Feb. 11, 1896
564,078	Paper Doll & Dress	M.T. Jones Boston, MA	July 14, 1896
565,994	Paper Doll	Paul B. King Buffalo, NY	Aug. 18, 1896
572,730	Articulated Toy Figure	F.M. Spiegle Philadelphia, PA	Dec. 8, 1896
575,384	Crib Box	Isidor Tahl	Jan. 19, 1897
575,749	Paper Doll	M.E. Wilmer Brooklyn, NY	Jan. 26, 1897
578,029	Cut-out Card	Nora M. Russell Hempstead, NY	Mar. 2, 1897
579,225	Doll House	Wm. H. Ferguson St. Louis, MO	Mar. 23, 1897
585,092	Paper Doll	E.T. Gibson Minneapolis, MN	June 22, 1897
589,173	Hot Air Toy	Fred E. Henke Lindenhurst, NY	Aug. 31, 1897
623,635	Animals	Nathan H. Sprague Lonsdale, RI	Apr. 25, 1899
635,994	Doll House	M.E. Cambell Baltimore, MD	Oct. 31, 1899
650,675	Cradle	Mary E. Eldridge Adamsford, PA	May 29, 1900
720,876	Cut & Stick Book	Jessie Atherton Philadelphia, PA	Feb. 17, 1903
723,438	Paper Doll	Kate V. Betts East Orange, NJ	Mar. 24, 1903
788,350	Doll	Dagobert Budwig Berlin, Germany	Apr. 25, 1905
814,340	Jointed Figure	T.E. Wood New York, NY	Mar. 6, 1906
859,280	Christmas Novelty	Herman Berg New York, NY	July 9, 1907
961,675	Surprise Book	James W. Bevans Washington, DC	June 14, 1910
969,309	Educational Device	G. Tuck, London A.E. Kennedy, Leyton	Sept. 6, 1910
984,735	Folding Rooms	L.C. Bailey Chicago, IL	Feb. 21, 1911
1,008,619	Head Mount	Carl Spear Nurenberg, Germany	Nov. 14, 1911
1,023,420	Animals	Drusilla E. Eaton Syracuse, NY	Apr. 16, 1912
1,026,624	Paper Doll	C.O. Chester New York, NY	May 14, 1912
1,041,917	Cut-out Figure	F. Waddington Baltimore, MD	Mar. 25, 1913
1,057,019	Figure Blank	F. Waddington Baltimore, MD	Mar. 25, 1913
1,067,923	Emboridery Pattern	W.T. Jefferson Chicago, IL	July 22, 1913
1,075,482	Paper Doll	Ella D. Lee Chicago, IL	Oct. 14, 1913
1,107,757	Theater	C. Catrevas Brooklyn, NY	Aug. 18, 1914
1,111,216	Horse & Wagon	C.C. Church Grand Rapids, MI	Sept. 22, 1914
1,150,792	Cut-out Doll	C.T. Switzler Newton, MA	Aug. 17, 1915
1,176,637	Paper Doll	Mary V. Anderson Washington, DC	Mar. 21, 1916
1,176,672	Paper Doll	George A. Fox Springfield, MA	Mar. 21, 1916
1,181,421	Elephant	Louis C. Apt New York, NY	May 2, 1916
1,205,386	Cut-out Picture	Desider & Perenyi Jersey City, NJ	Nov. 21, 1916
1,231,145	Paper Doll	G. Ferguson Waco, TX	June 26, 1917
1,232,601	Figure Toy	Wm. Pente Chicago, IL	July 10, 1917
1,255,677	Dress Fastener	A.G. Wilt Philadelphia, PA	Feb. 5, 1918

PATENT #	OBJECT	NAME & ADDRESS	DATE	PATENT #	OBJECT	NAME & ADDRESS	DATE
1,273,945	Paper Doll	F.W. Sooy Asbury Park, NJ	July 30, 1918	1,451,301	Paper Doll	T. Mathews Leicester, England	Apr. 10, 1923
1,287,399	Paper Doll	G.B. Murphy Jamestown, NJ	Dec. 10, 1918	1,475,070	Paper Doll	J.F. Johnston Berkley, CA	Nov. 20, 1923
1,305,071	Paper Doll	E.G.G. Davis Salt Lake City, UT	May 27, 1919	1,586,191	Shop	G.H. Fritzsche Brooklyn, NY	May 25, 1926
1,330,043	Paper Doll	Mary P. Offutt New York, NY	Feb. 3, 1920	1,601,393	Paper Cut-out	Nandor Honti Brooklyn, NY	Sept. 28, 1926
1,369,093	Seated Doll	A.F. Fisher Hempstown, NY	Feb. 22, 1921	1,621,231	Paper Doll	Mattie Basinger Kansas City, MO	Mar. 15, 1927
1,381,528	Doll Model	Mayme White Indianapolis, IN	June 14, 1921	2,028,120	Doll & Dress	B. Campbell New York, NY	Jan. 14, 1936
1,417,915	Doll	A.H. Hornsby Omaha, NE	May 30, 1922	2,050,556	Paper Doll	E.M. Bishop Minneapolis, MN	Aug. 11, 1936
1,438,337	Paper Doll	B.H. Scotford Atlantic City, NJ	Dec. 12, 1922	2,093,207	Doll & Costume	H.H. Munson, Jr. West Springfield, MA	Sept. 14, 1937

Index
Boldface numbers refer to illustration numbers